Cambridge School
Shakespeare

Hamlet

Edited by Richard Andrews and Rex Gibson

Series Editor: Rex Gibson
Director, Shakespeare and Schools Project

CAMBRIDGE
UNIVERSITY PRESS

CAMBRIDGE UNIVERSITY PRESS
Cambridge, New York, Melbourne, Madrid, Cape Town, Singapore,
São Paulo, Delhi, Dubai, Tokyo

Cambridge University Press
The Edinburgh Building, Cambridge CB2 8RU, UK

www.cambridge.org
Information on this title: www.cambridge.org/9780521618748

First published 1994
Second edition 2005
7th printing 2009

Printed in the United Kingdom at the University Press, Cambridge

A catalogue record for this publication is available from the British Library

ISBN 978-0-521-61874-8 Paperback

ACKNOWLEDGEMENTS
Thanks are due to the following for permission to reproduce illustrations:
Cover, v, vi, vii, viii, ix, x, xi, xii, 58, 84, 99*t*, 100, 118, 138, 155*t*, 162, 199, 208, 230,
240, 255, 257, 259, 260, 261, 263, 271, 272, 273, 275*b*, Donald Cooper/Photostage;
10, 202, Morris Newcombe; 26, Rex Gibson; 36, 155*b*, 186, Clive Barda/ArenaPAL;
42, 172, 236, licensed by Warner Bros. Entertainment Inc., all rights reserved; 57, 222,
Joe Cocks Studio Collection © Shakespeare Birthplace Trust; 66, Theatre Museum,
London © V/A Images; 99*b*, David Sim; 146, Raymond Mander & Joe Mitchenson
Theatre Collection; 166, 275*t*, Sovexport Film/photo by BFI; 180, Tom Holte Theatre
Photographic Collection © Shakespeare Birthplace Trust; 196, Millais, *Ophelia* (detail)
© Tate London 2005; 249, by permission of the Syndics of Cambridge University
Library; 274, Columbia/The Kobal Collection/Rosenthal, Zade.

Cover design by Smith

Contents

Cambridge School
Shakespeare

This edition of *Hamlet* is part of the **Cambridge School Shakespeare**
series. Like every other play in the series, it has been specially prepared to
help all students in schools and colleges.

This *Hamlet* aims to be different from other editions of the play. It invites
you to bring the play to life in your classroom, hall or drama studio through
enjoyable activities that will increase your understanding. Actors have
created their different interpretations of the play over the centuries.
Similarly, you are encouraged to make up your own mind about *Hamlet*,
rather than having someone else's interpretation handed down to you.

Cambridge School Shakespeare does not offer you a cut-down or
simplified version of the play. This is Shakespeare's language, filled with
imaginative possibilities. You will find on every left-hand page: a summary
of the action, an explanation of unfamiliar words, and a choice of activities
on Shakespeare's language, characters and stories.

Between the acts and in the pages at the end of the play, you will find
notes, illustrations and activities. These will help to increase your
understanding of the whole play.

There are a large number of activities to give you the widest choice to
suit your own particular needs. Please don't think you have to do every
one. Choose the activities that will help you most.

This edition will be of value to you whether you are studying for an
examination, reading for pleasure, or thinking of putting on the play to
entertain others. You can work on the activities on your own or in groups.
Many of the activities suggest a particular group size, but don't be afraid to
make up larger or smaller groups to suit your own purposes.

Although you are invited to treat *Hamlet* as a play, you don't need
special dramatic or theatrical skills to do the activities. By choosing your
activities, and by exploring and experimenting, you can make your own
interpretations of Shakespeare's language, characters and stories.
Whatever you do, remember that Shakespeare wrote his plays to be acted,
watched and enjoyed.

Rex Gibson

This edition of *Hamlet* uses the text of the play established by Philip Edwards in **The New
Cambridge Shakespeare**.

Hamlet dramatises the tragic story of the young prince of Denmark. His country is threatened with invasion by Norway, but Hamlet is obsessed by the recent death of his father and the marriage of his mother, Gertrude, to his uncle, Claudius, who has become king.

Hamlet's first appearance, dressed in black, conveys his isolation from the court. In both productions shown here his unhappiness about Gertrude's relationship with Claudius is evident. The outcome will be the destruction of two families: Hamlet's (Gertrude and Claudius, left above), and Polonius's (Laertes, Polonius and Ophelia, centre and right above).

Hamlet learns the truth from his father's Ghost. Claudius murdered old
Hamlet. Hamlet desires revenge, but is not sure if the Ghost has spoken
honestly.

To test the truth of the Ghost's story, Hamlet puts on 'an antic disposition'. His strange behaviour arouses the suspicion of Claudius.

Claudius sends for Hamlet's old school friends, Rosencrantz and Guildenstern, to spy on his stepson. Hamlet greets them joyfully, but discovers they are Claudius's agents.

Hamlet plans to discover Claudius's guilt. He orders a group of players to stage a play showing a king murdered by his brother, who then marries the queen. In this production 'The Mousetrap' was staged as a shadow play.

Hamlet's plan succeeds, and Claudius acknowledges his guilt as he prays. Hamlet is about to kill Claudius, but decides to wait until he can choose a moment when Claudius's soul will go direct to hell.

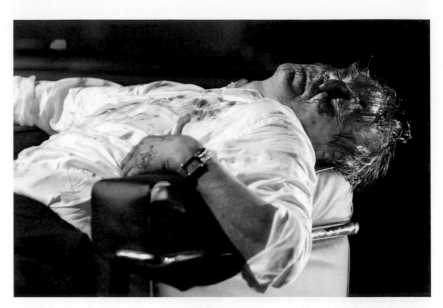

Polonius has concealed himself, wishing to overhear what Hamlet says to Gertrude. But Hamlet mistakes the hidden Polonius for Claudius, and kills him.

Hamlet rages at his mother, begging her to give up Claudius. But Claudius, wishing to be rid of his dangerous stepson, sends Hamlet to England, secretly ordering his execution there.

Claudius and Gertrude watch appalled as Ophelia's songs recall Hamlet's rejection and his killing of her father, Polonius. Her madness will shortly result in her death.

Hamlet has escaped execution in England, but has sent Rosencrantz and Guildenstern to their death there. In the graveyard, the sight of Yorick's skull prompts him to reflect on mortality.

Hamlet duels with Laertes, Polonius's son, who seeks revenge for his father's and sister's deaths. Claudius and Laertes have conspired to kill Hamlet by deceit. But their plot fails. Gertrude drinks the poison intended for Hamlet, Laertes is fatally wounded by the poisoned sword, and Hamlet kills Claudius.

List of characters

The Royal House of Denmark

HAMLET Prince of Denmark
CLAUDIUS King of Denmark, Hamlet's uncle
GERTRUDE Queen of Denmark, Hamlet's mother
GHOST of King Hamlet, Hamlet's father

The Court of Denmark

POLONIUS Counsellor to the king
OPHELIA his daughter
LAERTES his son
REYNALDO his servant

OSRIC
LORDS
GENTLEMAN
} Courtiers

MESSENGER and ATTENDANTS

VOLTEMAND
CORNELIUS
} Ambassadors to Norway

MARCELLUS
BARNARDO
FRANCISCO
} Officers of the Watch

SOLDIERS and GUARDS

Former fellow students of Hamlet

HORATIO Hamlet's friend
ROSENCRANTZ
GUILDENSTERN
} Sent for by Claudius to inform on Hamlet

Norway

FORTINBRAS Prince of Norway   CAPTAIN in Fortinbras's army

Other characters in the play

First PLAYER
Other players
} actors visiting Elsinore

English AMBASSADORS
SAILORS

CLOWN gravedigger and sexton
SECOND CLOWN his assistant
PRIEST at Ophelia's funeral

The action of the play is set in and around
the Danish royal palace at Elsinore.

Francisco is on sentry duty on the gun platform of Elsinore. It is midnight and freezing cold. Barnardo comes to relieve Francisco. Horatio and Marcellus arrive to join Barnardo.

1 Act it out! (in groups of four)

To experience the tense and uneasy atmosphere of the play's opening, the best thing to do is take parts and act out the first nineteen lines. You will find that speaking the lines helps you create the urgent and ominous mood that the short staccato exchanges establish. As you rehearse, talk together about the following points. Remember, your aim is to make the opening moments of the play gripping and dramatic.

a What will be the first thing the audience sees? For example, is Francisco on sentry duty, patrolling the stage, before the first members of the audience enter?

b Barnardo, the newcomer, challenges Francisco. This is contrary to military practice (Francisco should challenge him). How can you use that error to intensify the nervous atmosphere?

c How can you show the audience that the night is bitterly cold?

d Francisco is never seen again in the play, but his remark 'And I am sick at heart' forecasts the troubled melancholy that Hamlet feels when he appears in the next scene. How might Francisco speak and behave during his brief time on stage?

e In Shakespeare's day, the play was staged in broad daylight. Identify all the words and phrases in the script that help create the impression of night and darkness.

f What are the soldiers wearing? Sketch their costumes.

---

unfold yourself   identify yourself, give the password
Long live the king!   (the password, which will prove ironic as the play reveals the death of King Hamlet)
most carefully   precisely
rivals   partners
liegemen to the Dane   loyal followers of the Danish king

Hamlet, Prince of Denmark

Act 1 Scene 1
A gun platform on the battlements of Elsinore Castle

Enter BARNARDO *and* FRANCISCO, *two sentinels*

BARNARDO Who's there?

FRANCISCO Nay answer me. Stand and unfold yourself.

BARNARDO Long live the king!

FRANCISCO Barnardo?

BARNARDO He.   5

FRANCISCO You come most carefully upon your hour.

BARNARDO 'Tis now struck twelve, get thee to bed Francisco.

FRANCISCO For this relief much thanks, 'tis bitter cold
      And I am sick at heart.

BARNARDO Have you had quiet guard?

FRANCISCO   Not a mouse stirring.   10

BARNARDO Well, good night.
      If you do meet Horatio and Marcellus,
      The rivals of my watch, bid them make haste.

FRANCISCO I think I hear them.

Enter HORATIO *and* MARCELLUS

             Stand ho! Who is there?

HORATIO Friends to this ground.

MARCELLUS   And liegemen to the Dane.   15

FRANCISCO Give you good night.

MARCELLUS   Oh farewell honest soldier,
      Who hath relieved you?

FRANCISCO   Barnardo hath my place.
      Give you good night.   *Exit Francisco*

MARCELLUS   Holla, Barnardo!

BARNARDO   Say,
      What, is Horatio there?

HORATIO   A piece of him.

Marcellus reports that he and Barnardo have seen the Ghost twice. Horatio doesn't believe them, but is struck with fear and amazement when the Ghost of Hamlet's father appears.

1 Horatio's thoughts and feelings change (in pairs)

Horatio doesn't believe Marcellus's story, but then sees the Ghost with his own eyes. Horatio speaks five times on the opposite page. Talk together about the tone of his voice each time he speaks. Speak the lines to each other in an appropriate style. Afterwards, write down the range of emotions and attitudes that Horatio displays.

2 'Enter GHOST' – dead King Hamlet appears (in pairs)

The entry of the Ghost of Hamlet's father is a thrilling moment in the theatre. Each new production attempts to ensure that the entry is as electrifying and memorable as possible. Talk together and write notes on each of the following:

a What does the Ghost look like? Horatio gives a clue in lines 47–9 (and see the pictures in the colour section and on pp. 10, 26 and 146).

b Suggest how the Ghost might enter. Slowly or suddenly? From which direction? Decide whether he makes any gestures, what sound effects you might use, and how he leaves the stage.

c Sometimes, as the Ghost appears, the bell strikes. Would you have it strike if you were directing the play? Why? Or why not?

d In some productions the Ghost does not appear physically. The audience has to imagine its presence through lighting, sound and characters' reactions. How effective do you think this style of presenting the Ghost would be? Would you do the same?

Touching concerning
approve our eyes believe our story
assail your ears tell you forcefully
pole pole star (North Star)
scholar student (ghosts were believed to speak Latin)

harrows tortures, tears
usurp'st wrongfully seizes
buried Denmark the dead King Hamlet
charge order

BARNARDO Welcome Horatio, welcome good Marcellus.   20
MARCELLUS What, has this thing appeared again tonight?
BARNARDO I have seen nothing.
MARCELLUS Horatio says 'tis but our fantasy,
      And will not let belief take hold of him
      Touching this dreaded sight, twice seen of us.   25
      Therefore I have entreated him along
      With us to watch the minutes of this night,
      That if again this apparition come
      He may approve our eyes, and speak to it.
HORATIO Tush, tush, 'twill not appear.
BARNARDO   Sit down awhile,   30
      And let us once again assail your ears,
      That are so fortified against our story,
      What we two nights have seen.
HORATIO   Well, sit we down,
      And let us hear Barnardo speak of this.
BARNARDO Last night of all,   35
      When yond same star that's westward from the pole
      Had made his course t'illume that part of heaven
      Where now it burns, Marcellus and myself,
      The bell then beating one –

Enter GHOST

MARCELLUS Peace, break thee off. Look where it comes again.   40
BARNARDO In the same figure, like the king that's dead.
MARCELLUS Thou art a scholar, speak to it Horatio.
BARNARDO Looks a not like the king? Mark it Horatio.
HORATIO Most like. It harrows me with fear and wonder.
BARNARDO It would be spoke to.
MARCELLUS   Question it Horatio.   45
HORATIO What art thou that usurp'st this time of night,
      Together with that fair and warlike form
      In which the majesty of buried Denmark
      Did sometimes march? By heaven I charge thee speak.
MARCELLUS It is offended.
BARNARDO   See, it stalks away.   50
HORATIO Stay! Speak, speak, I charge thee speak!
                            Exit Ghost

Horatio agrees that the Ghost is the exact image of the dead King Hamlet. He thinks it foretells disasters for Denmark. Horatio begins to explain why there are so many urgent preparations for war.

1 A battle? Or an angry gesture? (in small groups)

Do lines 62–3 tell of Denmark's king defeating the Polish army ('Polacks') in a battle on the ice ('sledded' = on sledges)? Or do they mean that the king, in an angry discussion ('parle') with the Norwegians, struck his battle axe on the ice like a sledge hammer (= 'sledded'). Sometimes the word 'Polacks' is printed as 'polax' (poleaxe).

Work out two tableaux (frozen pictures) showing each interpretation. Decide which version is more imaginative and dramatic.

2 Denmark prepares for war (in pairs)

In lines 70–9 Marcellus questions why Denmark is feverishly preparing for war. Guards are mounted everywhere. 'Brazen' (brass) cannons roll off the production line daily. Weapons are bought in foreign countries and imported ('foreign mart for implements of war'). Ships are being built by forced labour ('impress'), working night and day, even on Sundays (unusual in a Christian country).

Write six additional lines listing more of Denmark's frantic war preparations. Use the same urgent style as Marcellus does.

3 'Doubling' – a feature of the play

Opposite are examples of a language device that recurs through the play. It is the use of 'and' to achieve a 'doubling' effect: 'tremble and look pale', 'sensible and true avouch', 'gross and scope', 'strict and most observant'. As you read on, list other examples (there are at least seven in Horatio's lines 80–107). The technical term is **hendiadys** (pronounced 'hen-die-a-dees'). You will find information about its dramatic importance on pages 268–9.

---

sensible and true avouch   evidence
jump   exactly
martial stalk   military stride
In what particular . . . work   how to
  think about it
gross and scope   general view

bodes . . . state   is ominous for us and
  for Denmark
toward   in preparation
emulate   jealous
sealed compact   treaty
law and heraldy   laws of chivalry

MARCELLUS 'Tis gone and will not answer.
BARNARDO How now Horatio? you tremble and look pale.
       Is not this something more than fantasy?
       What think you on't?   55
HORATIO Before my God, I might not this believe
       Without the sensible and true avouch
       Of mine own eyes.
MARCELLUS   Is it not like the king?
HORATIO As thou art to thyself.
       Such was the very armour he had on   60
       When he th'ambitious Norway combated;
       So frowned he once, when in an angry parle
       He smote the sledded Polacks on the ice.
       'Tis strange.
MARCELLUS Thus twice before, and jump at this dead hour,   65
       With martial stalk hath he gone by our watch.
HORATIO In what particular thought to work I know not,
       But in the gross and scope of mine opinion
       This bodes some strange eruption to our state.
MARCELLUS Good now sit down, and tell me he that knows,   70
       Why this same strict and most observant watch
       So nightly toils the subject of the land,
       And why such daily cast of brazen cannon,
       And foreign mart for implements of war,
       Why such impress of shipwrights, whose sore task   75
       Does not divide the Sunday from the week.
       What might be toward, that this sweaty haste
       Doth make the night joint-labourer with the day?
       Who is't that can inform me?
HORATIO   That can I –
       At least the whisper goes so. Our last king,   80
       Whose image even but now appeared to us,
       Was as you know by Fortinbras of Norway,
       Thereto pricked on by a most emulate pride,
       Dared to the combat; in which our valiant Hamlet –
       For so this side of our known world esteemed him –   85
       Did slay this Fortinbras; who by a sealed compact,
       Well ratified by law and heraldy,
       Did forfeit (with his life) all those his lands
       Which he stood seized of, to the conqueror;

Horatio says that young Fortinbras intends to regain the lands his father lost when killed by King Hamlet. The Ghost's appearance presages violence, just as Caesar's death was foretold by ominous events.

___

1 Act out Horatio's story! (in groups of six or more)

In lines 80–107 Horatio explains why Denmark is preparing for war. The king of Norway (old Fortinbras) had dared King Hamlet (Hamlet's father) to personal combat. Both men wagered ('gagèd') large areas of land on the outcome of the duel. Hamlet killed Fortinbras and so took over his territory. Now young Fortinbras, with an army of mercenaries ('landless resolutes'), seeks to recover his father's lost lands. The Danes are hastily preparing to defend themselves against the imminent invasion.

Bring Horatio's story to life. One person narrates, the others enact each episode. The lines contain over twenty-five separate actions that can be shown. (For instance, 'Sharked up' is a vivid image of a shark feeding indiscriminately.)

2 Predicting disasters – is Horatio superstitious?

'A mote it is to trouble the mind's eye' says Horatio (line 112): the appearance of the Ghost is an irritant ('mote') to the imagination. It suggests that disasters lie ahead. Shakespeare had written *Julius Caesar* shortly before *Hamlet*. The recollection of the sinister omens that preceded the death of Caesar was fresh in his mind. Horatio lists them: the living dead, comets, bloody rain, sunspots, an eclipse of the moon ('the moist star').

Is Horatio superstitious? He at first disbelieved the supernatural events that Marcellus had described. Now he seems to believe in omens and auguries. Explore different ways of speaking lines 112–25 (as obvious truth, sceptically, fearfully etc.). Which style seems most appropriate to Horatio's character?

___

moiety competent   equal amount
comart . . . design   treaty
unimprovèd mettle   untested
  bravery
a stomach in't   courage in it
terms compulsatory   forced
  agreement

post-haste and romage   frantic
  activity and turmoil
Neptune's empire   the sea
precurse   forewarning of doom
  (pre-curse)
harbingers   messengers
climatures   territories

Against the which a moiety competent   90
Was gagèd by our king, which had returned
To the inheritance of Fortinbras
Had he been vanquisher; as by the same comart
And carriage of the article design,
His fell to Hamlet. Now sir, young Fortinbras,   95
Of unimprovèd mettle hot and full,
Hath in the skirts of Norway here and there
Sharked up a list of landless resolutes
For food and diet to some enterprise
That hath a stomach in't; which is no other,   100
As it doth well appear unto our state,
But to recover of us by strong hand
And terms compulsatory those foresaid lands
So by his father lost. And this, I take it,
Is the main motive of our preparations,   105
The source of this our watch, and the chief head
Of this post-haste and romage in the land.

[BARNARDO I think it be no other but e'en so.
Well may it sort that this portentous figure
Comes armèd through our watch so like the king   110
That was and is the question of these wars.

HORATIO A mote it is to trouble the mind's eye.
In the most high and palmy state of Rome,
A little ere the mightiest Julius fell,
The graves stood tenantless and the sheeted dead   115
Did squeak and gibber in the Roman streets;
As stars with trains of fire, and dews of blood,
Disasters in the sun; and the moist star,
Upon whose influence Neptune's empire stands,
Was sick almost to doomsday with eclipse.   120
And even the like precurse of feared events,
As harbingers preceding still the fates
And prologue to the omen coming on,
Have heaven and earth together demonstrated
Unto our climatures and countrymen.]   125

Horatio five times demands that the reappearing Ghost speak to him. The cock crows and the Ghost vanishes without reply. Horatio says it cannot be harmed, but that it behaved like a criminal summoned to justice.

'. . . lo where it comes again!' Compare this presentation of the Ghost with those in the colour section and on pages 26 and 146.

1 Advise the actors

Horatio expresses three popular superstitions about why a ghost appears: it seeks someone whose action will enable it to rest in peace (lines 130–1); it knows of a future disaster in store for its country (lines 133–4); it seeks buried treasure, unjustly acquired ('Extorted') when alive (lines 136–7).

Step into role as director and write notes for the actors playing Horatio and the Ghost. Advise them, line by line, what they should do throughout lines 126–42. Give thought particularly to Horatio's five-times repeated demand that the Ghost should speak.

privy to   knowledgeable about
uphoarded   hoarded, hidden
partisan   pike, long-handled spear
invulnerable   impossible to hurt
vain blows   futile attempts to hit
a guilty thing . . . summons   an evildoer caught redhanded

extravagant and erring   wandering
hies . . . confine   hurries to his prison (cell, place of confinement)
present object   apparition (Ghost)
made probation   gave proof

Enter GHOST

But soft, behold, lo where it comes again!
I'll cross it though it blast me. Stay, illusion.

It spreads his arms

If thou hast any sound or use of voice,
Speak to me.
If there be any good thing to be done   130
That may to thee do ease, and grace to me,
Speak to me.
If thou art privy to thy country's fate,
Which happily foreknowing may avoid,
Oh speak.   135
Or if thou hast uphoarded in thy life
Extorted treasure in the womb of earth,
For which they say you spirits oft walk in death,   *The cock crows*
Speak of it. Stay and speak! Stop it Marcellus.
MARCELLUS Shall I strike at it with my partisan?   140
HORATIO Do if it will not stand.
BARNARDO   'Tis here.
HORATIO   'Tis here.
MARCELLUS 'Tis gone.

Exit Ghost

We do it wrong being so majestical
To offer it the show of violence,
For it is as the air invulnerable,   145
And our vain blows malicious mockery.
BARNARDO It was about to speak when the cock crew.
HORATIO And then it started like a guilty thing
Upon a fearful summons. I have heard,
The cock, that is the trumpet to the morn,   150
Doth with his lofty and shrill-sounding throat
Awake the god of day; and at his warning,
Whether in sea or fire, in earth or air,
Th'extravagant and erring spirit hies
To his confine. And of the truth herein   155
This present object made probation.

Marcellus claims that the cockerel crows all night long at Christmas, a time when no harm can be done. Horatio seems to agree. He proposes that they tell Hamlet about the Ghost.

1 Daybreak after darkness: a change of mood (in pairs)

Dawn is breaking. The mood of fear, tension and apprehension gives way to a different emotional climate. Lyrical, poetic language creates a sense of religious awe and wonder. To experience the atmosphere of these closing moments of Scene 1, try some or all of the following:

a Talk together about non-verbal ways in which the change of mood could be conveyed in the theatre (lighting, sound, posture etc.).

b Marcellus is a soldier. He may be dressed in armour for his night's vigil, but he speaks eloquently. His words are filled with poetic wonderment, and do not sound like the language of a no-nonsense military man. Experiment with ways of speaking lines 157–64: full of religious awe; bluntly and factually; conspiratorially, as a great secret. Decide how you think the lines should be spoken on stage.

c After Marcellus's eloquent description of how Christmastime prevents any evil, Horatio responds with 'So have I heard, and do in part believe it.' His remark seems tinged with scepticism. Speak line 165 emphasising 'in part'. See if you can agree on whether the actor should use the line to show that Horatio does not really believe what Marcellus says.

d Horatio uses a vivid image to describe the red glow spreading across the horizon at dawn. He likens daybreak to a traveller dressed in a reddish coloured cloak (lines 166–7). The image is an example of personification (see p. 265). Use the same expressive style to invent two other images which describe daybreak.

---

ever 'gainst always before (or, in expectation of)
our Saviour Jesus Christ
bird of dawning cockerel
strike have an evil influence

takes bewitches, does harm
hallowed holy
russet mantle reddish-coloured cloak
most conveniently very easily

MARCELLUS It faded on the crowing of the cock.
        Some say that ever 'gainst that season comes
        Wherein our Saviour's birth is celebrated,
        This bird of dawning singeth all night long,   160
        And then, they say, no spirit dare stir abroad,
        The nights are wholesome, then no planets strike,
        No fairy takes, nor witch hath power to charm,
        So hallowed and so gracious is that time.
HORATIO So have I heard, and do in part believe it.   165
        But look, the morn in russet mantle clad
        Walks o'er the dew of yon high eastward hill.
        Break we our watch up, and by my advice
        Let us impart what we have seen tonight
        Unto young Hamlet, for upon my life   170
        This spirit, dumb to us, will speak to him.
        Do you consent we shall acquaint him with it,
        As needful in our loves, fitting our duty?
MARCELLUS Let's do't I pray, and I this morning know
        Where we shall find him most conveniently.   175
                                    Exeunt

Claudius announces to the court that, although he grieves for his dead brother, he has, with joy, married Gertrude. He turns his attention to the political situation: young Fortinbras is threatening Denmark.

---

1 Claudius: honest or devious? (in small groups)

King Hamlet has recently died. Claudius, his brother, has become king of Denmark and has married Gertrude. Claudius now possesses his dead brother's throne and his widow. He explains his marriage to his sister-in-law Gertrude so soon after her first husband's death (lines 1–16), and then turns to political affairs (lines 17–39).

a **Stage the entry**   Explore different stagings of the entry of Claudius. One version could show Claudius respected by the courtiers. Another might show he is feared: his courtiers suspect he may become a tyrant.

b **Honest or devious?**   Some critics argue that Claudius's eloquence is appropriate to the occasion. His carefully constructed long sentences suggest he is self-assured and honest. But other critics argue that the speech reveals his insincerity. Its fluency makes it sound rehearsed and false. His constant references to himself using the royal 'we', 'us', 'our' suggest he is anxious about whether his kingship is legal. Take turns to speak lines 1–39 to show Claudius as: confident and in control, uneasy and insecure, devious and crafty, honest and sincere. Afterwards, talk together about what you feel Claudius's language reveals about his character.

c **Oppositions**   Lines 10–14 display another characteristic of the play's language, antithesis (setting words against each other: 'defeated' versus 'joy', 'mirth' versus 'funeral'). Speak the lines using an action to accompany each antithesis (see p. 266 for more on antithesis).

d **Love?**   Might Claudius kiss or embrace Gertrude? Why? Or why not?

---

green   young, fresh
us befitted   was appropriate
imperial jointress   joint ruler of the
  state
auspicious   promising happiness
dirge   sad song
dole   sadness

barred   rejected, disregarded
Holding . . . worth   underestimating us
Colleaguèd   linked
Importing   concerning
bands of law   legally binding
  agreements

Act 1 Scene 2
The Great Hall of Elsinore Castle

Trumpet Call   Enter CLAUDIUS *King of Denmark,* GERTRUDE
the Queen, HAMLET, POLONIUS, LAERTES, OPHELIA,
VOLTEMAND, CORNELIUS, LORDS *attendant*

CLAUDIUS Though yet of Hamlet our dear brother's death
The memory be green, and that it us befitted
To bear our hearts in grief, and our whole kingdom
To be contracted in one brow of woe,
Yet so far hath discretion fought with nature   5
That we with wisest sorrow think on him,
Together with remembrance of ourselves.
Therefore our sometime sister, now our queen,
Th'imperial jointress to this warlike state,
Have we, as 'twere with a defeated joy,   10
With one auspicious and one dropping eye,
With mirth in funeral and with dirge in marriage,
In equal scale weighing delight and dole,
Taken to wife; nor have we herein barred
Your better wisdoms, which have freely gone   15
With this affair along – for all, our thanks.
Now follows that you know: young Fortinbras,
Holding a weak supposal of our worth,
Or thinking by our late dear brother's death
Our state to be disjoint and out of frame,   20
Colleaguèd with this dream of his advantage,
He hath not failed to pester us with message
Importing the surrender of those lands
Lost by his father, with all bands of law,
To our most valiant brother. So much for him.   25
Now for ourself and for this time of meeting
Thus much the business is: we have here writ
To Norway, uncle of young Fortinbras,

Claudius sends messengers to the king of Norway to prevent Fortinbras from attacking Denmark. He asks Laertes to state his request. Laertes wishes to return to France. Polonius says he has reluctantly agreed.

1 Is it a sneer to underline Claudius's manliness?

The king of Norway is, like Claudius, a brother who has succeeded to his brother's throne. Claudius describes him as 'impotent and bed-rid' (line 29). Suggest a way of speaking the line to give the audience an insight into Claudius's character. For example, might he embrace Gertrude as he speaks, to stress his own virility and manhood?

2 Write 'these dilated articles'

Write the 'dilated articles' (clear, full statements) that Claudius sends to 'old Norway'. Begin with a formal greeting from one king to another. Set out a list of statements to clarify the political situation. Then make your demand: the king of Norway must put an end to Fortinbras's attempt to reclaim Danish territory. Include Danish place-names in your 'articles'. You may wish to add authenticity to the document that Cornelius and Voltemand will deliver to the king of Norway, for example by sealing it with wax and tying it with ribbon.

3 Can you agree? (in groups of eight)

Everyone takes a part: Claudius, Gertrude, Hamlet, Polonius, Laertes, Ophelia, Cornelius and Voltemand. Line up in order of social status in Denmark. Do you all agree on who is socially superior to whom? Argue any differences in view. As you work through the play, you can use this ranking activity in other ways (order of 'dramatic importance', or 'age', or 'most moral . . . least moral' etc.). It produces helpful discussion.

---

impotent   powerless (in politics and sex)

further gait herein   going further

in that   because

levies, lists   soldiers

full proportions   army necessary for this campaign

subject   people

suit   request

native   related

instrumental   serviceable

bend again   turn again

slow leave   reluctant permission

laboursome petition   persistent asking

hard consent   grudging agreement

Who, impotent and bed-rid, scarcely hears
Of this his nephew's purpose, to suppress   30
His further gait herein, in that the levies,
The lists, and full proportions, are all made
Out of his subject; and we here dispatch
You, good Cornelius, and you, Voltemand,
For bearers of this greeting to old Norway,   35
Giving to you no further personal power
To business with the king, more than the scope
Of these dilated articles allow.
Farewell, and let your haste commend your duty.

CORNELIUS
VOLTEMAND } In that and all things will we show our duty.   40

CLAUDIUS We doubt it nothing, heartily farewell.

Exeunt Voltemand and Cornelius

And now Laertes, what's the news with you?
You told us of some suit, what is't Laertes?
You cannot speak of reason to the Dane
And lose your voice. What wouldst thou beg Laertes,   45
That shall not be my offer, not thy asking?
The head is not more native to the heart,
The hand more instrumental to the mouth,
Than is the throne of Denmark to thy father.
What wouldst thou have Laertes?

LAERTES   My dread lord,   50
Your leave and favour to return to France,
From whence though willingly I came to Denmark
To show my duty in your coronation,
Yet now I must confess, that duty done,
My thoughts and wishes bend again toward France,   55
And bow them to your gracious leave and pardon.

CLAUDIUS Have you your father's leave? What says Polonius?

POLONIUS He hath my lord wrung from me my slow leave
By laboursome petition, and at last
Upon his will I sealed my hard consent.   60
I do beseech you give him leave to go.

Claudius grants Laertes's request to return to France. He asks Hamlet why he is so melancholy. Gertrude urges Hamlet to cease grieving for the death of his father. Hamlet replies that his mourning is truly felt.

1 Hamlet: the master listener (in pairs)

You will discover that everything Hamlet says throughout the play reveals his acute alertness to language. He listens carefully to everything that is said to him, and often plays or puns on the words he has heard, giving them different meaning and significance (see p. 254).

a **Listening to Claudius**   Hamlet immediately picks up the kinship implications of Claudius's use of 'cousin' and 'son'. He detests the close kinship that Claudius's marriage to his mother has created. His first line puns on 'kin' and 'kind', saying in effect that he feels too closely related, and does not have the same nature as his new stepfather. His second line plays on 'sun' and 'son', again rejecting any close relationship to Claudius.

Talk together, then write notes for the actor playing Hamlet about how to speak line 65 (To himself? To the audience? In a sardonic tone? Or bitterly? Or . . . ?). The line is an Aside, not heard by other characters. Also write advice on line 67: which word or words might Hamlet stress to question his kinship to Claudius, for example?

b **Listening to Gertrude**   Hamlet seizes on Gertrude's 'seems' (line 75) and insists that his appearance *does* match the way he feels. Indeed, his black clothes and mournful behaviour only partly reflect his sorrow for his father's death. He is not playing a part by wearing the 'trappings' of mourning, but is genuinely grief-stricken.

To gain an insight into Hamlet's feelings, one person slowly reads aloud lines 76–86, pausing after each line. In each pause, the other person says, 'I know not seems', stressing whichever of the four words seems appropriate to what has just been spoken.

thy best graces   your good characteristics
nighted   dark, gloomy
Denmark   the king (Claudius)
vailèd lids   downcast eyes
windy suspiration   sighs
haviour of the visage   facial expression

filial obligation   a son's duty
obsequious   dutiful, as required by funeral rites (obsequies)
persever / In obstinate condolement   keep up this stubborn mourning
impious   unholy

CLAUDIUS Take thy fair hour Laertes, time be thine,
And thy best graces spend it at thy will.
But now my cousin Hamlet, and my son –
HAMLET (*Aside*) A little more than kin, and less than kind.   65
CLAUDIUS How is it that the clouds still hang on you?
HAMLET Not so my lord, I am too much i'th'sun.
GERTRUDE Good Hamlet cast thy nighted colour off,
And let thine eye look like a friend on Denmark.
Do not forever with thy vailèd lids   70
Seek for thy noble father in the dust.
Thou know'st 'tis common, all that lives must die,
Passing through nature to eternity.
HAMLET Ay madam, it is common.
GERTRUDE   If it be,
Why seems it so particular with thee?   75
HAMLET Seems madam? nay it is, I know not seems.
'Tis not alone my inky cloak, good mother,
Nor customary suits of solemn black,
Nor windy suspiration of forced breath,
No, nor the fruitful river in the eye,   80
Nor the dejected haviour of the visage,
Together with all forms, moods, shapes of grief,
That can denote me truly. These indeed seem,
For they are actions that a man might play,
But I have that within which passes show –   85
These but the trappings and the suits of woe.
CLAUDIUS 'Tis sweet and commendable in your nature Hamlet,
To give these mourning duties to your father;
But you must know, your father lost a father,
That father lost, lost his, and the survivor bound   90
In filial obligation for some term
To do obsequious sorrow; but to persever
In obstinate condolement is a course
Of impious stubbornness, 'tis unmanly grief,

Claudius criticises Hamlet's continued grief, declares him next in line to the throne, but refuses him permission to return to Wittenberg University. Gertrude pleads with Hamlet to stay. He agrees to her request.

1 Rebuke, assurance and refusal (in small groups)

In an extended speech, Claudius first delivers a long criticism of Hamlet's grief; next, briefly pleads with him to abandon his mourning and declares him heir to the throne; then abruptly refuses Hamlet permission to return to Wittenberg. Claudius's speech offers opportunities to the actor to establish the king's character and his attitude to Hamlet. Take turns to speak the three sections:

The rebuke (lines 87–106, to 'This must be so')   Use a commanding tone. Emphasise repetitions ('father', 'father', 'father'; 'a fault', 'A fault', 'a fault'), and the critical expressions ('persever', 'obstinate condolement' etc.).

The assurance (lines 106–12, to 'toward you')   Use a cordial tone, and make much of declaring Hamlet as 'most immediate to our throne' (the next king).

The refusal (lines 112–17)   Abrupt and sharp, but end using a seemingly friendly, reassuring tone.

Afterwards, work on how the speech could be delivered on stage.

2 Exploring motives and feelings (in small groups)

Actors always discuss characters' motives and feelings. Step into role as actors preparing a production of *Hamlet* and discuss:

- Why does Claudius rebuke Hamlet so strongly for his grief?
- Why does he now declare Hamlet his heir (line 109)?
- Why does he refuse Hamlet leave to return to Wittenberg?
- What does Claudius feel towards Hamlet (dislike, fear or . . .)?
- Is Hamlet's agreement to obey his mother (line 120) sincere?
- Does Claudius *really* think Hamlet gives 'a loving and a fair reply'?

---

heart unfortified weak will
peevish irritable
fault offence
corse corpse
unprevailing useless
most immediate next in line, heir

retrograde opposite
bend you accept the idea
accord agreement
jocund health happy toast in wine
rouse toast
bruit noisily announce

It shows a will most incorrect to heaven, 95
A heart unfortified, a mind impatient,
An understanding simple and unschooled.
For what we know must be, and is as common
As any the most vulgar thing to sense,
Why should we in our peevish opposition 100
Take it to heart? Fie, 'tis a fault to heaven,
A fault against the dead, a fault to nature,
To reason most absurd, whose common theme
Is death of fathers, and who still hath cried,
From the first corse till he that died today, 105
'This must be so.' We pray you throw to earth
This unprevailing woe, and think of us
As of a father, for let the world take note
You are the most immediate to our throne,
And with no less nobility of love 110
Than that which dearest father bears his son,
Do I impart toward you. For your intent
In going back to school in Wittenberg,
It is most retrograde to our desire,
And we beseech you bend you to remain 115
Here in the cheer and comfort of our eye,
Our chiefest courtier, cousin, and our son.
GERTRUDE Let not thy mother lose her prayers Hamlet.
    I pray thee stay with us, go not to Wittenberg.
HAMLET I shall in all my best obey you madam. 120
CLAUDIUS Why, 'tis a loving and a fair reply.
    Be as ourself in Denmark. Madam, come.
    This gentle and unforced accord of Hamlet
    Sits smiling to my heart, in grace whereof,
    No jocund health that Denmark drinks today 125
    But the great cannon to the clouds shall tell,
    And the king's rouse the heaven shall bruit again,
    Re-speaking earthly thunder. Come away.
                  Flourish. Exeunt all but Hamlet

Hamlet longs for death but knows that suicide is forbidden by God. He is disgusted that his mother has married so soon after his father's death, but feels he must keep silent. He greets Horatio and Marcellus.

---

1 Obsessed by family matters (in small groups)

A soliloquy is spoken by a character who is alone (or thinks they are alone) on stage. It reveals the speaker's true thoughts and feelings. Hamlet's soliloquy exposes his deep depression. In turn he expresses weariness, despair, grief, anger, nausea, loathing and disgust, and resignation. He has no thoughts about political matters, about becoming king, or about being forbidden to return to Wittenberg. His troubled mind is obsessed solely with family matters: his father, his uncle and – above all – his mother. His thoughts move as follows:

Lines 129–32 He wishes to die, but the law ('canon') of God ('the Everlasting') forbids suicide.

Lines 133–7 He thinks of life as tedious and foul ('rank').

Lines 138–40 He recalls his dead father, who was infinitely superior to Claudius ('Hyperion' = the sun-god, 'satyr' = lecherous creature, half-man, half-goat).

Lines 140–2 He recalls his father's powerful love for his mother.

Lines 143–5 He recalls how passionately Gertrude loved his father.

Lines 146–57 He is disgusted by his mother's speedy marriage to the inferior Claudius so shortly after his father's death.

Lines 158–9 He condemns the marriage but, sorrowfully, vows silence.

To experience Hamlet's intensity of feeling, use the information above and experiment with different styles of delivery (e.g. speaking to himself, speaking directly to the audience, sharing out the soliloquy with each person speaking a small section in turn).

---

all the uses of everything in
merely completely
beteem permit
or ere before
Niobe Queen of Thebes, who wept for her dead children even when she was turned to stone

wants . . . reason lacks brains
Hercules mythical Greek hero, enormously strong
gallèd sore from weeping
post hurry
incestuous sheets her husband's brother's bed

HAMLET O that this too too solid flesh would melt,
Thaw and resolve itself into a dew, 130
Or that the Everlasting had not fixed
His canon 'gainst self-slaughter. O God, God,
How weary, stale, flat and unprofitable
Seem to me all the uses of this world!
Fie on't, ah fie, 'tis an unweeded garden 135
That grows to seed, things rank and gross in nature
Possess it merely. That it should come to this!
But two months dead – nay not so much, not two –
So excellent a king, that was to this
Hyperion to a satyr, so loving to my mother 140
That he might not beteem the winds of heaven
Visit her face too roughly – heaven and earth,
Must I remember? why, she would hang on him
As if increase of appetite had grown
By what it fed on, and yet within a month – 145
Let me not think on't; frailty, thy name is woman –
A little month, or ere those shoes were old
With which she followed my poor father's body
Like Niobe, all tears, why she, even she –
O God, a beast that wants discourse of reason 150
Would have mourned longer – married with my uncle,
My father's brother, but no more like my father
Than I to Hercules – within a month,
Ere yet the salt of most unrighteous tears
Had left the flushing in her gallèd eyes, 155
She married. Oh most wicked speed, to post
With such dexterity to incestuous sheets.
It is not, nor it cannot come to good.
But break, my heart, for I must hold my tongue.

Enter HORATIO, MARCELLUS *and* BARNARDO

HORATIO Hail to your lordship.
HAMLET   I am glad to see you well. 160
Horatio – or I do forget myself.
HORATIO The same, my lord, and your poor servant ever.
HAMLET Sir, my good friend, I'll change that name with you.
And what make you from Wittenberg, Horatio?
Marcellus. 165

Hamlet does not believe Horatio returned to Denmark as a truant or to attend King Hamlet's funeral, but to see Gertrude's marriage. Horatio reports that he thinks he saw Hamlet's father the previous night.

---

1 Hamlet's changing moods

Hamlet's mood changes dramatically between lines 167 and 195. Identify his shifts in mood and write down a brief description for each (e.g. line 167 'welcoming'; lines 170–3 'disbelieving but friendly').

2 An embittered joke? Or just bitter?

'Thrift, thrift', says Hamlet bitterly, commenting on how quickly his mother remarried after his father's death (lines 180–1). He implies that the leftovers from King Hamlet's funeral feast were used for the wedding breakfast of Gertrude and Claudius. Sometimes Hamlet delivers the two lines as a sour joke, sometimes entirely without humour. Which style do you prefer? Why?

3 A conversation – but private thoughts intrude (in pairs)

Take parts as Hamlet and Horatio and read lines 168–95. There are two moments where Hamlet might appear to be speaking to himself, rather than to Horatio. Identify them, and suggest how Hamlet might deliver those lines to show how memories of his dead father still preoccupy him.

4 'I saw him once' – Where? When?

When and where did Horatio see King Hamlet? It may have been on a battlefield, or at a state visit or some sport or recreation. There is, of course, no 'true' answer, but write Horatio's account of an imagined occasion when he saw the king. Your account should reveal something of Horatio's character and experience.

---

make you   brings you
disposition   nature
truster   believer
hard upon   quickly
Thrift   penny-pinching, money-saving
coldly   as cold meats (or leftovers)

furnish forth   were served on
Or ever   before
a was   he was
all in all   weighing all his qualities
Season your admiration   control your amazement

MARCELLUS My good lord.

HAMLET I am very glad to see you. (*To Barnardo*) Good even sir.
　　　　But what in faith make you from Wittenberg.

HORATIO A truant disposition, good my lord.

HAMLET I would not hear your enemy say so,   170
　　　　Nor shall you do my ear that violence
　　　　To make it truster of your own report
　　　　Against yourself. I know you are no truant.
　　　　But what is your affair in Elsinore?
　　　　We'll teach you to drink deep ere you depart.   175

HORATIO My lord, I came to see your father's funeral.

HAMLET I pray thee do not mock me fellow student,
　　　　I think it was to see my mother's wedding.

HORATIO Indeed my lord, it followed hard upon.

HAMLET Thrift, thrift, Horatio. The funeral baked meats   180
　　　　Did coldly furnish forth the marriage tables.
　　　　Would I had met my dearest foe in heaven
　　　　Or ever I had seen that day, Horatio.
　　　　My father, methinks I see my father –

HORATIO Where my lord?

HAMLET 　　　　　　　　In my mind's eye, Horatio.   185

HORATIO I saw him once, a was a goodly king.

HAMLET A was a man, take him for all in all.
　　　　I shall not look upon his like again.

HORATIO My lord, I think I saw him yesternight.

HAMLET Saw? Who?   190

HORATIO My lord, the king your father.

HAMLET 　　　　　　　　　　　The king my father!

HORATIO Season your admiration for a while
　　　　With an attent ear, till I may deliver
　　　　Upon the witness of these gentlemen
　　　　This marvel to you.

HAMLET 　　　　　　　For God's love let me hear.   195

Horatio reports the sightings of the Ghost: how it was clad in armour and how it vanished at daybreak. Hamlet is troubled by what he hears. He closely questions Marcellus and Barnardo.

'A figure like your father, / Armèd at point exactly, cap-a-pe'. In 1989 the Royal National Theatre used a 3-metre high statue of the Ghost. Compare it with the images in the colour section and on page 10. Which most matches your imagined version of the Ghost?

dead waste desolation
at point correct in every detail
cap-a-pe from head to foot
truncheon military baton
impart they did they told
as they had delivered exactly as they described it

platform gun emplacement
address / Itself to motion began to move
Hold you the watch tonight? Are you on guard duty tonight?

HORATIO Two nights together had these gentlemen,
       Marcellus and Barnardo, on their watch
       In the dead waste and middle of the night,
       Been thus encountered. A figure like your father,
       Armèd at point exactly, cap-a-pe,   200
       Appears before them, and with solemn march
       Goes slow and stately by them. Thrice he walked
       By their oppressed and fear-surprisèd eyes
       Within his truncheon's length, whilst they, distilled
       Almost to jelly with the act of fear,   205
       Stand dumb and speak not to him. This to me
       In dreadful secrecy impart they did,
       And I with them the third night kept the watch,
       Where, as they had delivered, both in time,
       Form of the thing, each word made true and good,   210
       The apparition comes. I knew your father,
       These hands are not more like.
HAMLET   But where was this?
MARCELLUS My lord, upon the platform where we watched.
HAMLET Did you not speak to it?
HORATIO   My lord, I did,
       But answer made it none. Yet once methought   215
       It lifted up it head and did address
       Itself to motion like as it would speak;
       But even then the morning cock crew loud,
       And at the sound it shrunk in haste away
       And vanished from our sight.
HAMLET   'Tis very strange.   220
HORATIO As I do live my honoured lord 'tis true,
       And we did think it writ down in our duty
       To let you know of it.
HAMLET Indeed, indeed sirs, but this troubles me.
       Hold you the watch tonight?
MARCELLUS ⎫
BARNARDO ⎭   We do, my lord.   225
HAMLET Armed say you?
MARCELLUS ⎫
BARNARDO ⎭   Armed my lord.
HAMLET   From top to toe?

Hamlet continues his close questioning about the Ghost. He resolves to join the others on watch that night and to speak to the Ghost. He commands the others not to talk about what they've seen.

---

1 Very fast exchanges? Or . . .? (in groups of four)

Take parts and speak lines 224–42, in which Hamlet questions the three men. Theatrical convention is that when speeches follow each other in single lines, or when a line is shared between speakers, the dialogue should be spoken very quickly, without pauses (in a staccato or 'rat-a-tat-tat' way). Read the exchanges in that manner, then experiment by using pauses. Afterwards, discuss whether the actors should follow dramatic custom here, or use pauses.

2 A choice of writing activities

a **Marcellus and Barnardo compare notes**   Marcellus and Barnardo have seen the Ghost three times. They have told their news to Hamlet. Imagine they have returned to their quarters. They talk about their sightings of the Ghost, and about Hamlet's response. Write the script of their conversation, using your knowledge of Scenes 1 and 2.

b **Hamlet writes about his day's experience**   Hamlet's final four lines express surprise, apprehension, suspicion, impatience and the certainty that evil actions cannot remain concealed. As you will discover in Scene 5, Hamlet keeps a notebook ('tables') in which he writes down what he learns. Write Hamlet's notebook entry for this day. It will describe his behaviour at the court, his feelings about Claudius and Gertrude and his own moodiness, what he makes of Horatio's story, and his speculations about why his father's Ghost appears to be haunting Elsinore. He is probably also puzzled about why the Ghost had a 'countenance [look] more in sorrow than in anger'.

---

beaver visor	**tenable** held, kept secret
tell count	**hap** happen
grizzled grey	**requite** reward
sable silvered black with a few white	**doubt** fear, suspect
hairs	**Though all the earth . . . eyes**
warrant promise, guarantee	however deeply buried

MARCELLUS ⎱ My lord, from head to foot.
BARNARDO ⎰

HAMLET Then saw you not his face?

HORATIO Oh yes my lord, he wore his beaver up.

HAMLET What, looked he frowningly?   230

HORATIO A countenance more in sorrow than in anger.

HAMLET Pale, or red?

HORATIO Nay very pale.

HAMLET   And fixed his eyes upon you?

HORATIO Most constantly.

HAMLET   I would I had been there.

HORATIO It would have much amazed you.   235

HAMLET Very like, very like. Stayed it long?

HORATIO While one with moderate haste might tell a hundred.

MARCELLUS ⎱ Longer, longer.
BARNARDO ⎰

HORATIO Not when I saw 't.

HAMLET   His beard was grizzled, no?

HORATIO It was as I have seen it in his life,   240
          A sable silvered.

HAMLET   I will watch tonight,
          Perchance 'twill walk again.

HORATIO   I warrant it will.

HAMLET If it assume my noble father's person,
          I'll speak to it though hell itself should gape
          And bid me hold my peace. I pray you all,   245
          If you have hitherto concealed this sight,
          Let it be tenable in your silence still,
          And whatsomever else shall hap tonight,
          Give it an understanding but no tongue.
          I will requite your loves. So fare you well: 250
          Upon the platform 'twixt eleven and twelve
          I'll visit you.

ALL   Our duty to your honour.

HAMLET Your loves, as mine to you. Farewell.

                                        Exeunt all but Hamlet

          My father's spirit, in arms! All is not well.
          I doubt some foul play. Would the night were come.   255
          Till then sit still my soul. Foul deeds will rise
          Though all the earth o'erwhelm them to men's eyes.   *Exit*

Laertes warns Ophelia against Hamlet's love, saying it is merely youthful infatuation. As a prince, Hamlet is not free to choose his own wife; he must marry in the interest of the state.

1 Advice to a sister (in pairs)

Laertes hands out much advice to his sister. His elaborate style may make him sound pompous, even overbearing. An activity on his character is on page 32. The following activities are on the lines opposite.

a **Young love won't last** In lines 5–10, Laertes stresses Hamlet's youth and the fickleness of young love. It won't last, he tells Ophelia, and he makes comparisons with short-lived things: 'fashion' (passing mood), 'toy in blood' (whim of passionate youth), 'violet' (a flower of early spring) and so on. One person reads lines 5–10, pausing at each punctuation mark. In the pause, the other person repeats what has just been said, but with scornful emphasis. How many comparisons with short-lasting love does Laertes make?

b **Maturity comes with age** When Ophelia questions Laertes's assertion that Hamlet's love will be short-lived, he replies very formally: the body ('this temple') does not only increase ('waxes') in sinews and size ('thews and bulk'), but in wisdom too. Take turns reading Laertes's lines 10–14 to each other. Use actions to bring out the meaning.

c **Princes can't choose** Can a prince choose to marry whoever he wants? Laertes doesn't think so. He tells Ophelia that 'his [Hamlet's] will is not his own'. In lines 17–28, he gives reasons why a prince, unlike an ordinary person, is not free to marry anyone he chooses; he must bear in mind the needs and interests of his country. Discuss whether you think what Laertes says was true in past times – and whether it is true for princes and other royalty today.

---

necessaries luggage
convoy is assistant ships are available
the youth of primy nature the spring
suppliance pastime
crescent growing

no soil nor cautel no blemish or deceit
Carve choose
peculiar sect and force high status
give . . . deed turn into action
main voice majority opinion

Act 1 Scene 3
Elsinore A private room

Enter LAERTES and his sister OPHELIA

LAERTES My necessaries are embarked, farewell.
        And sister, as the winds give benefit
        And convoy is assistant, do not sleep
        But let me hear from you.
OPHELIA   Do you doubt that?
LAERTES For Hamlet, and the trifling of his favour,   5
        Hold it a fashion, and a toy in blood,
        A violet in the youth of primy nature,
        Forward, not permanent, sweet, not lasting,
        The perfume and suppliance of a minute,
        No more.
OPHELIA   No more but so?
LAERTES   Think it no more.   10
        For nature crescent does not grow alone
        In thews and bulk, but as this temple waxes
        The inward service of the mind and soul
        Grows wide withal. Perhaps he loves you now,
        And now no soil nor cautel doth besmirch   15
        The virtue of his will; but you must fear,
        His greatness weighed, his will is not his own,
        For he himself is subject to his birth.
        He may not, as unvalued persons do,
        Carve for himself, for on his choice depends   20
        The sanctity and health of this whole state,
        And therefore must his choice be circumscribed
        Unto the voice and yielding of that body
        Whereof he is the head. Then if he says he loves you,
        It fits your wisdom so far to believe it   25
        As he in his peculiar sect and force
        May give his saying deed, which is no further
        Than the main voice of Denmark goes withal.

Laertes continues to warn Ophelia not to trust Hamlet, because young women are vulnerable and face many dangers. She reminds him to follow his own advice. Polonius urges Laertes to leave.

---

1 Is Laertes pompous, or sincerely caring, or . . .? (in pairs)

Opposite, Laertes uses images of treasure, war, masks and disease to warn Ophelia against losing her virginity to Hamlet. How does Laertes speak all his advice to his sister? Pompously? Lovingly? Imploringly? And how does Ophelia react as her brother lectures her on the briefness of young love, Hamlet's high status, and the dangers that face young women?

Take parts and experiment with different ways of speaking lines 1–44, and of showing Ophelia's reactions. Afterwards, jointly write a paragraph saying what you think is Laertes's attitude to his sister. For example, is he genuinely affectionate or is he sexist and condescending?

2 Practise what you preach (in pairs)

In lines 45–51 Ophelia agrees to follow Laertes's advice, but then reminds him to practise what he preaches. Is her first sentence (agreeing) spoken ironically or submissively? Experiment with speaking the lines and decide which style best fits your view of Ophelia's character.

3 'Steep and thorny way' – 'primrose path' (in small groups)

Prepare two mimes to show the difference between 'the steep and thorny way to heaven', and 'the primrose path of dalliance' that 'a puffed and reckless libertine' (pleasure seeker) treads. It will help if you think of the first as refusing all temptations, and the second as happily accepting every temptation that comes your way.

---

credent trustful
list his songs listen to his love talk
chaste treasure virginity
unmastered importunity
 uncontrolled harassment
chariest most modest
prodigal lavish, wasteful

calumnious slandering
buttons buds
Contagious blastments infectious
 diseases
recks not his own rede disregards
 his own advice, doesn't practise what
 he preaches

Then weigh what loss your honour may sustain
If with too credent ear you list his songs,   30
Or lose your heart, or your chaste treasure open
To his unmastered importunity.
Fear it Ophelia, fear it my dear sister,
And keep you in the rear of your affection,
Out of the shot and danger of desire.   35
The chariest maid is prodigal enough
If she unmask her beauty to the moon.
Virtue itself scapes not calumnious strokes.
The canker galls the infants of the spring
Too oft before their buttons be disclosed,   40
And in the morn and liquid dew of youth
Contagious blastments are most imminent.
Be wary then, best safety lies in fear:
Youth to itself rebels, though none else near.

OPHELIA I shall th'effect of this good lesson keep   45
As watchman to my heart. But good my brother,
Do not as some ungracious pastors do,
Show me the steep and thorny way to heaven,
Whiles like a puffed and reckless libertine
Himself the primrose path of dalliance treads,   50
And recks not his own rede.

LAERTES   Oh fear me not.

Enter POLONIUS

I stay too long – But here my father comes.
A double blessing is a double grace;
Occasion smiles upon a second leave.

POLONIUS Yet here Laertes? Aboard, aboard for shame!   55
The wind sits in the shoulder of your sail,
And you are stayed for. There, my blessing with thee,

Polonius gives Laertes fatherly advice on speech, friendship, quarrelling, judgement, dress, money and consistency. He questions Ophelia about her relationship with Hamlet, saying she has met him often.

1 A father gives advice to his son (in pairs)

a How does Polonius deliver his advice to his son? On stage his style has been variously comic, authoritarian, lovingly sincere, pompously aloof and so on. Try speaking lines 58–81 in such styles, then talk together about what the lines suggest about his character.

b In lines 59–80, Polonius hands out eight pieces of advice. Imagine Laertes dares to ask his father to give a practical example of each principle. One person reads Polonius's lines, pausing at each full stop. In the pause, Laertes asks 'concrete example, please'. Reply, providing an actual instance (there is an example in lines 72–4).

c How do Laertes and Ophelia react? In some productions Polonius's children listen dutifully and respectfully. In others they make faces behind Polonius's back, mocking his advice. In yet others they silently mouth his words, showing they have heard it all many times before. Advise Laertes and Ophelia how to react to each sentence of counsel.

d Write out the eight pieces of advice in order of importance to you. Then write eight pieces of advice for a father to give to a son or daughter today.

2 Why does Ophelia so quickly break her promise?

In lines 85–6, Ophelia promises to keep Laertes's advice secret. But three lines later she begins to tell Polonius what the advice was about. Suggest one or two reasons for her so quickly breaking her promise.

---

precepts moral principles
character engrave, imprint
unproportioned ill-considered
adoption tried worthiness tested
dull thy palm squander your hospitality
courage comrade

censure opinion
habit clothes
husbandry good housekeeping, thrift
Marry by St Mary
audience time, attention
put on me reported to me

And these few precepts in thy memory
Look thou character. Give thy thoughts no tongue,
Nor any unproportioned thought his act.   60
Be thou familiar, but by no means vulgar.
Those friends thou hast, and their adoption tried,
Grapple them unto thy soul with hoops of steel,
But do not dull thy palm with entertainment
Of each new-hatched, unfledged courage. Beware   65
Of entrance to a quarrel, but being in,
Bear't that th'opposèd may beware of thee.
Give every man thy ear, but few thy voice;
Take each man's censure, but reserve thy judgement.
Costly thy habit as thy purse can buy,   70
But not expressed in fancy: rich, not gaudy.
For the apparel oft proclaims the man,
And they in France of the best rank and station
Are of a most select and generous chief in that.
Neither a borrower nor a lender be,   75
For loan oft loses both itself and friend,
And borrowing dulls the edge of husbandry.
This above all, to thine own self be true,
And it must follow, as the night the day,
Thou canst not then be false to any man.   80
Farewell, my blessing season this in thee.
LAERTES Most humbly do I take my leave, my lord.
POLONIUS The time invites you. Go, your servants tend.
LAERTES Farewell Ophelia, and remember well
What I have said to you.
OPHELIA   'Tis in my memory locked,   85
And you yourself shall keep the key of it.
LAERTES Farewell.   *Exit Laertes*
POLONIUS What is't Ophelia he hath said to you?
OPHELIA So please you, something touching the Lord Hamlet.
POLONIUS Marry, well bethought.   90
'Tis told me he hath very oft of late
Given private time to you, and you yourself
Have of your audience been most free and bounteous.
If it be so, as so 'tis put on me,
And that in way of caution, I must tell you   95
You do not understand yourself so clearly

Polonius, scornful of Hamlet's love, remonstrates with Ophelia. He orders her not to believe Hamlet's love-talk. She must give up seeing him because of his royal position and his merely lustful desire.

Polonius picks up words Ophelia uses and interprets them differently: 'affection' (love/lust), 'tenders' (offers / look after / make), 'fashion' (manner/pretence). But does he speak harshly or affectionately?

1 Images of deceit (and see 'Imagery', pp. 264–5)

Line 115 'springes to catch woodcocks' – 'springes' are traps. Elizabethans thought woodcocks to be foolish birds.

Lines 127–31 false appearance – Hamlet's love promises are pimps ('brokers'), like false-coloured clothes ('dye', 'investments'). They plan to do mischief ('implorators of unholy suits') when they vow true marriage ('sanctified and pious bonds').

behooves is appropriate to	**prodigal** lavishly
Unsifted inexperienced	**blazes** passionate flare-ups
sterling of true value	**scanter** less free, more grudging
Roaming playing with	**command to parley** invitation to talk
fool baby, simpleton	of love
importuned addressed, solicited	**tedder** tether (rope)
countenance strength, support	**In few** briefly

As it behooves my daughter, and your honour.
What is between you? Give me up the truth.

OPHELIA He hath my lord of late made many tenders
Of his affection to me.   100

POLONIUS Affection? Puh! You speak like a green girl,
Unsifted in such perilous circumstance.
Do you believe his tenders as you call them?

OPHELIA I do not know my lord what I should think.

POLONIUS Marry I'll teach you. Think yourself a baby   105
That you have tane these tenders for true pay,
Which are not sterling. Tender yourself more dearly,
Or – not to crack the wind of the poor phrase,
Roaming it thus – you'll tender me a fool.

OPHELIA My lord, he hath importuned me with love   110
In honourable fashion.

POLONIUS Ay, fashion you may call it. Go to, go to.

OPHELIA And hath given countenance to his speech, my lord,
With almost all the holy vows of heaven.

POLONIUS Ay, springes to catch woodcocks. I do know,   115
When the blood burns, how prodigal the soul
Lends the tongue vows. These blazes daughter,
Giving more light than heat, extinct in both
Even in their promise as it is a-making,
You must not take for fire. From this time   120
Be something scanter of your maiden presence.
Set your entreatments at a higher rate
Than a command to parley. For Lord Hamlet,
Believe so much in him, that he is young
And with a larger tedder may he walk   125
Than may be given you. In few Ophelia,
Do not believe his vows, for they are brokers,
Not of that dye which their investments show,
But mere implorators of unholy suits,
Breathing like sanctified and pious bonds,   130
The better to beguile. This is for all:
I would not in plain terms from this time forth
Have you so slander any moment leisure
As to give words or talk with the Lord Hamlet.
Look to't I charge you. Come your ways.   135

OPHELIA I shall obey, my lord.

Exeunt

Just after midnight. Trumpets and gun salutes are heard. Hamlet condemns the drunkenness of the Danes and reflects that some men have a particular character fault that overwhelms reason and dignity.

1 Danish revelry: a custom best broken?

Hamlet explains that '*A flourish of trumpets and two pieces* [cannons] *goes off*' means that Claudius is celebrating with revelry ('wake'), drinking ('rouse', 'wassail') and wild dances ('swaggering up–spring reels'). As Claudius drinks his draughts of 'Rhenish' (German wine), loud music accompanies his toast ('pledge'). In Scene 2, lines 125–8, Claudius had promised such noisy revelry.

Hamlet deplores this tradition of the Danes, saying more honour results from *not* following the custom ('More honoured in the breach than the observance.'). Write down, giving reasons, the tone in which you think Hamlet speaks lines 8–22. Also give an example of, and discuss, a custom that is practised today that you think would be more honoured in the breach than the observance.

2 Fatal flaw: 'some vicious mole of nature' (in pairs)

In lines 23–36, Hamlet reflects on how a single character flaw ('complexion') can corrupt a person entirely. In some of his plays, Shakespeare shows the destructive effect of such a character defect. Macbeth is destroyed by ambition, Othello by jealousy, Coriolanus by pride. Laurence Olivier began his film of *Hamlet* (see picture on p. 84, and text on p. 274) with these lines as a voice-over, and added: 'This is the tragedy of a man who could not make up his mind'.

Talk together about whether you agree with Hamlet's view that some people are born with a character fault that will overwhelm all their virtues. Give examples. Then discuss what you think about Olivier's beginning his film with these lines.

---

shrewdly sharply
held his wont is accustomed
breach breaking of it
heavy-headed drunken
traduced and taxed of slandered and
 criticised by
clepe call

Soil our addition dirty our good name
pith and marrow . . . attribute
 essence of our reputation
pales boundaries
**o'erleavens / The form of plausive
 manners** unbalances good behaviour

Act 1 Scene 4
The gun platform

Enter HAMLET, HORATIO and MARCELLUS

HAMLET The air bites shrewdly, it is very cold.
HORATIO It is a nipping and an eager air.
HAMLET What hour now?
HORATIO   I think it lacks of twelve.
MARCELLUS No, it is struck.
HORATIO Indeed? I heard it not. It then draws near the season   5
   Wherein the spirit held his wont to walk.
    A flourish of trumpets and two pieces goes off
   What does this mean, my lord?
HAMLET The king doth wake tonight and takes his rouse,
   Keeps wassail, and the swaggering up-spring reels,
   And as he drains his draughts of Rhenish down,   10
   The kettle-drum and trumpet thus bray out
   The triumph of his pledge.
HORATIO   Is it a custom?
HAMLET Ay marry is't,
   But to my mind, though I am native here
   And to the manner born, it is a custom   15
   More honoured in the breach than the observance.
   [This heavy-headed revel east and west
   Makes us traduced and taxed of other nations.
   They clepe us drunkards, and with swinish phrase
   Soil our addition; and indeed it takes   20
   From our achievements, though performed at height,
   The pith and marrow of our attribute.
   So, oft it chances in particular men,
   That for some vicious mole of nature in them,
   As in their birth, wherein they are not guilty,   25
   Since nature cannot choose his origin,
   By their o'ergrowth of some complexion,
   Oft breaking down the pales and forts of reason,
   Or by some habit that too much o'erleavens
   The form of plausive manners – that these men,   30

The Ghost appears, interrupting Hamlet's reflections on human nature. Hamlet addresses it as his dead father, asking why it has returned from the grave. Marcellus urges Hamlet not to follow the Ghost.

1 'The dram of eale . . .' – what does it mean?

Lines 36–8 are obscure and probably incomplete. No one knows what Shakespeare actually wrote. Maybe the original printer made a mistake. The meaning might be that a small quantity ('dram') of 'eale' (some kind of rotting agent?) corrupts the whole of a noble enterprise, bringing discredit ('scandal') on a man, however good.

Imagine you are editing *Hamlet*. You have reached this point at the end of Hamlet's meditation on human nature. Write about how you would edit the three lines (you can change words if you think it sensible; for example, 'eale' might become 'evil').

2 A good spirit? Or an evil goblin? (in pairs)

Hamlet is unsure about what kind of apparition he sees. Is it a good spirit from heaven or an evil goblin from hell, tempting him to eternal damnation? He expresses his uncertainty in vivid antitheses (see p. 266):

'spirit of health' versus 'goblin damned'
'airs from heaven' versus 'blasts from hell'
'wicked' versus 'charitable'.

The problem of knowing whether the Ghost is good or bad will preoccupy Hamlet for much of the play. You will find notes on pages 249–51 to help you understand why he speaks of 'Angels', 'goblin damned', 'heaven' and 'hell' here. Take turns to read lines 39–57 to each other. Emphasise the antitheses, and try different pacings: fast, slow, varying. Experiment with different tones: amazed, questioning, fearful or pleading.

---

stamp imprint
livery costume (inheritance)
fortune's star bad luck
censure opinion, judgement
canonised buried in holy fashion
hearsèd coffined
cerements shrouds, grave-clothes

enurned buried
corse corpse
complete steel armour
glimpses of the moon moonlight
impartment message
removèd ground remote place

Carrying I say the stamp of one defect,
Being nature's livery or fortune's star,
His virtues else be they as pure as grace,
As infinite as man may undergo,
Shall in the general censure take corruption   35
From that particular fault. The dram of eale
Doth all the noble substance of a doubt
To his own scandal.]

Enter GHOST

HORATIO   Look my lord, it comes!
HAMLET Angels and ministers of grace defend us!
Be thou a spirit of health, or goblin damned,   40
Bring with thee airs from heaven or blasts from hell,
Be thy intents wicked or charitable,
Thou com'st in such a questionable shape
That I will speak to thee. I'll call thee Hamlet,
King, father, royal Dane. Oh answer me.   45
Let me not burst in ignorance, but tell
Why thy canonised bones, hearsèd in death,
Have burst their cerements; why the sepulchre,
Wherein we saw thee quietly enurned,
Hath oped his ponderous and marble jaws   50
To cast thee up again. What may this mean,
That thou, dead corse, again in complete steel
Revisits thus the glimpses of the moon,
Making night hideous, and we fools of nature
So horridly to shake our disposition   55
With thoughts beyond the reaches of our souls?
Say, why is this? wherefore? What should we do?
Ghost beckons Hamlet
HORATIO It beckons you to go away with it,
As if it some impartment did desire
To you alone.
MARCELLUS   Look with what courteous action   60
It wafts you to a more removèd ground.
But do not go with it.
HORATIO   No, by no means.

Horatio tries to persuade Hamlet not to follow the Ghost. Hamlet is determined to follow. He threatens Horatio and Marcellus with death if they try to restrain him. He follows the Ghost.

'Go on, I'll follow thee.' A strong tradition has developed of Hamlet following the Ghost using his sword hilt as a cross to defend himself against evil. That gesture, the ambiguous nature of the Ghost, and Marcellus's line 90 ('Something is rotten in the state of Denmark') create a sense of corruption that grows increasingly through the play.

a pin's fee the value of a pin
flood sea
beetles hangs
toys of desperation suicidal thoughts
petty arture drop of blood (little artery)
As hardy as brave as
Nemean lion's nerve terrifying lion's sinews (Hercules strangled the lion

terrorising Nemea because weapons could not hurt it)
waxes increases
Have after let's follow him
Something is rotten in the state of Denmark (see pp. 244 and 265)

HAMLET It will not speak. Then I will follow it.

HORATIO Do not my lord.

HAMLET   Why, what should be the fear?
    I do not set my life at a pin's fee,   65
    And for my soul, what can it do to that,
    Being a thing immortal as itself?
    It waves me forth again. I'll follow it.

HORATIO What if it tempt you toward the flood my lord,
    Or to the dreadful summit of the cliff   70
    That beetles o'er his base into the sea,
    And there assume some other horrible form
    Which might deprive your sovereignty of reason,
    And draw you into madness? Think of it.
    [The very place puts toys of desperation,   75
    Without more motive, into every brain
    That looks so many fathoms to the sea
    And hears it roar beneath.]

HAMLET It wafts me still. Go on, I'll follow thee.

MARCELLUS You shall not go my lord.

HAMLET   Hold off your hands.   80

HORATIO Be ruled, you shall not go.

HAMLET   My fate cries out,
    And makes each petty arture in this body
    As hardy as the Nemean lion's nerve.
    Still am I called. Unhand me gentlemen!
    By heaven I'll make a ghost of him that lets me.   85
    I say away! – Go on, I'll follow thee.
                            Exit Ghost and Hamlet

HORATIO He waxes desperate with imagination.

MARCELLUS Let's follow, 'tis not fit thus to obey him.

HORATIO Have after. To what issue will this come?

MARCELLUS Something is rotten in the state of Denmark.   90

HORATIO Heaven will direct it.

MARCELLUS   Nay let's follow him.
                                    Exeunt

The Ghost says it must shortly return to its suffering but is forbidden to tell mortals of the horrors it endures. Otherwise it would speak of appalling torments. The Ghost commands Hamlet to revenge.

---

1 An agent of the devil? Chill the audience! (in small groups)

The Ghost hints at the terrors of its suffering. It cannot go to heaven because it died before it could confess its sins. So it must suffer dreadfully in purgatory. According to Roman Catholic belief, purgatory is the place where unconfessed sinners experience indescribable remorse as their sins are burnt and purged away before they can see God in heaven (see pp. 249–51). But the Ghost says it is forbidden to tell of its terrifying ordeal ('this eternal blazon must not be').

The majority of Shakespeare's audiences were Protestants, and they would have two reasons for suspecting that the Ghost was an evil agent of the devil: first, because Protestantism had abolished the notion of purgatory; second, because the Protestant Church judged revenge as a sin, for which the revenger's soul was damned.

But the Ghost's words make thrilling theatre. Experiment with readings of lines 9–22 that will make the audience shrink back in their seats. The lines are packed with vivid phrases suggesting horrors and torments. Make the most of them! Add sound effects as you think appropriate.

A hint: search in the library or on the web for pictures by Hieronymus Bosch (1450–1516). He painted haunting images of the tortures of the dead. They will help you imagine what the Ghost endures.

2 'Revenge his foul and most unnatural murder'

Work in pairs to construct a tableau to show how the Ghost and Hamlet appear at line 25. Use whatever space you have available to make it as dramatically striking as possible.

My hour daybreak
render up myself return
bound compelled, ready
term period
harrow cruelly rip

locks hair
porpentine porcupine
eternal blazon telling of what
  happens after death
List listen

Act 1 Scene 5
The walls of Elsinore Castle

Enter GHOST and HAMLET

HAMLET Whither wilt thou lead me? Speak, I'll go no further.
GHOST Mark me.
HAMLET   I will.
GHOST   My hour is almost come
         When I to sulph'rous and tormenting flames
         Must render up myself.
HAMLET   Alas poor ghost!
GHOST Pity me not, but lend thy serious hearing   5
         To what I shall unfold.
HAMLET   Speak, I am bound to hear.
GHOST So art thou to revenge, when thou shalt hear.
HAMLET What?
GHOST I am thy father's spirit,
         Doomed for a certain term to walk the night,   10
         And for the day confined to fast in fires,
         Till the foul crimes done in my days of nature
         Are burnt and purged away. But that I am forbid
         To tell the secrets of my prison house,
         I could a tale unfold whose lightest word   15
         Would harrow up thy soul, freeze thy young blood,
         Make thy two eyes like stars start from their spheres,
         Thy knotted and combinèd locks to part
         And each particular hair to stand an end
         Like quills upon the fretful porpentine.   20
         But this eternal blazon must not be
         To ears of flesh and blood. List, list, oh list!
         If thou didst ever thy dear father love –
HAMLET O God!
GHOST Revenge his foul and most unnatural murder.   25
HAMLET Murder?

Hamlet is eager to take immediate revenge for his father's murder. The Ghost reveals he was killed by Claudius, and expresses disgust that Gertrude now sleeps with his brother.

1 Family matters again

Like Hamlet (in his soliloquy in Scene 2, lines 129–59), the Ghost seems little concerned with affairs of state. His mind is full of family matters. He expresses revulsion at the thought of Gertrude's sexual relationship with Claudius ('that incestuous, that adulterate beast'). He is sickened at the thought of his betrayal by his 'seeming virtuous queen', and speaks bitterly of 'lust' and 'garbage'.

Actors often speculate about the past lives of their characters. Join in the speculation by writing a paragraph on these two questions:

- Had Gertrude been unfaithful while her husband was still alive?
- Had Hamlet earlier suspected that Claudius had killed his father (when he says 'O my prophetic soul! My uncle?')?

Afterwards, write another paragraph reflecting on whether addressing such questions is helpful to your understanding of the play.

2 Portray the vivid images (in small groups)

The opposite page is full of strikingly imaginative images. Here are just two:

Lines 29–31 'I with wings as swift / As meditation or the thoughts of love / May sweep to my revenge.'

Lines 39–40 'The serpent that did sting thy father's life / Now wears his crown.'

Choose one of these images (or another of your choice). Work out a way of portraying it as a mime. Prepare by talking together about each element in the image (e.g. lines 29–31: how can you relate 'wings as swift / As meditation' and 'thoughts of love' to 'revenge'?).

---

as in the best it is   even if done for good reason
meditation   thought, contemplation
apt   ready to act
fat weed   huge banks of weeds

Lethe   a river in Hades, the world of the dead; drinking the river's water caused forgetfulness
forgèd process   false account
lewdness court   lust tempt
sate   greedily satisfy, satiate

GHOST   Murder most foul, as in the best it is,
        But this most foul, strange, and unnatural.
HAMLET Haste me to know't, that I with wings as swift
        As meditation or the thoughts of love   30
        May sweep to my revenge.
GHOST   I find thee apt,
        And duller shouldst thou be than the fat weed
        That rots itself in ease on Lethe wharf,
        Wouldst thou not stir in this. Now Hamlet, hear.
        'Tis given out that, sleeping in my orchard,   35
        A serpent stung me. So the whole ear of Denmark
        Is by a forgèd process of my death
        Rankly abused; but know, thou noble youth,
        The serpent that did sting thy father's life
        Now wears his crown.
HAMLET   O my prophetic soul!   40
        My uncle?
GHOST   Ay, that incestuous, that adulterate beast,
        With witchcraft of his wits, with traitorous gifts –
        O wicked wit and gifts that have the power
        So to seduce – won to his shameful lust   45
        The will of my most seeming virtuous queen.
        O Hamlet, what a falling off was there,
        From me whose love was of that dignity
        That it went hand in hand even with the vow
        I made to her in marriage, and to decline   50
        Upon a wretch whose natural gifts were poor
        To those of mine.
        But virtue as it never will be moved,
        Though lewdness court it in a shape of heaven,
        So lust, though to a radiant angel linked,   55
        Will sate itself in a celestial bed,
        And prey on garbage.
        But soft, methinks I scent the morning air;

The Ghost tells how Claudius murdered him by pouring poison in his ear. He died with no chance to confess his sins. He urges Hamlet to revenge, but without harming Gertrude.

---

1 Act out the Ghost's story (in groups of four)

Take parts as narrator, Hamlet's father, Claudius, Gertrude. The narrator reads lines 59–80, pausing often. The others act what is described.

2 'Oh horrible, oh horrible, most horrible!' (in small groups)

a The Ghost is horrified at having no chance before death to settle his account with God through proper religious ceremony:

'Unhouseled': without sacrament (the bread and wine of Holy Communion)

'disappointed': unprepared for death (by confession and absolution)

'unaneled': unanointed (not blessed by being anointed with holy oil).

Talk together about whether this horror at the lack of preparation for death is widely shared today. If an atheist (someone who doesn't believe in God) said, 'I just can't experience that horror, and so this aspect of the play doesn't grip me', what would you reply?

b In some productions, Hamlet speaks line 80. Discuss what you think are the dramatic gains and losses of that transfer.

3 'This distracted globe' – Head? World? Globe?

In line 97, do you think Hamlet refers to his own 'distracted' head; to the disturbed world; to Shakespeare's Globe Theatre; or to all, some or none of these? Advise the actor what to do as he says 'this distracted globe'.

---

secure unguarded, carefree
cursèd hebenon poison
leperous distilment evil mixture causing leprosy
posset curdle (clotting the blood)
tetter skin disease
lazar-like like leprosy

blossoms full bloom, height
luxury lust
matin morning
gins . . . fire begins to lose its glow
couple include (with heaven and earth: Hamlet suspects the Ghost may be an evil spirit)

Brief let me be. Sleeping within my orchard,
My custom always of the afternoon,   60
Upon my secure hour thy uncle stole,
With juice of cursèd hebenon in a vial,
And in the porches of my ears did pour
The leperous distilment, whose effect
Holds such an enmity with blood of man   65
That swift as quicksilver it courses through
The natural gates and alleys of the body,
And with a sudden vigour it doth posset
And curd, like eager droppings into milk,
The thin and wholesome blood. So did it mine,   70
And a most instant tetter barked about,
Most lazar-like, with vile and loathsome crust,
All my smooth body.
Thus was I, sleeping, by a brother's hand,
Of life, of crown, of queen, at once dispatched;   75
Cut off even in the blossoms of my sin,
Unhouseled, disappointed, unaneled;
No reckoning made, but sent to my account
With all my imperfections on my head –
Oh horrible, oh horrible, most horrible!   80
If thou hast nature in thee bear it not;
Let not the royal bed of Denmark be
A couch for luxury and damnèd incest.
But howsomever thou pursues this act
Taint not thy mind, nor let thy soul contrive   85
Against thy mother aught. Leave her to heaven
And to those thorns that in her bosom lodge
To prick and sting her. Fare thee well at once.
The glow-worm shows the matin to be near,
And gins to pale his uneffectual fire.   90
Adieu, adieu, adieu. Remember me.   *Exit*

HAMLET O all you host of heaven! O earth! what else?
And shall I couple hell? Oh fie! Hold, hold, my heart,
And you my sinews grow not instant old
But bear me stiffly up. Remember thee?   95
Ay thou poor ghost, whiles memory holds a seat
In this distracted globe. Remember thee?

Hamlet determines to remember only the Ghost's commandment to revenge. He writes in his notebook. When Horatio and Marcellus find him, he avoids telling them what he knows.

1 '. . . smiling damnèd villain!'

Shakespeare's imagination was haunted by the image of the smiling villain. He used it to express the theme of deceptive appearances:

'There's daggers in men's smiles' (*Macbeth*)
'I can smile, and murder whiles I smile' (*King Henry VI, Part 3*)
'Some that smile have in their hearts, I fear, millions of mischief' (*Julius Caesar*)
'I did but smile till now' (false Angelo in *Measure for Measure*)
'. . . one may smile, and smile, and be a villain' (line 108 opposite).

Would playing Claudius as a 'smiler' add to or lessen dramatic impact? Write a paragraph giving your views and reasons.

2 Hamlet's 'tables' – his notebook

Hamlet determines to forget book learning and trivial matters (lines 98–104). In some productions he writes down his thoughts about Claudius in his notebook ('table'). In Elizabethan times, this would probably be made up of two tablets of slate or wood.

You may have already written an entry in Hamlet's tables (Activity 2, p. 28). Write what he now enters in them. You might include the partly obliterated proverbs ('saws'), the fresh thought of line 108 and the determination to revenge.

3 'There needs no ghost . . .'

Horatio's lines 125–6 often make the audience laugh. If you were playing Horatio, would you hope for audience laughter? Why? Or why not?

---

fond foolish
saws conventional sayings, platitudes
forms general ideas
all pressures past impressions
baser cruder

word watchword
Illo, ho, ho the falconer's cry to his hawk
arrant absolute, complete

Yea, from the table of my memory
I'll wipe away all trivial fond records,
All saws of books, all forms, all pressures past,　　　　　100
That youth and observation copied there,
And thy commandment all alone shall live
Within the book and volume of my brain,
Unmixcd with baser matter: yes, by heaven!
O most pernicious woman!　　　　　105
O villain, villain, smiling damnèd villain!
My tables – meet it is I set it down
That one may smile, and smile, and be a villain;
At least I'm sure it may be so in Denmark. [*Writing*]
So uncle, there you are. Now to my word:　　　　　110
It is 'Adieu, adieu, remember me.'
I have sworn't.

HORATIO (*Within*) My lord, my lord!
MARCELLUS (*Within*)　　　　　Lord Hamlet!

Enter HORATIO *and* MARCELLUS

HORATIO　　　　　Heavens secure him!
HAMLET So be it.
MARCELLUS Illo, ho, ho, my lord!　　　　　115
HAMLET Hillo, ho, ho, boy! Come bird, come.
MARCELLUS How is't, my noble lord?
HORATIO　　　　　What news my lord?
HAMLET Oh, wonderful!
HORATIO Good my lord, tell it.
HAMLET　　　　　No, you will reveal it.
HORATIO Not I my lord, by heaven.
MARCELLUS　　　　　Nor I my lord.　　　　　120
HAMLET How say you then, would heart of man once think it –
　　　But you'll be secret?
HORATIO　⎫
MARCELLUS　⎰　　　　　Ay, by heaven, my lord.
HAMLET There's ne'er a villain dwelling in all Denmark
　　　But he's an arrant knave.
HORATIO There needs no ghost, my lord, come from the grave,　　　　　125
　　　To tell us this.

Hamlet's replies puzzle Horatio. Hamlet asks the two men to keep secret all they have seen. They promise to do so. He demands they swear an oath of silence on his sword. The Ghost echoes his words.

---

1 '. . . wild and whirling words' (in groups of three)

In performance, Hamlet usually delivers lines 126–32 very quickly indeed, shaking hands vigorously, then making to go off to pray. Horatio expresses puzzlement at the hectic pace and seeming meaninglessness of Hamlet's words.

To gain a sense of the rapid changes in Hamlet's language, take parts as Hamlet, Marcellus and Horatio and read lines 115–52. As you read, move around the room, with Hamlet frequently changing direction. The other two try to keep up with him.

Afterwards, talk together about how the physical movement gives additional meaning to Horatio's claim of 'wild and whirling words'. Also discuss how the activity reveals a good deal about the state of Hamlet's mind.

2 Does only Hamlet hear the Ghost?

In most productions only Hamlet hears the Ghost. But what would be the dramatic effect if Marcellus and Horatio also heard the Ghost's demand 'Swear' (line 149)? Imagine you are directing the play. Write notes for yourself listing the dramatic gains and losses if all three characters hear the Ghost's 'Swear'.

3 Swearing the oath of silence

Imagine the hilt of Hamlet's sword is shaped like a cross. Work out how he would hold it so the other two men could swear their promise of silence upon it. Decide whether you think Horatio and Marcellus are willing or unwilling to swear the oath (see line 147). Suggest what they might be thinking at this moment.

---

circumstance formality
desire pleasure
Saint Patrick (who, in legend,
  released sinners from purgatory)
Touching concerning

O'ermaster't overcome it
truepenny honest fellow
in the cellarage underground
  (beneath the stage)

HAMLET   Why right, you are i'th'right,
And so without more circumstance at all
I hold it fit that we shake hands and part –
You as your business and desire shall point you,
For every man hath business and desire,   130
Such as it is, and for my own poor part,
Look you, I'll go pray.

HORATIO These are but wild and whirling words, my lord.

HAMLET I'm sorry they offend you, heartily,
Yes faith, heartily.

HORATIO   There's no offence my lord.   135

HAMLET Yes by Saint Patrick but there is Horatio,
And much offence too. Touching this vision here,
It is an honest ghost, that let me tell you.
For your desire to know what is between us,
O'ermaster't as you may. And now good friends,   140
As you are friends, scholars, and soldiers,
Give me one poor request.

HORATIO What is't my lord? we will.

HAMLET Never make known what you have seen tonight.

HORATIO
MARCELLUS } My lord we will not.

HAMLET   Nay but swear't.

HORATIO   In faith   145
My lord not I.

MARCELLUS   Nor I my lord in faith.

HAMLET Upon my sword.

MARCELLUS   We have sworn my lord already.

HAMLET Indeed, upon my sword, indeed.

GHOST Swear.   *Ghost cries under the stage*

HAMLET Ha, ha, boy, sayst thou so? art thou there truepenny?   150
Come on, you hear this fellow in the cellarage,
Consent to swear.

HORATIO   Propose the oath my lord.

HAMLET Never to speak of this that you have seen,
Swear by my sword.

GHOST Swear.   155

Hamlet demands that Horatio and Marcellus swear they will not reveal what has happened. They must also promise not to put on a show of knowing the true nature of any future strange behaviour by Hamlet.

1 Stage directions for Hamlet

Hamlet shifts position to swear the oath as the Ghost's voice is again heard from beneath the stage. Often in the theatre this 'swearing' episode results in audience laughter.

Hamlet then orders his friends not to look knowing if they see him behaving oddly (lines 173–9). His instructions contain detailed stage directions about how he could behave as he speaks. There are more stage directions in Hamlet's final speech as he expresses friendship, again orders the two men to keep silent, and ends with 'let's go together'.

Imagine you are about to play Hamlet. Write detailed notes about how you will behave as you speak all the lines opposite. Add reasons justifying that behaviour. Ensure you cover these points:

- Should I attempt to gain audience laughter as I order the others to move around the stage to 'swear'?
- What actions should accompany my instructions in lines 173–9 and 188?
- How might I show friendship in my final line?

2 Famous sayings – still relevant

Lines 166–7 'There are more things in heaven and earth . . .'. Hamlet reminds Horatio that philosophy does not know everything.

Lines 189–90 'The time is out of joint . . .'. Hamlet acknowledges the troubled times. He regrets that it is he who must restore order.

Suggest aspects of society today for which (or persons for whom) each quotation could be appropriately used.

Hic et ubique? Here and everywhere?
worthy pioneer brave miner
meet appropriate
put an antic disposition on pretend
 to be mad
doubtful phrase broad hint

list wished
giving out hinting
aught anything
still always
cursèd spite damned malice, evil
 fortune

HAMLET   *Hic et ubique?* then we'll shift our ground.
    Come hither gentlemen,
    And lay your hands again upon my sword.
    Never to speak of this that you have heard,
    Swear by my sword.   160
GHOST   Swear.
HAMLET   Well said old mole, canst work i'th'earth so fast?
    A worthy pioneer. Once more remove, good friends.
HORATIO   O day and night, but this is wondrous strange.
HAMLET   And therefore as a stranger give it welcome.   165
    There are more things in heaven and earth, Horatio,
    Than are dreamt of in your philosophy.
    But come –
    Here as before, never so help you mercy,
    How strange or odd some'er I bear myself,   170
    As I perchance hereafter shall think meet
    To put an antic disposition on –
    That you at such times seeing me never shall,
    With arms encumbered thus, or this head-shake,
    Or by pronouncing of some doubtful phrase,   175
    As 'Well, well, we know,' or 'We could and if we would,'
    Or 'If we list to speak,' or 'There be and if they might,'
    Or such ambiguous giving out, to note
    That you know aught of me: this not to do,
    So grace and mercy at your most need help you, 180
    Swear.
GHOST   Swear.
HAMLET   Rest, rest, perturbèd spirit. So gentlemen,
    With all my love I do commend me to you,
    And what so poor a man as Hamlet is   185
    May do t'express his love and friending to you,
    God willing shall not lack. Let us go in together,
    And still your fingers on your lips I pray. –
    The time is out of joint: O cursèd spite,
    That ever I was born to set it right. –   190
    Nay come, let's go together.
                 Exeunt

Looking back at Act 1
Activities for groups or individuals

1 'Who's there?' – Does appearance match reality?

The opening line of the play is the first of many anxious questions which establish the tone of uncertainty that runs through the play. It symbolises the search for personal identity, and for the reality that lies behind outward appearance. Write down one example from each of the five scenes where you feel that appearance does not match reality.

2 Disordered society, disturbed individuals

Suggestions of the disordered state of society and of individuals run through Act 1: 'Something is rotten in the state of Denmark' (Scene 4, line 90); 'The time is out of joint' (Scene 5, line 189). Identify one or two moments in each scene which show evidence of disorder. Find a way of representing your findings (perhaps as a set of drawings, in tableaux, or as an extended essay).

3 Political matters – family matters

Hamlet begins as if it will be a play centrally concerned with politics and affairs of state (descriptions of feverish preparations for war; Claudius's dispatch of ambassadors to old Fortinbras). But Hamlet, Laertes, Polonius and the Ghost appear to be obsessed with family matters, particularly the sexuality of Gertrude and Ophelia. Divide a sheet of paper (or a computer screen) into two columns. Head one column 'Political matters'. Head the other 'Family matters'. Work through Act 1, noting in the appropriate column events and quotations relevant to the heading. Which column contains most entries?

4 A sister and daughter gives advice

Ophelia is given much advice by her brother and father. Both men attempt to control her emotions, thoughts and actions. Both are intensely concerned with her sexual behaviour. But what if the roles were reversed? As Ophelia, write eight to sixteen lines of advice to Laertes and to Polonius. Try to include images which are as striking as those used by her brother and father.

5 Horatio's point of view

Horatio has come to Denmark from Wittenberg University. He appears in four of the five scenes in Act 1, and seems to know a great deal about state affairs (Is he a Dane?). Remind yourself quickly of all he says in this act, then write his account of what has happened to him since he returned to Denmark.

Gertrude and Claudius, Royal Shakespeare Company, 1984. Choose a line from Scene 2 that would make an appropriate caption for this picture.

6 'To put an antic disposition on'

Hamlet tells his friends that his future behaviour may appear strange, even mad (Scene 5, lines 171–2). Jot down several reasons why you think Hamlet has decided to act as if he were mad.

7 Court circular

Imagine that a daily court circular is issued recording the activities of the royal family. Write the court circular for one day in Act 1.

Polonius gives Reynaldo money for Laertes in Paris. He orders Reynaldo to spy on Laertes's behaviour using devious, indirect methods. Even lies may be used to discover what Laertes is doing.

Polonius (right) tells Reynaldo that roundabout ways of questioning ('encompassment . . . question') will yield better information than direct approaches ('come you more nearer . . . touch it'). Think about how you would advise Polonius to speak in this scene to suggest his character and his role in the Danish court. Pages 243–4 and 262 may help you.

make inquire ask after
Marry by St Mary
Danskers Danes
means resources
keep live

Take you show, assume
Addicted given to vices
forgeries slanders, lies
wanton carefree, loose behaviour
drabbing whoring, using prostitutes

Act 2 Scene 1
A state room in the castle

Enter POLONIUS and REYNALDO

POLONIUS Give him this money, and these notes, Reynaldo.
REYNALDO I will my lord.
POLONIUS You shall do marvellous wisely, good Reynaldo,
    Before you visit him, to make inquire
    Of his behaviour.
REYNALDO   My lord, I did intend it.   5
POLONIUS Marry well said, very well said. Look you sir,
    Inquire me first what Danskers are in Paris,
    And how, and who, what means, and where they keep,
    What company, at what expense; and finding
    By this encompassment and drift of question   10
    That they do know my son, come you more nearer
    Than your particular demands will touch it.
    Take you as 'twere some distant knowledge of him,
    As thus, 'I know his father and his friends,
    And in part him' – do you mark this Reynaldo?   15
REYNALDO Ay, very well, my lord.
POLONIUS 'And in part him, but' – you may say – 'not well,
    But if't be he I mean, he's very wild,
    Addicted so and so' – and there put on him
    What forgeries you please; marry, none so rank   20
    As may dishonour him, take heed of that,
    But sir, such wanton, wild, and usual slips
    As are companions noted and most known
    To youth and liberty.
REYNALDO   As gaming my lord?
POLONIUS Ay, or drinking, fencing, swearing,   25
    Quarrelling, drabbing – you may go so far.
REYNALDO My lord, that would dishonour him.

Polonius continues to advise Reynaldo to use indirect methods to find out whether Laertes is guilty of improper behaviour in Paris. But Polonius loses the thread of his argument.

1 Reynaldo – the fox? (in pairs)

This is Reynaldo's only appearance in the play. The actor playing him will wish to establish his character, even though he has such a small part. He might be guided by the knowledge that Reynaldo (Reynard) means 'the fox', an animal with a reputation for cunning. Take parts and read lines 1–72 in several ways to discover which works best:

- Reynaldo is an experienced secret agent.
- Reynaldo thinks that Polonius is a rambling old fool.
- Reynaldo is genuinely puzzled about what he's being asked to do, but wishes to be a loyal servant.

2 Losing the drift of his argument

Identify the line where Polonius begins to lose the thread of his argument. Advise the actor on how he should play this 'forgetful' episode to help establish the character of Polonius. For example, should he try to win audience sympathy for an old man's failing memory, or should he aim to get a laugh at Polonius's expense? In performance, the forgetfulness is often played for laughs.

3 Polonius, the spymaster = Lord Burghley?

Many people think that Shakespeare had Lord Burghley, Queen Elizabeth's chief minister, in mind when he created Polonius. There was a popular rumour that Burghley had not only given his son a set of precepts, but had sent spies to keep watch on him (see p. 244). Improvise a scene in Paris where Reynaldo is talking with two people, trying to find out information about Laertes.

---

season it in the charge   modify the accusation
incontinency   rampant sexual misbehaviour
quaintly   cleverly
unreclaimèd blood   untamed passion

Of general assault   that attacks everyone
fetch of warrant   trick that is legitimate
prenominate   already mentioned
o'ertook in's rouse   drunk
Videlicet   that is to say

POLONIUS Faith no, as you may season it in the charge.
       You must not put another scandal on him,
       That he is open to incontinency,   30
       That's not my meaning. But breathe his faults so quaintly
       That they may seem the taints of liberty,
       The flash and outbreak of a fiery mind,
       A savageness in unreclaimèd blood,
       Of general assault.
REYNALDO   But my good lord –   35
POLONIUS Wherefore should you do this?
REYNALDO   Ay my lord,
       I would know that.
POLONIUS   Marry sir, here's my drift,
       And I believe it is a fetch of warrant.
       You laying these slight sullies on my son,
       As 'twere a thing a little soiled i'th'working,   40
       Mark you,
       Your party in converse, him you would sound,
       Having ever seen in the prenominate crimes
       The youth you breathe of guilty, be assured
       He closes with you in this consequence,   45
       'Good sir', or so, or 'friend', or 'gentleman',
       According to the phrase and the addition
       Of man and country.
REYNALDO   Very good my lord.
POLONIUS And then sir does a this – a does – what was I about to say?
    By the mass I was about to say something. Where did I leave?   50
REYNALDO At 'closes in the consequence', at 'friend, or so', and
    'gentleman'.
POLONIUS At 'closes in the consequence' – ay marry,
       He closes with you thus: 'I know the gentleman,
       I saw him yesterday, or th'other day,   55
       Or then, or then, with such or such, and as you say,
       There was a gaming, there o'ertook in's rouse,
       There falling out at tennis', or perchance,
       'I saw him enter such a house of sale' –
       Videlicet, a brothel – or so forth. See you now,   60
       Your bait of falsehood takes this carp of truth,

Polonius dispatches Reynaldo on his spying mission to Paris. Ophelia comes to report that she has been frightened by Hamlet's strange appearance. His clothing was dishevelled and his behaviour odd.

---

1 A father spies on his son (in pairs)

Talk together about what you think of Polonius as a father. Is there any justification for what he orders Reynaldo to do?

2 'Your bait of falsehood takes this carp of truth . . .'

From line 61 to 64, Shakespeare gives Polonius a number of metaphors by which to make his point. Identify each metaphor, write down what each implies, and work out what it suggests about his character. Which is the most important of these metaphors? As a director, would you have the actor playing Polonius speak these lines with gestures, or without?

3 Act Hamlet's 'antic disposition' (in groups of three)

Some films of the play add a scene showing Hamlet's appearance to Ophelia. Lines 75–98 are heard as a voice-over to Hamlet's behaviour. Act out your own version of this 'absent scene'. As one person slowly narrates the lines, the other two mime them.

4 Points of view on Hamlet's madness (in groups of four)

Take parts as Claudius, Gertrude, Polonius and Ophelia. In role, offer your explanation of Hamlet's appearance from your character's point of view. Begin by saying whether you think Hamlet is really mad or just putting on an act. Then go on to say why you think he is behaving as he is. Are there any points on which all four characters agree?

---

of wisdom and of reach   who are wise and perceptive
windlasses   roundabout ways (like hunters circling their prey)
assays of bias   indirect attempts (as, in a game of bowls, a bowl curves towards its target)

ply his music   go his own way
closet   private room
down-gyvèd   fallen (like fetters around his ankles)
in purport   in expression
perusal   study

> And thus do we of wisdom and of reach,
> With windlasses and with assays of bias,
> By indirections find directions out.
> So, by my former lecture and advice,   65
> Shall you my son. You have me, have you not?
REYNALDO My lord, I have.
POLONIUS   God buy ye, fare ye well.
REYNALDO Good my lord.
POLONIUS Observe his inclination in yourself.
REYNALDO I shall my lord.   70
POLONIUS And let him ply his music.
REYNALDO   Well my lord.
POLONIUS Farewell.

Exit Reynaldo

Enter OPHELIA

>   How now Ophelia, what's the matter?
OPHELIA Oh my lord, my lord, I have been so affrighted.
POLONIUS With what, i'th'name of God?
OPHELIA My lord, as I was sewing in my closet,   75
> Lord Hamlet with his doublet all unbraced,
> No hat upon his head, his stockings fouled,
> Ungartered, and down-gyvèd to his ankle,
> Pale as his shirt, his knees knocking each other,
> And with a look so piteous in purport   80
> As if he had been loosèd out of hell
> To speak of horrors – he comes before me.
POLONIUS Mad for thy love?
OPHELIA   My lord I do not know,
> But truly I do fear it.
POLONIUS   What said he?
OPHELIA He took me by the wrist, and held me hard;   85
> Then goes he to the length of all his arm,
> And with his other hand thus o'er his brow
> He falls to such perusal of my face
> As a would draw it. Long stayed he so;

Ophelia says how strangely Hamlet behaved. Polonius guesses that Hamlet has been driven mad by Ophelia's rejection of his love. He decides to tell all to Claudius.

---

1 'I am sorry' (in pairs)

These three words from line 104 could have different meanings. Decide which of the following you prefer, because of your view of Polonius:

- Polonius is genuinely sorry for his daughter
- he feels sorry for Hamlet
- he doesn't care at all about Ophelia's or Hamlet's feelings
- he is worried about his own position as a state official who should know about such matters
- an interpretation of your own.

2 Write one of Hamlet's letters

From what you know of the relationship of Hamlet and Ophelia so far, compose a letter from Hamlet to her, revealing some of the concerns, suspicions and melancholy that he has exhibited, but also including other aspects of their relationship. Be prepared to defend your letter by reference to the script.

3 Safer to tell – a clue to Polonius's character?

Polonius seems to think in lines 115–17 that it is safer to tell his suspicions to Claudius about Hamlet's love, rather than keeping them secret ('close'). Although it might make trouble ('move / More grief'), it is better to tell.

Look back over the scene and pick out as many examples as you can that suggest Polonius is a very cautious man, always weighing up what will bring him advantage.

---

bulk body		**quoted** observed	
ecstasy madness		**trifle** play	
property quality, nature		**wrack** dishonour, seduce	
fordoes destroys		**beshrew** a curse on	
undertakings deeds		**proper to** characteristic of	

At last, a little shaking of mine arm,   90
And thrice his head thus waving up and down,
He raised a sigh so piteous and profound
As it did seem to shatter all his bulk,
And end his being. That done, he lets me go,
And with his head over his shoulder turned   95
He seemed to find his way without his eyes,
For out-a-doors he went without their helps
And to the last bended their light on me.
POLONIUS Come, go with me, I will go seek the king.
This is the very ecstasy of love,   100
Whose violent property fordoes itself,
And leads the will to desperate undertakings
As oft as any passion under heaven
That does afflict our natures. I am sorry.
What, have you given him any hard words of late?   105
OPHELIA No my good lord; but as you did command,
I did repel his letters, and denied
His access to me.
POLONIUS   That hath made him mad.
I am sorry that with better heed and judgement
I had not quoted him. I feared he did but trifle,   110
And meant to wrack thee, but beshrew my jealousy.
By heaven, it is as proper to our age
To cast beyond ourselves in our opinions
As it is common for the younger sort
To lack discretion. Come, go we to the king.   115
This must be known, which being kept close, might move
More grief to hide than hate to utter love.
Come.
                                            Exeunt

Claudius has sent for Hamlet's fellow students. They are to find out the cause of Hamlet's strange behaviour. Gertrude promises Rosencrantz and Guildenstern they will be royally rewarded if they stay.

Rosencrantz and Guildenstern as portrayed in Tom Stoppard's play *Rosencrantz and Guildenstern Are Dead*. Is this how you picture them? Do you think they should look and dress alike? See also page viii (bottom).

1 Both spies – but different characters?

On page 68 is an activity that asks you to consider these characters' similarities. But, as you read on, can you find evidence in the script for their differences?

Moreover that not only	**glean** gather, pick up
Sith nor since neither	**opened** revealed
neighboured to familiar with	**gentry** courtesy
haviour behaviour	**supply and profit** help and benefit
vouchsafe your rest agree to stay	**fits** befits
occasion favourable opportunities	

Act 2 Scene 2
The Great Hall of Elsinore Castle

Trumpet Call Enter KING and QUEEN, ROSENCRANTZ and
     GUILDENSTERN, with others

CLAUDIUS Welcome dear Rosencrantz and Guildenstern!
  Moreover that we much did long to see you,
  The need we have to use you did provoke
  Our hasty sending. Something have you heard
  Of Hamlet's transformation – so call it,   5
  Sith nor th'exterior nor the inward man
  Resembles that it was. What it should be,
  More than his father's death, that thus hath put him
  So much from th'understanding of himself,
  I cannot dream of. I entreat you both,   10
  That being of so young days brought up with him,
  And sith so neighboured to his youth and haviour,
  That you vouchsafe your rest here in our court
  Some little time, so by your companies
  To draw him on to pleasures, and to gather   15
  So much as from occasion you may glean,
  Whether aught to us unknown afflicts him thus,
  That opened lies within our remedy.
GERTRUDE Good gentlemen, he hath much talked of you,
  And sure I am, two men there is not living   20
  To whom he more adheres. If it will please you
  To show us so much gentry and good will
  As to expend your time with us a while,
  For the supply and profit of our hope,
  Your visitation shall receive such thanks   25
  As fits a king's remembrance.
ROSENCRANTZ   Both your majesties
  Might by the sovereign power you have of us
  Put your dread pleasures more into command
  Than to entreaty.

Guildenstern promises that he and Rosencrantz will do whatever Claudius commands. Polonius announces the ambassadors' return. He says he has discovered the cause of Hamlet's madness.

1 Tweedledum and Tweedledee?

Many directors seize on Gertrude's line 34 as an opportunity to make the audience laugh and to make a point about the similarity between Rosencrantz and Guildenstern. These directors advise Gertrude to speak the line in one of two ways:

Either she is unable to distinguish which man is which, and so speaks the line as an uncertain question, unsure whether she is addressing the right person.

Or she corrects a mistake by Claudius, who has misidentified the two courtiers.

How would you advise Gertrude to speak line 34 in order to help members of the audience form their impression of Rosencrantz and Guildenstern? Would you want to get a laugh on the line by having the king or queen (or both) unable to differentiate between the two men?

2 Public and private (in pairs)

Gertrude and Claudius share a brief private moment together in lines 54–8 when Gertrude expresses her unease about how quickly they married after King Hamlet's death. How would you stage the lines to emphasise the difference between their public life (as king and queen) and their domestic life (as mother and stepfather, and wife and husband)? Remember, the rest of the court on stage will be watching their every move, and hoping to overhear what they are saying.

How significant is the distinction between private and public life in *Hamlet*? From what you have read so far, would you say it is an important theme of the play? (See pp. 24, 56.)

---

in the full bent completely (like a fully drawn archery bow)
practices behaviour (or deceits)
still always
trail of policy affairs of state (or deceptions)

fruit final course of a meal
distemper illness
main major matter
sift him question Polonius (or Hamlet?) closely
brother fellow king

GUILDENSTERN   But we both obey,
    And here give up ourselves in the full bent   30
    To lay our service freely at your feet
    To be commanded.
CLAUDIUS Thanks Rosencrantz, and gentle Guildenstern.
GERTRUDE Thanks Guildenstern, and gentle Rosencrantz.
    And I beseech you instantly to visit   35
    My too much changèd son. Go some of you
    And bring these gentlemen where Hamlet is.
GUILDENSTERN Heavens make our presence and our practices
    Pleasant and helpful to him.
GERTRUDE   Ay, amen.
    Exeunt Rosencrantz and Guildenstern [and some Attendants]

Enter POLONIUS

POLONIUS Th'ambassadors from Norway, my good lord,   40
    Are joyfully returned.
CLAUDIUS Thou still hast been the father of good news.
POLONIUS Have I my lord? Assure you, my good liege,
    I hold my duty, as I hold my soul,
    Both to my God and to my gracious king;   45
    And I do think, or else this brain of mine
    Hunts not the trail of policy so sure
    As it hath used to do, that I have found
    The very cause of Hamlet's lunacy.
CLAUDIUS Oh speak of that, that do I long to hear.   50
POLONIUS Give first admittance to th'ambassadors;
    My news shall be the fruit to that great feast.
CLAUDIUS Thyself do grace to them and bring them in.
                                  [Exit Polonius]
    He tells me, my dear Gertrude, he hath found
    The head and source of all your son's distemper.   55
GERTRUDE I doubt it is no other but the main:
    His father's death, and our o'erhasty marriage.
CLAUDIUS Well, we shall sift him.

Enter POLONIUS, VOLTEMAND *and* CORNELIUS

               Welcome my good friends.
    Say Voltemand, what from our brother Norway?

Voltemand reports that the king of Norway has prevented Fortinbras from attacking Denmark, sending him instead to invade Poland. Polonius embarks on a long-winded explanation of Hamlet's madness.

1 Voltemand's report (in small groups)

Much political activity has happened. To help your understanding of Voltemand's report, try one or more of the following activities:

a Point it out! One person slowly reads aloud lines 60–85 (to 'Most welcome home.'). At every mention of a person, everyone in the group points to a group member as that person (allocate parts as you read). It sounds complicated, but you will very quickly pick it up and find it helps you understand who's who. The first 'point' is in line 61, 'our' (Voltemand and Cornelius); the next is on 'he' (king of Norway). Don't worry if you do not have sufficient group members for everyone mentioned. Just point to objects (e.g. a chair or table) to represent characters.

b Act it out! One person reads aloud, pausing at each punctuation mark. The others act out each section of Voltemand's speech.

c Write it out! The king of Norway has sent a formal letter to Claudius. Among other things, it asks for safe passage through Denmark for Fortinbras's army as it marches to invade Poland. Write the document in full.

2 '. . . brevity is the soul of wit' (individually, then in threes)

In the spirit of Polonius's famous phrase, write down three or four statements each that sum up the action of the play so far. Then, in threes, compare notes and order the statements in terms of their wittiness and appropriateness for *Hamlet*. Present your best three statements to the class, deciding further which are the most succinct and witty insights into the play and its characters.

---

desires good wishes
Upon our first when we raised the matter
levies troops
Polack Polish nation
impotence powerlessness

borne in hand deceived
in fine in conclusion
th'assay of arms battle
allowance permission
expostulate discuss, expound
flourishes decorations

VOLTEMAND   Most fair return of greetings and desires.   60
          Upon our first, he sent out to suppress
          His nephew's levies, which to him appeared
          To be a preparation 'gainst the Polack;
          But better looked into, he truly found
          It was against your highness; whereat grieved   65
          That so his sickness, age and impotence
          Was falsely borne in hand, sends out arrests
          On Fortinbras, which he in brief obeys,
          Receives rebuke from Norway, and in fine
          Makes vow before his uncle never more   70
          To give th'assay of arms against your majesty.
          Whereon old Norway, overcome with joy,
          Gives him three thousand crowns in annual fee,
          And his commission to employ those soldiers,
          So levied as before, against the Polack;   75
          With an entreaty, herein further shown,
          That it might please you to give quiet pass
          Through your dominions for this enterprise,
          On such regards of safety and allowance
          As therein are set down.
                        [Gives a document]
CLAUDIUS   It likes us well,   80
          And at our more considered time we'll read,
          Answer, and think upon this business.
          Meantime, we thank you for your well-took labour.
          Go to your rest; at night we'll feast together.
          Most welcome home.
                            Exeunt Ambassadors
POLONIUS   This business is well ended.   85
          My liege, and madam, to expostulate
          What majesty should be, what duty is,
          Why day is day, night night, and time is time,
          Were nothing but to waste night, day, and time.
          Therefore, since brevity is the soul of wit   90
          And tediousness the limbs and outward flourishes,
          I will be brief. Your noble son is mad.

Polonius rambles on, even though Gertrude urges him to come to the point. He reads aloud Hamlet's letter to Ophelia, and says his daughter has told him all about Hamlet's attempts to woo her.

---

1 Focus on Polonius (in pairs)

a 'More matter with less art'   Ironically, Polonius forgets his own comment that 'brevity is the soul of wit'. In spite of Gertrude's impatience, he continues to play pompously with language. Find a way of speaking lines 85–108 that you think matches his character. For example, try speaking pompously, or poetically, or with embarrassment.

b '*Et cetera*'   No one can be quite sure why Polonius says '*et cetera*' (line 112). Is it to cover up some very personal words of love that are embarrassing for a father to read? Or is it just to summarise some formal phrases in Hamlet's letter (such as 'warm greetings')? Talk together about why you think Polonius says '*et cetera*'. Then write the missing words that Polonius has declined to read.

c Tell me everything   Polonius says Ophelia has told him of all her encounters with Hamlet. But how did he get the story out of her? Did she offer it willingly? Or did he bully or wheedle it out? Improvise a meeting between father and daughter where he learns all about Hamlet's 'solicitings . . . by time, by means, and place'.

d Is it good poetry?   Hamlet clearly doesn't think much of himself as a poet ('I am ill at these numbers'). Critics are divided about the poetic quality of his four lines of verse in the letter (lines 115–18). Continue his four lines in two ways: first, in the style of the verses written in the letter; then, in a parody of them. Do you think Hamlet is right about his own writing?

More matter with less art   more information and less playing with language
figure   figure of speech
Perpend   consider carefully
gather and surmise   draw your own conclusions

numbers   verses
whilst this machine is to him   as long as I live ('machine' = body)
solicitings   pleadings, importunings

	Mad call I it, for to define true madness,
	What is't but to be nothing else but mad?
	But let that go.
GERTRUDE	More matter with less art.	95
POLONIUS	Madam, I swear I use no art at all.

POLONIUS Madam, I swear I use no art at all.
　　　　That he is mad, 'tis true; 'tis true 'tis pity,
　　　　And pity 'tis 'tis true – a foolish figure,
　　　　But farewell it, for I will use no art.
　　　　Mad let us grant him then, and now remains　　100
　　　　That we find out the cause of this effect,
　　　　Or rather say, the cause of this defect,
　　　　For this effect defective comes by cause.
　　　　Thus it remains, and the remainder thus.
　　　　Perpend.　　105
　　　　I have a daughter – have while she is mine –
　　　　Who in her duty and obedience, mark,
　　　　Hath given me this. Now gather and surmise.

　　　　　　　　Reads the letter

'To the celestial, and my soul's idol, the most beautified Ophelia,' –
That's an ill phrase, a vile phrase, 'beautified' is a vile phrase – but　　110
you shall hear. Thus:
'In her excellent white bosom, these, *et cetera.*'
GERTRUDE Came this from Hamlet to her?
POLONIUS Good madam stay awhile, I will be faithful.
　　　　'Doubt thou the stars are fire,　　115
　　　　Doubt that the sun doth move,
　　　　Doubt truth to be a liar,
　　　　But never doubt I love.
'O dear Ophelia, I am ill at these numbers, I have not art to reckon
my groans; but that I love thee best, O most best, believe it. Adieu.　　120
　　　　　'Thine evermore, most dear lady, whilst this machine is
　　　　　　　to him, Hamlet.'
　　　　This in obedience hath my daughter shown me,
　　　　And, more above, hath his solicitings,
　　　　As they fell out, by time, by means, and place,　　125
　　　　All given to mine ear.
CLAUDIUS　　　　　　　　But how hath she
　　　　Received his love?
POLONIUS　　　　　　　　What do you think of me?
CLAUDIUS As of a man faithful and honourable.

Polonius reports that he ordered Ophelia to reject Hamlet's love, so causing the prince's madness. Polonius suggests a plan: he and Claudius will spy on an arranged meeting between Ophelia and Hamlet.

---

1 'Lord Hamlet is a prince out of thy star . . .'

Whereas Romeo and Juliet came from families of equal social status in Verona, Hamlet and Ophelia are from different social levels in Danish society. To what extent do you think this is an issue for you in today's society, and to what extent might it have been an issue for Hamlet, Ophelia and their families?

2 Show what happened (in small groups)

In lines 141–9, Polonius describes at least eleven distinct actions. One person slowly narrates the lines, the others act out each event.

3 'Not that I know' – Trust? Suspicion? (in pairs)

In what tone of voice does Claudius speak line 153? Talk together about what the line suggests about Claudius's attitude to Polonius.

4 'Take this from this' (in pairs)

Shakespeare often builds stage directions into his language. But just what does Polonius do at line 154? Does he touch his head and shoulder ('chop off my head')? Or does he touch his official staff of office and his hand ('dismiss me')? Work out an appropriate action to accompany the line.

5 'I'll loose my daughter to him'

'Loose' sounds like releasing a farmyard animal. Write down what line 160 suggests to you about Polonius's view of Ophelia. Consider also how he refers to her in line 138. As you read on, collect further images of entrapment and release in the play.

---

fain gladly
given my heart a winking shut my eyes to the love-affair
round directly
out of thy star far above you socially
prescripts orders

watch sleeplessness
lightness delirium, light-headedness
declension decline
arras hanging tapestry (like a curtain covering a wall)

POLONIUS I would fain prove so. But what might you think,
      When I had seen this hot love on the wing – 130
      As I perceived it, I must tell you that,
      Before my daughter told me – what might you,
      Or my dear majesty your queen here, think,
      If I had played the desk, or table-book,
      Or given my heart a winking, mute and dumb, 135
      Or looked upon this love with idle sight –
      What might you think? No, I went round to work,
      And my young mistress thus I did bespeak:
      'Lord Hamlet is a prince out of thy star.
      This must not be.' And then I prescripts gave her, 140
      That she should lock herself from his resort,
      Admit no messengers, receive no tokens.
      Which done, she took the fruits of my advice,
      And he, repulsed – a short tale to make –
      Fell into a sadness, then into a fast, 145
      Thence to a watch, thence into a weakness,
      Thence to a lightness, and by this declension
      Into the madness wherein now he raves,
      And all we mourn for.
CLAUDIUS   Do you think 'tis this?
GERTRUDE It may be, very like. 150
POLONIUS Hath there been such a time, I'ld fain know that,
      That I have positively said, 'tis so,
      When it proved otherwise?
CLAUDIUS   Not that I know.
POLONIUS Take this from this, if this be otherwise.
      If circumstances lead me, I will find 155
      Where truth is hid, though it were hid indeed
      Within the centre.
CLAUDIUS   How may we try it further?
POLONIUS You know sometimes he walks four hours together
      Here in the lobby.
GERTRUDE   So he does indeed.
POLONIUS At such a time I'll loose my daughter to him. 160
      Be you and I behind an arras then.

Claudius agrees to Polonius's plan to spy on Hamlet. Polonius tries to make sense of Hamlet's puzzling replies and questions.

---

1 '*Enter* HAMLET *reading on a book*'

Each new production of the play takes decisions on the following questions. Write a paragraph in response to each, explaining the dramatic effect of your decisions:

a Does Hamlet see Polonius plotting with Claudius?

b How is Hamlet dressed, and how does he behave? (This is his first appearance since he was reported mad.)

c Is Hamlet aware of others on stage before Polonius greets him?

d Why, and to whom, does Polonius say 'Oh give me leave' (line 168)? To Claudius? Gertrude? The Attendants? Hamlet?

2 Cross-talk comics? (in pairs)

Some critics argue that Hamlet treats Polonius as a 'straight man' in a cross-talk comedy team. Take parts and read lines 169–212 in a variety of ways to discover if Hamlet and Polonius really do sound like a pair of comedians.

3 '. . . y'are a fishmonger'

A 'fishmonger' (line 172) could be a prostitute's pimp, a fisher for information, a person whose daughters would be both beautiful and prolific breeders of children, a bit of nonsense by Hamlet, or something Hamlet reads out of the book he is holding. Which suggestion do you prefer? Why?

---

thereon   because of his disappointment in love
assistant for a state   important civil servant
board him presently   greet him immediately
God-a-mercy   thank you ('God have mercy on you', a conventional reply to a social inferior)

carrion   dead flesh (see p. 244)
Conception   becoming pregnant
harping on   talking only of (like a harpist playing one string only)
a   he

Mark the encounter: if he love her not,
And be not from his reason fallen thereon,
Let me be no assistant for a state,
But keep a farm and carters.
CLAUDIUS   We will try it.   165

Enter HAMLET *reading on a book*

GERTRUDE But look where sadly the poor wretch comes reading.
POLONIUS Away, I do beseech you both, away.
          I'll board him presently.
                              Exeunt Claudius and Gertrude [and Attendants]
                              Oh give me leave.
          How does my good Lord Hamlet?
HAMLET Well, God-a-mercy.   170
POLONIUS Do you know me, my lord?
HAMLET Excellent well, y'are a fishmonger.
POLONIUS Not I my lord.
HAMLET Then I would you were so honest a man.
POLONIUS Honest my lord?   175
HAMLET Ay sir. To be honest, as this world goes, is to be one man
          picked out of ten thousand.
POLONIUS That's very true my lord.
HAMLET For if the sun breed maggots in a dead dog, being a good
          kissing carrion   Have you a daughter?   180
POLONIUS I have my lord.
HAMLET Let her not walk i'th'sun. Conception is a blessing, but as your
          daughter may conceive – Friend, look to't.
POLONIUS (*Aside*) How say you by that? Still harping on my daughter.
          Yet he knew me not at first, a said I was a fishmonger – a is far   185
          gone, far gone. And truly, in my youth I suffered much extremity
          for love, very near this. I'll speak to him again. – What do you read
          my lord?
HAMLET Words, words, words.
POLONIUS What is the matter, my lord?   190
HAMLET Between who?
POLONIUS I mean the matter that you read, my lord.

Hamlet insults Polonius who none the less persists in finding good sense in Hamlet's words. Polonius leaves, and Hamlet welcomes Rosencrantz and Guildenstern, exchanging sexual puns with them.

1 'The satirical rogue'

To ridicule Polonius, Hamlet quotes the author of the book he is reading. Two well-known writers mocked the handicaps of old age. Juvenal was a Roman satirist of the first century AD who ridiculed folly. Erasmus (1466–1536) was a Dutch Christian humanist who wrote *In Praise of Folly*.

Research either Juvenal or Erasmus. Report on whether you think their writings would appeal to Hamlet, and why.

2 Polonius writes his report (in pairs)

As the senior officer of state in Denmark, Polonius would write or dictate a report of all his encounters with royalty. Write his report (based on lines 170–211) in which he attempts to discover 'method' (logic) in Hamlet's madness.

3 Young men joking together

Hamlet greets Rosencrantz and Guildenstern warmly. He joins in the kind of wordplay and sexual innuendo that was probably typical of most male students. Fortune is turned into a female prostitute. So 'her privates we' might mean her genitals (private parts), but it could simply mean 'we are intimate with Fortune'. Similarly, 'favours' and 'secret parts' could also be *double entendres*, though their surface meanings are 'help' and 'private affairs' respectively. Shakespeare often indulges in such wordplay for fun (see *Shakespeare's Bawdy* by Eric Partridge). What are the dramatic purposes of its inclusion here, do you think?

Slanders defamatory and false reports
purging discharging, exuding
hams thighs
pregnant meaningful, apt

suddenly immediately
withal with
indifferent ordinary
button topmost
strumpet prostitute

HAMLET Slanders sir, for the satirical rogue says here that old men have grey beards, that their faces are wrinkled, their eyes purging thick amber and plumtree gum, and that they have a plentiful lack of wit, together with most weak hams. All which sir, though I most powerfully and potently believe, yet I hold it not honesty to have it thus set down. For yourself sir shall grow old as I am, if like a crab you could go backward. 195

POLONIUS (*Aside*) Though this be madness, yet there is method in't. – Will you walk out of the air, my lord? 200

HAMLET Into my grave?

POLONIUS Indeed that's out of the air. (*Aside*) How pregnant sometimes his replies are! a happiness that often madness hits on, which reason and sanity could not so prosperously be delivered of. I will leave him, and suddenly contrive the means of meeting between him and my daughter. – My honourable lord, I will most humbly take my leave of you. 205

HAMLET You cannot sir take from me anything that I will more willingly part withal; except my life, except my life, except my life. 210

POLONIUS Fare you well my lord.

HAMLET These tedious old fools!

Enter GUILDENSTERN *and* ROSENCRANTZ

POLONIUS You go to seek the Lord Hamlet, there he is.

ROSENCRANTZ God save you sir.

[*Exit Polonius*]

GUILDENSTERN My honoured lord! 215

ROSENCRANTZ My most dear lord!

HAMLET My excellent good friends! How dost thou Guildenstern? Ah, Rosencrantz. Good lads, how do you both?

ROSENCRANTZ As the indifferent children of the earth.

GUILDENSTERN Happy in that we are not over-happy; on Fortune's cap we are not the very button. 220

HAMLET Nor the soles of her shoe?

ROSENCRANTZ Neither, my lord.

HAMLET Then you live about her waist, or in the middle of her favours?

GUILDENSTERN Faith, her privates we. 225

HAMLET In the secret parts of Fortune? Oh most true, she is a strumpet. What news?

Hamlet, Rosencrantz and Guildenstern continue their banter, but Hamlet becomes more serious. He challenges the courtiers about why they have come to Elsinore. Have they come freely or been sent for?

1 'Denmark's a prison'

Do you think Hamlet is joking or serious in claiming 'Denmark's a prison'? Identify three possible reasons why Hamlet makes his remark.

2 True or false? (in small groups)

Hamlet says 'for there is nothing either good / or bad but thinking makes it so' (lines 239–40). Do you believe that? Talk together about whether you agree with Hamlet's claim. Use practical examples from your own experience.

3 Verbal fencing (in groups of three)

On three or four occasions in lines 241–9, Rosencrantz and Guildenstern try to encourage Hamlet to talk about 'ambition'. Presumably they are following Claudius's instructions to discover what afflicts Hamlet. If they can get him to talk about his ambition, they will have something of real importance to report to the king. But Hamlet pushes their reasoning to an absurd conclusion. He says that if ambitions are shadows, then beggars (who have no ambitions) are more substantial ('bodies') than kings (who are filled with ambition).

The conversation between Hamlet and the courtiers might just be another example of the quick-fire wordplay that students at Wittenberg indulged in. Take parts and experiment with ways of speaking the lines. Bring out how Rosencrantz and Guildenstern are trying to get Hamlet to reveal his secret thoughts (e.g. they might stress 'ambition'). Show how Hamlet warily fends them off. Have the image of a sword-fencing match in your mind as you speak.

---

doomsday the Day of Judgement
Fortune goddess of chance
confines, wards cells in a prison
bodies people without ambition
outstretched heroes great men, or ambitious actors

fay faith
sort associate
am most / dreadfully attended have useless servants
in the beaten way of friendship as old friends

ROSENCRANTZ None my lord, but that the world's grown honest.

HAMLET Then is doomsday near – but your news is not true. Let me
question more in particular. What have you, my good friends,   230
deserved at the hands of Fortune, that she sends you to prison
hither?

GUILDENSTERN Prison, my lord?

HAMLET Denmark's a prison.

ROSENCRANTZ Then is the world one.   235

HAMLET A goodly one, in which there are many confines, wards, and
dungeons; Denmark being one o'th'worst.

ROSENCRANTZ We think not so my lord.

HAMLET Why then 'tis none to you, for there is nothing either good
or bad but thinking makes it so. To me it is a prison.   240

ROSENCRANTZ Why then your ambition makes it one; 'tis too narrow
for your mind.

HAMLET O God, I could be bounded in a nutshell, and count myself
a king of infinite space, were it not that I have bad dreams.

GUILDENSTERN Which dreams indeed are ambition, for the very   245
substance of the ambitious is merely the shadow of a dream.

HAMLET A dream itself is but a shadow.

ROSENCRANTZ Truly, and I hold ambition of so airy and light a quality
that it is but a shadow's shadow.

HAMLET Then are our beggars bodies, and our monarchs and out-   250
stretched heroes the beggars' shadows. Shall we to th'court? for by
my fay I cannot reason.

BOTH We'll wait upon you.

HAMLET No such matter. I will not sort you with the rest of my
servants; for to speak to you like an honest man, I am most   255
dreadfully attended. But in the beaten way of friendship, what make
you at Elsinore?

ROSENCRANTZ To visit you my lord, no other occasion.

HAMLET Beggar that I am, I am even poor in thanks, but I thank
you – and sure, dear friends, my thanks are too dear a halfpenny.   260
Were you not sent for? Is it your own inclining? Is it a free
visitation? Come, deal justly with me. Come, come. Nay, speak.

GUILDENSTERN What should we say my lord?

HAMLET Why, anything but to the purpose. You were sent for – and
there is a kind of confession in your looks which your modesties   265
have not craft enough to colour. I know the good king and queen
have sent for you.

Guildenstern admits that he and Rosencrantz were sent for by Claudius. Hamlet reflects on his melancholy and on the contrasting splendour of man and the heavens. Rosencrantz says the players are about to arrive.

1 From friendship to suspicion (in groups of three)

Hamlet becomes increasingly suspicious of his two friends. Why have they come to Denmark? He decides to 'conjure' (seriously ask) them to tell, appealing to their 'consonancy' (youthful friendship). Take parts and read lines 215–77. Identify where you feel Hamlet's suspicions begin, and explain the reasons for your choices of line(s).

2 Hamlet's melancholy (individually or in pairs)

In lines 280–90, Hamlet reflects that he has 'lost all my mirth'. He speaks of the wonderful nature both of the world and of humankind, but says that nothing now gives him pleasure. Earth seems 'a sterile / promontory'; the heavens 'a foul and pestilent / congregation of vapours'; and humankind, though the 'paragon' (ideal of excellence) of animals, is merely 'dust', offering him no delight. It is possible that Shakespeare is referring ironically to the Globe Theatre: 'majestical roof' = the painted canopy over the stage; 'foul and pestilent . . . vapours' = the audience (see p. 272).

Every actor who plays Hamlet spends many hours deciding how to speak the lines. Is Hamlet's tone sincere, ironical, sarcastic, bitter, awe-struck – or does the mood vary from line to line? There is no single 'right' way to deliver these lines, so explore ways of speaking, then write notes on the version you would recommend.

3 Identify the players

Hamlet lists some members of the acting company: the king, the knight, the lover, the humorous man (not a comic, but a man driven by his 'humour' or moods), and the clown. Identify which of these characters might be shown in the picture on page 84.

---

what more dear what greater reasons
a better proposer a more skilful
  speaker
moult no feather remain intact
express well made
apprehension understanding

lenten frugal, thin
coted overtook
foil and target sword and shield
gratis without reward
tickle o'th'sere easily tickled to
  laughter (sere = gun trigger)

ROSENCRANTZ To what end my lord?

HAMLET That you must teach me. But let me conjure you, by the rights
of our fellowship, by the consonancy of our youth, by the obligation   270
of our ever-preserved love, and by what more dear a better proposer
can charge you withal, be even and direct with me, whether you
were sent for or no.

ROSENCRANTZ (*To Guildenstern*) What say you?

HAMLET (*Aside*) Nay then I have an eye of you. – If you love me, hold   275
not off.

GUILDENSTERN My lord, we were sent for.

HAMLET I will tell you why. So shall my anticipation prevent your
discovery, and your secrecy to the king and queen moult no feather.
I have of late, but wherefore I know not, lost all my mirth, forgone   280
all custom of exercises; and indeed it goes so heavily with my
disposition that this goodly frame, the earth, seems to me a sterile
promontory; this most excellent canopy the air, look you, this brave
o'erhanging firmament, this majestical roof fretted with golden
fire – why, it appeareth no other thing to me but a foul and pestilent   285
congregation of vapours. What a piece of work is a man! How noble
in reason, how infinite in faculties, in form and moving how express
and admirable, in action how like an angel, in apprehension how
like a god! The beauty of the world, the paragon of animals – and
yet to me, what is this quintessence of dust? Man delights not   290
me – no, nor woman neither, though by your smiling you seem to
say so.

ROSENCRANTZ My lord, there was no such stuff in my thoughts.

HAMLET Why did ye laugh then, when I said man delights not me?

ROSENCRANTZ To think, my lord, if you delight not in man, what   295
lenten entertainment the players shall receive from you. We coted
them on the way, and hither are they coming to offer you service.

HAMLET He that plays the king shall be welcome, his majesty shall have
tribute of me; the adventurous knight shall use his foil and target,
the lover shall not sigh gratis, the humorous man shall end his part   300
in peace, the clown shall make those laugh whose lungs are tickle
o'th'sere, and the lady shall say her mind freely – or the blank verse
shall halt for't. What players are they?

ROSENCRANTZ Even those you were wont to take such delight in, the
tragedians of the city.   305

HAMLET How chances it they travel? their residence, both in reputation
and profit, was better both ways.

Hamlet asks many questions about the travelling actors. Rosencrantz explains that the popularity of a company of child actors has forced the players to travel. Hamlet reflects on the fickleness of fashion.

The arrival of the players. Their 'inhibition' (ban on acting in their own theatre) has been caused by 'the late innovation' (recent political changes, see pp. 243–4). The players' reputation ('estimation') has declined because of 'an eyrie of children, little eyases, that cry out on the / top of question' (a nest of child actors, as noisy as unfledged hawks). The lines refer to the 'war of the theatres' in 1600, when the success of a company of boy actors threatened the adult acting companies in London. The boys specialised in bitter satire. Some noblemen were afraid to visit the theatre for fear of mockery ('many wearing rapiers are afraid of goose-quills').

wonted pace   usual standard
escoted   financed
quality   profession (of acting)
no longer than they can sing   until their voices break
tar   provoke
went to cuffs   fought
Hercules and his load   Hercules with the heavens on his back (the emblem of the Globe Theatre)

make mouths   sneer
ducats   gold coins
picture in little   miniature picture
Th'appurtenance of   what is appropriate to
comply with you   show you a proper welcome

ROSENCRANTZ I think their inhibition comes by the means of the late innovation.

HAMLET Do they hold the same estimation they did when I was in the city? Are they so followed? 310

ROSENCRANTZ No indeed are they not.

HAMLET How comes it? Do they grow rusty?

ROSENCRANTZ Nay, their endeavour keeps in the wonted pace, but there is sir an eyrie of children, little eyases, that cry out on the 315 top of question and are most tyrannically clapped for't. These are now the fashion, and so be-rattle the common stages (so they call them) that many wearing rapiers are afraid of goose-quills, and dare scarce come thither.

HAMLET What, are they children? Who maintains 'em? How are they 320 escoted? Will they pursue the quality no longer than they can sing? Will they not say afterwards, if they should grow themselves to common players – as it is most like if their means are no better, their writers do them wrong to make them exclaim against their own succession? 325

ROSENCRANTZ Faith, there has been much to do on both sides, and the nation holds it no sin to tar them to controversy. There was for a while no money bid for argument unless the poet and the player went to cuffs in the question.

HAMLET Is't possible? 330

GUILDENSTERN Oh there has been much throwing about of brains.

HAMLET Do the boys carry it away?

ROSENCRANTZ Ay that they do my lord, Hercules and his load too.

HAMLET It is not very strange, for my uncle is king of Denmark, and those that would make mouths at him while my father lived give 335 twenty, forty, fifty, a hundred ducats apiece for his picture in little. 'Sblood, there is something in this more than natural, if philosophy could find it out.

A flourish

GUILDENSTERN There are the players.

HAMLET Gentlemen, you are welcome to Elsinore. Your hands, come 340 then. Th'appurtenance of welcome is fashion and ceremony. Let me comply with you in this garb, lest my extent to the players, which I tell you must show fairly outwards, should more appear like entertainment than yours. You are welcome – but my uncle-father and aunt-mother are deceived. 345

Polonius enters to tell Hamlet of the players' arrival. Hamlet mocks him. Polonius praises the actors in high-flown language. Hamlet taunts Polonius about his daughter.

---

1 Appearance versus reality – and hawks and handsaws

The talk about the players (lines 295–345) may seem to have little to do with the concerns of the play. But it is important because acting reflects Hamlet's preoccupation with the theme of appearance versus reality (and Hamlet will shortly devise a scheme using the players to expose Claudius's guilt). Hamlet uses the change in acting fashions to make a barbed comment on Denmark: courtiers now buy Claudius's picture (lines 334–6).

He ends with an enigmatic comment: 'I know a hawk from a handsaw' (line 348). A 'hawk' might be a bird of prey, or a plasterer's board for mortar. A 'handsaw' could be a 'hernshaw' (heron), or a carpenter's saw. Hamlet might be saying, 'I know the difference between one thing and another – I'm not mad.' Or he may merely be talking nonsense to bewilder Rosencrantz and Guildenstern.

Suggest what you think Hamlet's words might mean. For example, 'I can recognise a bird of prey [Guildenstern?] when I see one.' Trying out hand gestures to accompany the lines might help you explore the possible meanings.

2 '. . . tragical-comical-historical-pastoral' (in small groups)

In lines 363–5, Shakespeare may be satirising Elizabethan scholars' classification of plays. Polonius shows off his theatrical knowledge in a way that invites audience laughter at the absurdity of his long-winded list. To explore the comic potential, one person speaks the words slowly while the others mime, in fast motion, each category he mentions ('pastoral' is a play with a country theme). You'll find 'tragical-comical-historical-pastoral' quite a challenge!

---

swaddling clouts   baby clothes
scene individable, **law of writ**   rules of drama
Seneca, **Plautus**   tragic/comic Roman dramatists
Jephtha   a military leader and judge who sacrificed his daughter to God

One fair daughter . . .   Hamlet quotes from a song of the time
wot   knows
row   verse
pious chanson   religious song
abridgement   entertainment, or interruption

GUILDENSTERN In what my dear lord?

HAMLET I am but mad north-north-west. When the wind is southerly, I know a hawk from a handsaw.

Enter POLONIUS

POLONIUS Well be with you gentlemen.

HAMLET Hark you Guildenstern, and you too – at each ear a hearer. 350
That great baby you see there is not yet out of his swaddling clouts.

ROSENCRANTZ Happily he's the second time come to them, for they say an old man is twice a child.

HAMLET I will prophesy: he comes to tell me of the players, mark
it. – You say right sir, a Monday morning, 'twas then indeed. 355

POLONIUS My lord, I have news to tell you.

HAMLET My lord, I have news to tell you. When Roscius was an actor in Rome –

POLONIUS The actors are come hither my lord.

HAMLET Buzz, buzz! 360

POLONIUS Upon my honour.

HAMLET Then came each actor on his ass –

POLONIUS The best actors in the world, either for tragedy, comedy,
history, pastoral, pastoral-comical, historical-pastoral, tragical-
historical, tragical-comical-historical-pastoral, scene individable or 365
poem unlimited. Seneca cannot be too heavy, nor Plautus too light.
For the law of writ and the liberty, these are the only men.

HAMLET O Jephtha judge of Israel, what a treasure hadst thou!

POLONIUS What a treasure had he my lord?

HAMLET Why – 370
  'One fair daughter and no more,
  The which he lovèd passing well.'

POLONIUS Still on my daughter.

HAMLET Am I not i'th'right, old Jephtha?

POLONIUS If you call me Jephtha my lord, I have a daughter that I 375
love passing well.

HAMLET Nay, that follows not.

POLONIUS What follows then my lord?

HAMLET Why –
  'As by lot God wot,' 380
And then you know –
  'It came to pass, as most like it was,' –
the first row of the pious chanson will show you more, for look where
my abridgement comes.

Hamlet welcomes the players, some of whom he recognises. He asks the
principal actor to declaim a speech about Pyrrhus. Hamlet begins with the
speech which tells how Pyrrhus entered Troy in the wooden horse.

1 A soliloquy – or a debate

Either make a list giving as many reasons as you can for Hamlet's
enthusiasm for the arrival of the players. Work this list into a soliloquy
or an Aside in which Hamlet reveals his inner thoughts on the arrival
of the players. It is at about this time that his plans for revenge on
Claudius begin to hatch. Where exactly in this scene would you insert
the soliloquy/Aside?

Or Hamlet says (line 397) that the play he is thinking of was 'caviary
to the general', caviare (expensive food) to ordinary people (that is,
too good for them). Some people today have the same view of Shakespeare's plays. They think that they are wasted on 'ordinary' people,
and can be properly appreciated only by an élite, a small minority.
What do you think? Is the play *Hamlet* 'caviary to the general' –
beyond the reach of all but a select few? Organise a class debate on
the question.

2 The story of Pyrrhus

Pyrrhus, like Hamlet, was a son who vowed to avenge his dead father.
Lines 404–6 refer to Virgil's *Aeneid*, in which Aeneas tells Queen
Dido the story of Pyrrhus, whose father Achilles was killed at the
siege of Troy. Pyrrhus was one of the Greek warriors in the wooden
horse ('the ominous horse') which was used to defeat the Trojans.
Hamlet begins the tale of how the 'rugged' (long-haired) Pyrrhus,
like a savage tiger ('th'Hyrcanian beast'), clad in black armour ('sable
arms'), but covered in blood ('total gules', 'o'er-sizèd with coagulate
gore'), sought out Priam, king of Troy, to kill him in revenge for his
own father. See Activity 1 on page 90.

---

valanced bearded
beard challenge
byrlady by Our Lady (the Virgin Mary)
chopine high-heeled shoe
uncurrent gold valueless cracked
coins
fly . . . see have a go at anything

sallets salads
indict prove guilty
tricked decorated (a heraldic term,
like 'sable', 'arms', 'gules')
impasted made into paste
carbuncles fire-red precious stones

Enter the PLAYERS

Y'are welcome masters, welcome all. I am glad to see thee well. 385
Welcome good friends. Oh, my old friend! why, thy face is valanced
since I saw thee last; com'st thou to beard me in Denmark? What,
my young lady and mistress – byrlady, your ladyship is nearer to
heaven than when I saw you last by the altitude of a chopine. Pray
God your voice like a piece of uncurrent gold be not cracked within 390
the ring. Masters, you are all welcome. We'll e'en to't like French
falconers, fly at anything we see: we'll have a speech straight. Come
give us a taste of your quality: come, a passionate speech.

I PLAYER What speech, my good lord?

HAMLET I heard thee speak me a speech once, but it was never acted, 395
or if it was, not above once, for the play I remember pleased not
the million: 'twas caviary to the general. But it was, as I received
it, and others whose judgements in such matters cried in the top
of mine, an excellent play, well digested in the scenes, set down with
as much modesty as cunning. I remember one said there were no 400
sallets in the lines to make the matter savoury, nor no matter in
the phrase that might indict the author of affectation, but called it
an honest method, as wholesome as sweet and by very much more
handsome than fine. One speech in't I chiefly loved, 'twas Aeneas'
tale to Dido, and thereabout of it especially where he speaks of 405
Priam's slaughter. If it live in your memory, begin at this line, let
me see, let me see –
       'The rugged Pyrrhus, like th'Hyrcanian beast' –
'Tis not so, it begins with Pyrrhus –
       'The rugged Pyrrhus, he whose sable arms, 410
       Black as his purpose, did the night resemble
       When he lay couchèd in the ominous horse,
       Hath now this dread and black complexion smeared
       With heraldy more dismal. Head to foot
       Now is he total gules, horridly tricked 415
       With blood of fathers, mothers, daughters, sons,
       Baked and impasted with the parching streets,
       That lend a tyrannous and a damnèd light
       To their lord's murder. Roasted in wrath and fire,
       And thus o'er-sizèd with coagulate gore, 420
       With eyes like carbuncles, the hellish Pyrrhus
       Old grandsire Priam seeks –'
So, proceed you.

The first player continues the speech from where Hamlet leaves off. He declaims how Pyrrhus finds Priam, pauses for a long moment, then slays him. The player is interrupted by Polonius, but Hamlet urges him on.

---

1 Bombast: go for it!

Shakespeare may be 'sending up' an older stage tradition of acting and speaking. He gives the player a speech full of high-flown language. Work out a dramatic way of reading aloud lines 426–55 (and Hamlet's lines 410–22). Try a bombastic, over-the-top, declamatory style, to match the highly coloured language. Add exaggerated gestures and formal movements to match the style.

2 Bombast: act it out! (in small groups)

As one person reads the player's speech, the others act out what they describe. The following may help you:

'Repugnant to command' = resisting orders
'fell' = cruel
'senseless Ilium' = unfeeling Troy
'Stoops to his base' = crashes to the ground
'Takes prisoner Pyrrhus' ear' = dazes him
'neutral to his will and matter' = unable to think or act
'Cyclops' = one-eyed giants who worked as blacksmiths
'Mars' = god of war.

3 'Did nothing': Pyrrhus and Hamlet both delay

Both Hamlet and Pyrrhus are sons who seek revenge for the killing of their fathers. The player's speech contains another parallel. Pyrrhus stood still and 'Did nothing' (line 440). His inability to act forecasts Hamlet's own inaction as he delays avenging his father's murder. Some productions heavily emphasise this moment, and Hamlet echoes 'Did nothing.' Explain the dramatic effect of that echo.

---

discretion taste
milky white-haired
as a painted tyrant like a tyrant in a portrait
rack clouds
orb Earth
proof eterne eternal protection

strumpet Fortune unpredictable floozy
synod gathering
fellies part of the rim of the wheel of Fortune
nave hub
mobled veiled

POLONIUS 'Fore God my lord, well spoken, with good accent and good
    discretion. 425
I PLAYER   'Anon he finds him,
    Striking too short at Greeks; his antique sword,
    Rebellious to his arm, lies where it falls,
    Repugnant to command. Unequal matched,
    Pyrrhus at Priam drives, in rage strikes wide, 430
    But with the whiff and wind of his fell sword
    Th'unnervèd father falls. Then senseless Ilium,
    Seeming to feel this blow, with flaming top
    Stoops to his base, and with a hideous crash
    Takes prisoner Pyrrhus' ear; for lo, his sword, 435
    Which was declining on the milky head
    Of reverend Priam, seemed i'th'air to stick.
    So, as a painted tyrant, Pyrrhus stood,
    And like a neutral to his will and matter,
    Did nothing. 440
    But as we often see against some storm,
    A silence in the heavens, the rack stand still,
    The bold winds speechless, and the orb below
    As hush as death, anon the dreadful thunder
    Doth rend the region; so after Pyrrhus' pause, 445
    A rousèd vengeance sets him new a-work,
    And never did the Cyclops' hammers fall
    On Mars's armour, forged for proof eterne,
    With less remorse than Pyrrhus' bleeding sword
    Now falls on Priam. 450
    Out, out, thou strumpet Fortune! All you gods,
    In general synod take away her power,
    Break all the spokes and fellies from her wheel,
    And bowl the round nave down the hill of heaven
    As low as to the fiends.' 455
POLONIUS This is too long.
HAMLET It shall to th' barber's with your beard. Prithee say on.
    He's for a jig or a tale of bawdry, or he sleeps. Say on, come to
    Hecuba.
I PLAYER 'But who – ah woe! – had seen the mobled queen –' 460
HAMLET The mobled queen?
POLONIUS That's good, 'mobled queen' is good.

The player, with tears in his eyes, ends his tale of Hecuba. Hamlet orders Polonius to treat the actors hospitably. He asks the player to perform a play the next night, including a specially written speech.

---

1 The shift from high poetry to prose

The actors speak in a formalised, high-flown diction and style; much of the rest of *Hamlet* is in freer blank verse; and there is a good deal of prose in *Hamlet* too (see p. 267). Using the examples opposite, prepare director's notes for an actor as to how they should speak the different kinds of lines. Look particularly at transitions between two kinds of language, as at lines 476–7.

2 Actors reveal society (in small groups)

Polonius stresses the low social status of the actors, saying he will 'use them according to their desert'. But for Hamlet, actors are 'the abstract and brief chronicles / of the time' (lines 481–2). They show, in a dramatic form, the nature of society. Their performances are summaries and shortened stories of certain events that occur in the time in which they live. Test out that claim in two ways:

- By discussing how any television programme of your choice is an 'abstract and brief chronicle of the time'.
- By making up and acting out a short play that is somehow a mirror of today's society.

3 'Mock him not': is Hamlet serious?

Read line 497 in various ways: tongue-in-check, forcefully, as a genuine warning, or in some other tone. Decide which seems most appropriate to match what is in Hamlet's mind at this moment. See page 88, Activity 1, which asks you to try to get inside Hamlet's mind and intentions during this scene.

---

bisson rheum blinding tears
clout piece of cloth
diadem crown
o'er-teemèd worn out (Hecuba was said to have had a hundred children)
milch milky

passion in the gods won sympathy from the gods
desert deservings
bounty generosity
for a need if necessary

1 PLAYER 'Run barefoot up and down, threat'ning the flames
        With bisson rheum, a clout upon that head
        Where late the diadem stood, and, for a robe,   465
        About her lank and all o'er-teemèd loins
        A blanket, in th'alarm of fear caught up –
        Who this had seen, with tongue in venom steeped
        'Gainst Fortune's state would treason have pronounced.
        But if the gods themselves did see her then,   470
        When she saw Pyrrhus make malicious sport
        In mincing with his sword her husband's limbs,
        The instant burst of clamour that she made,
        Unless things mortal move them not at all,
        Would have made milch the burning eyes of heaven,   475
        And passion in the gods.
POLONIUS Look where he has not turned his colour, and has tears in's
    eyes. Prithee no more.
HAMLET 'Tis well, I'll have thee speak out the rest of this soon. – Good
    my lord, will you see the players well bestowed? Do you hear, let   480
    them be well used, for they are the abstract and brief chronicles
    of the time. After your death you were better have a bad epitaph
    than their ill report while you live.
POLONIUS My lord, I will use them according to their desert.
HAMLET God's bodkin man, much better. Use every man after his   485
    desert, and who shall scape whipping? Use them after your own
    honour and dignity; the less they deserve, the more merit is in your
    bounty. Take them in.
POLONIUS Come sirs.   *Exit Polonius*
HAMLET Follow him friends, we'll hear a play tomorrow. – Dost thou   490
    hear me old friend, can you play *The Murder of Gonzago*?
1 PLAYER Ay my lord.
HAMLET We'll ha't tomorrow night. You could for a need study a
    speech of some dozen or sixteen lines, which I would set down and
    insert in't, could you not?   495
1 PLAYER Ay my lord.
HAMLET Very well. Follow that lord, and look you mock him not.
                                            Exeunt Players
    My good friends, I'll leave you till night. You are welcome to
    Elsinore.
ROSENCRANTZ Good my lord.   500
                  Exeunt Rosencrantz and Guildenstern

Hamlet wonders at the player's ability to weep for a fictional character. He berates himself for doing nothing, even though he has real reasons for revenge. He curses Claudius, and cries for vengeance.

---

1 Self-reproach: 'And all for nothing?' (in pairs)

'What's Hecuba to him, or he to Hecuba . . . ?' demands Hamlet as he sees the player weeping for the sufferings of Hecuba. Faced with an actor who can cry at the imagined torments of a fictional character in a play, Hamlet reproaches himself for his own lack of action. The actor can weep 'for nothing', but Hamlet, with a murdered father, is incapable of taking revenge ('unpregnant of my cause'). Like a day-dreamer ('John-a-dreams') he does nothing.

a Talk together about whether you are sometimes more moved by a work of fiction (a play or a novel) than by what happens to you in real life.

b Do you think that Hamlet is being too hard on himself? Consider in turn each of the things he calls himself and decide if they are true ('rogue', 'peasant slave', 'dull and muddy-mettled rascal', 'John-a-dreams', 'coward', 'pigeon-livered'). Why does he level these accusations at himself?

c Consider each of the seven things Hamlet calls Claudius in lines 532–3 and discuss how justified you think each description is.

d Shakespeare often inserts lists into his plays (a literary device called **copiousness**). The accumulation of items helps to increase the intensity of the mood being created. Pick out the following lists: the player's reactions (lines 506–9); what the player would do if he played Hamlet (lines 514–18); what Hamlet imagines a bully would do to him (lines 524–7); what Hamlet calls Claudius (lines 532–3). Write a new list to insert into the soliloquy opposite (e.g. a list concerning his mother, or his false friends).

---

conceit imagination	**peak** mope
visage wanned face paled	**pate** skull, top of the head
in's aspect in his look	**i'th'throat** deep down
cleave split	**'swounds** God's wounds
Confound confuse	**gall** courage
muddy-mettled cowardly and sluggish	**kites** scavenging birds
	offal guts

HAMLET Ay so, God bye to you. Now I am alone.
          O what a rogue and peasant slave am I!
          Is it not monstrous that this player here,
          But in a fiction, in a dream of passion,
          Could force his soul so to his own conceit   505
          That from her working all his visage wanned,
          Tears in his eyes, distraction in's aspect,
          A broken voice, and his whole function suiting
          With forms to his conceit? And all for nothing?
          For Hecuba!   510
          What's Hecuba to him, or he to Hecuba,
          That he should weep for her? What would he do,
          Had he the motive and the cue for passion
          That I have? He would drown the stage with tears,
          And cleave the general ear with horrid speech,   515
          Make mad the guilty and appal the free,
          Confound the ignorant, and amaze indeed
          The very faculties of eyes and ears. Yet I,
          A dull and muddy-mettled rascal, peak
          Like John-a-dreams, unpregnant of my cause,   520
          And can say nothing – no, not for a king,
          Upon whose property and most dear life
          A damned defeat was made. Am I a coward?
          Who calls me villain, breaks my pate across,
          Plucks off my beard and blows it in my face,   525
          Tweaks me by th'nose, gives me the lie i'th'throat
          As deep as to the lungs? Who does me this?
          Ha, 'swounds, I should take it, for it cannot be
          But I am pigeon-livered, and lack gall
          To make oppression bitter, or ere this   530
          I should ha' fatted all the region kites
          With this slave's offal. Bloody, bawdy villain!
          Remorseless, treacherous, lecherous, kindless villain!
          Oh, vengeance!

Hamlet rebukes himself for his emotional outburst. He resolves to stage a play showing a murder similar to his father's. If the watching Claudius reveals his guilt, it will prove that the Ghost has spoken truly.

1 Changing moods (in groups of three or four)

Hamlet goes through several changes of mood in lines 501–58. His soliloquy contains the following sections:

Line 501   dismissing Rosencrantz and Guildenstern

Line 502   self-criticism

Lines 503–12   wondering at the player's tears for Hecuba

Lines 512–18   imagining the player's reactions to real grievances

Lines 518–32   deepening self-disgust

Lines 532–4   rage against Claudius

Lines 535–40   self-reproach for his emotional outburst

Lines 541–51   working out a plan to test the Ghost's word

Lines 551–6   fear that the Ghost may be a devil, telling lies to tempt him to eternal damnation by killing Claudius

Lines 557–8   elation at the thought that he will prove Claudius's guilt.

Make notes on each section, advising Hamlet on how to communicate his changes of mood through tone, pace, rhythm, volume, movement and gesture. Then speak your own version of the soliloquy.

2 'The play's the thing' – Is it? (in pairs)

Is theatre as powerful as Hamlet claims? Talk together about whether you think a criminal, watching a play with a similar theme to their own crime, will feel guilty and remorseful. Try to think of instances you have experienced or have read about when a play literally *moves* an audience, or incites demonstrations, violence or other actions.

---

the dear murderèd   a murdered father
drab, **scullion**   low-ranking servants
 (or prostitutes)
presently   immediately
malefactions   evil deeds

organ   voice
tent   probe
quick   most tender part
a do blench   he flinches
relative   relevant, conclusive

Why, what an ass am I! This is most brave,   535
That I, the son of the dear murderèd,
Prompted to my revenge by heaven and hell,
Must like a whore unpack my heart with words,
And fall a-cursing like a very drab,
A scullion!   540
Fie upon't, foh! About, my brains. Hum, I have heard
That guilty creatures sitting at a play
Have by the very cunning of the scene
Been struck so to the soul, that presently
They have proclaimed their malefactions;   545
For murder, though it have no tongue, will speak
With most miraculous organ. I'll have these players
Play something like the murder of my father
Before mine uncle. I'll observe his looks,
I'll tent him to the quick. If a do blench,   550
I know my course. The spirit that I have seen
May be a devil – and the devil hath power
T'assume a pleasing shape. Yea, and perhaps,
Out of my weakness and my melancholy,
As he is very potent with such spirits,   555
Abuses me to damn me. I'll have grounds
More relative than this. The play's the thing
Wherein I'll catch the conscience of the king.   *Exit*

Looking back at Act 2
Activities for groups or individuals

1 Appearance versus reality

One of the themes in *Hamlet* (and in all Shakespeare's plays) is that of appearance versus reality. Identify instances of this theme in Act 2. Rank them in order of importance to the play as a whole, as you see it so far.

2 Nine episodes

A great deal happens in Scene 2. You will find that a new action begins at the following lines: 1, 40, 85, 166, 213, 295, 339, 490 and 501. Use these lines to identify the separate events in the scene, and write a single sentence about each. Choose one line from each section that you think best expresses the dramatic action. Use your chosen lines to work out a very short enactment of the whole scene.

3 Emotional range

Hamlet appears at line 165 in Scene 2. Follow him through the scene and list ten words to show the range of emotions he experiences. Link each of your 'mood' words to a line in the script.

4 '. . . there is nothing either good / or bad but thinking makes it so'

In Activity 2 on page 80 you were asked to reflect on whether you thought the above statement was true or false. Now list each character in Act 2. For each suggest at least one thing they think 'good', but which another character would probably think 'bad'. For example, Polonius has no doubts about the moral justification of spying on his son, but Laertes would probably see it otherwise.

5 'Denmark's a prison'

Design a set for Scene 2 based on line 234.

6 Surveillance

Act 2 begins and ends with someone proposing to spy on someone else. Identify each occasion in the act which involves surveillance (observation or spying) of some kind.

Two versions of the first player declaiming the story of Pyrrhus and Priam.
Identify Hamlet in each picture and write a paragraph on what the body
language of each actor suggests about Hamlet's mood and thoughts at this
moment.

Rosencrantz and Guildenstern report Hamlet's unwillingness to talk about the reasons for his madness, and his joy at news of the players. Claudius asks them to encourage Hamlet's theatrical interests.

Rosencrantz is here shown reporting on his and Guildenstern's meeting with Hamlet. But how truthfully do they describe that conversation? Turn back to page 79 and refresh your memory by quickly reading lines 215–348. Then read aloud what they say opposite and decide if Rosencrantz and Guildenstern give Claudius a true and full account of their meeting.

1 Does Claudius suspect Hamlet? The evidence

In line 2, Claudius says Hamlet 'puts on' his mad act. Draw up a list that Claudius might have made, with evidence for Hamlet's madness in one column, and against it in another.

---

drift of circumstance   indirect talk
distracted   mad
forward   ready, willing
sounded   questioned
disposition   inclination

Niggard   sparse (Hamlet was unwilling to talk)
assay   urge
o'er-raught   overtook
a further edge   more encouragement

Act 3 Scene 1
The Great Hall of Elsinore Castle

Enter KING, QUEEN, POLONIUS, OPHELIA, ROSENCRANTZ,
GUILDENSTERN, LORDS

CLAUDIUS And can you by no drift of circumstance
           Get from him why he puts on this confusion,
           Grating so harshly all his days of quiet
           With turbulent and dangerous lunacy?
ROSENCRANTZ He does confess he feels himself distracted,   5
           But from what cause a will by no means speak.
GUILDENSTERN Nor do we find him forward to be sounded,
           But with a crafty madness keeps aloof
           When we would bring him on to some confession
           Of his true state.
GERTRUDE   Did he receive you well?   10
ROSENCRANTZ Most like a gentleman.
GUILDENSTERN But with much forcing of his disposition.
ROSENCRANTZ Niggard of question, but of our demands
           Most free in his reply.
GERTRUDE   Did you assay him
           To any pastime?   15
ROSENCRANTZ Madam, it so fell out that certain players
           We o'er-raught on the way; of these we told him,
           And there did seem in him a kind of joy
           To hear of it. They are about the court,
           And as I think, they have already order   20
           This night to play before him.
POLONIUS   'Tis most true,
           And he beseeched me to entreat your majesties
           To hear and see the matter.
CLAUDIUS With all my heart, and it doth much content me
           To hear him so inclined.   25
           Good gentlemen, give him a further edge,
           And drive his purpose on to these delights.
ROSENCRANTZ We shall my lord.
                    Exeunt Rosencrantz and Guildenstern

Claudius and Polonius prepare to spy on Hamlet to discover if his love for Ophelia has really driven him mad. Claudius's guilty conscience surfaces and reminds him of the murder of King Hamlet.

1 Does Ophelia overhear? (in pairs)

Every production must decide whether Ophelia overhears Claudius's lines 28–37. Imagine that she does overhear. One person slowly reads Claudius's lines, pausing frequently. In each pause, the partner, as Ophelia, speaks her thoughts. Change roles and repeat. Then discuss whether, if you were directing the play, you would have Ophelia overhear, and the dramatic implications of each alternative.

2 Catching the conscience of the king

Line 50 reveals that the Ghost's story is true. Claudius is guilty of murder. His conscience pricks him as he hears Polonius say that a pious appearance often covers evil. Design a mask for lines 47–9, or line 50, or lines 51–3. As you read on, think about where masks might be appropriate in other parts of the play.

3 Parents spy on children (in small groups)

a **The men's view** Claudius and Polonius will spy on Hamlet and Ophelia: stepson and daughter. The two men have no doubts about such surveillance. They see themselves as 'lawful espials': legitimate spies. Talk together about what this action suggests about the character of each man. Are there times when parents may legitimately spy on their children?

b **The women's view** Do you think Gertrude and Ophelia also fully accept spying as a legitimate practice? Discuss whether you think the two women are fully consenting participants in the plot to spy on Hamlet.

---

closely secretly
Affront meet
bestow hide
wonted way usual behaviour, sanity
To both your honours to the credit of you both

Gracious your grace
colour explain
devotion's visage the show of praying
sugar o'er conceal, sweetly cover
plastering art make-up
painted deceitful

CLAUDIUS   Sweet Gertrude, leave us too,
    For we have closely sent for Hamlet hither,
    That he, as 'twere by accident, may here   30
    Affront Ophelia. Her father and myself,
    Lawful espials,
    Will so bestow ourselves, that seeing unseen,
    We may of their encounter frankly judge,
    And gather by him, as he is behaved,   35
    If 't be th'affliction of his love or no
    That thus he suffers for.
GERTRUDE   I shall obey you.
    And for your part Ophelia, I do wish
    That your good beauties be the happy cause
    Of Hamlet's wildness. So shall I hope your virtues   40
    Will bring him to his wonted way again,
    To both your honours.
OPHELIA   Madam, I wish it may.
                   [Exit Gertrude with Lords]
POLONIUS Ophelia walk you here. – Gracious, so please you,
    We will bestow ourselves. – Read on this book,
    That show of such an exercise may colour   45
    Your loneliness. – We are oft to blame in this:
    'Tis too much proved, that with devotion's visage,
    And pious action, we do sugar o'er
    The devil himself.
CLAUDIUS (*Aside*)   Oh, 'tis too true.
    How smart a lash that speech doth give my conscience!   50
    The harlot's cheek, beautied with plastering art,
    Is not more ugly to the thing that helps it
    Than is my deed to my most painted word.
    O heavy burden!
POLONIUS I hear him coming. Let's withdraw, my lord.   55
                   Exeunt Claudius and Polonius

Hamlet reflects on death. Is it better to live or die, to endure suffering or to fight against it? The fear of what might happen after death makes us bear with life. Thought prevents us from acting.

---

1 'To be, or not to be . . .' (in groups)

Line 56   Hamlet wonders whether to commit suicide.

Lines 57–60   He wonders whether to endure or fight.

Lines 60–4   He looks forward to the sleep of death.

Lines 64–8   He is troubled with thoughts of what happens after death.

Lines 68–82   What stops people committing suicide, in spite of all oppressions in this life, is the fear of terrors that await the dead.

Lines 83–8   He decides that thinking stops us from acting.

Choose one or more of the following activities on the soliloquy:

An exercise in persuasion   Share the reading, each group member speaking in turn a short sense unit. Quietly persuade your group each time you read, so that the soliloquy builds up as a developing argument.

Echo   One person echoes 'To be, or not to be, that is the question' every few lines throughout a shared reading.

Speak it aloud in different ways   As if Hamlet has only suicide in mind; as if Hamlet has only killing Claudius in mind; as a philosophy lecture to a group of students; as if every line, phrase or thought is a question.

A dramatic reading for radio   Use sound effects, music, and short phrases from elsewhere in the play.

A set of tableaux of lines 70–4   To show the six or seven injustices of human life that Hamlet considers.

Afterwards, write notes on how to speak the soliloquy on stage.

---

consummation   ending
rub   obstacle
shuffled off . . . coil   died (shaken off the confusions of human life)
contumely   humiliating insults
disprized   unvalued
office   people in authority

quietus   release
a bare bodkin   a mere dagger
fardels   burdens
native hue of resolution   natural determination to act
sicklied o'er   unhealthily covered
orisons   prayers

Enter HAMLET

HAMLET To be, or not to be, that is the question –
Whether 'tis nobler in the mind to suffer
The slings and arrows of outrageous fortune,
Or to take arms against a sea of troubles,
And by opposing end them. To die, to sleep – 60
No more; and by a sleep to say we end
The heart-ache and the thousand natural shocks
That flesh is heir to – 'tis a consummation
Devoutly to be wished. To die, to sleep –
To sleep, perchance to dream. Ay, there's the rub, 65
For in that sleep of death what dreams may come,
When we have shuffled off this mortal coil,
Must give us pause. There's the respect
That makes calamity of so long life,
For who would bear the whips and scorns of time, 70
Th'oppressor's wrong, the proud man's contumely,
The pangs of disprized love, the law's delay,
The insolence of office, and the spurns
That patient merit of th'unworthy takes,
When he himself might his quietus make 75
With a bare bodkin? Who would fardels bear,
To grunt and sweat under a weary life,
But that the dread of something after death,
The undiscovered country from whose bourn
No traveller returns, puzzles the will, 80
And makes us rather bear those ills we have
Than fly to others that we know not of?
Thus conscience does make cowards of us all,
And thus the native hue of resolution
Is sicklied o'er with the pale cast of thought, 85
And enterprises of great pitch and moment
With this regard their currents turn awry
And lose the name of action. Soft you now,
The fair Ophelia. – Nymph, in thy orisons
Be all my sins remembered.
OPHELIA   Good my lord, 90
How does your honour for this many a day?

Ophelia attempts to return Hamlet's gifts. Hamlet taunts her, saying that he once loved her, then denying it. He orders her to a nunnery and self-loathingly accuses himself of vices. Ophelia lies about her father.

1 Different stresses = different meanings (in pairs)

Try five different ways of speaking line 96 ('I never gave you aught.'). Each time, heavily stress a different word. Talk together about how each version results in different possible interpretations.

2 Does Hamlet know he is watched? (in small groups)

Talk together about whether you think Hamlet knows he is being watched. If you think he is aware of watchers, identify the line where the realisation dawns on him and suggest who he thinks is spying on him (Claudius? Polonius? Gertrude?). Make notes on how you would stage this part of the scene to maximise dramatic effect.

3 Three decisions – no 'right' answers!

a But why? Draw up a list of possible reasons that might explain Hamlet's bitter treatment of Ophelia. Put them in order of 'most likely' to 'least likely'. What is your evidence?

b 'Get thee to a nunnery'. Does Hamlet urge Ophelia to go to a convent because there she will be safe from (or renounce) the temptations and corruption of the world? Or is Hamlet being sarcastic, and by 'nunnery' means 'brothel'? Which interpretation seems more likely to you, and why?

c Beauty will corrupt virtue more easily than virtue can make beautiful people virtuous or pure, asserts Hamlet (lines 111–14). Is he thinking mainly of Ophelia or of Gertrude at this moment? Is his pessimism characteristic? Give evidence for your decisions.

---

remembrances gifts, love-tokens
aught anything
wax grow
honest pure, a virgin
discourse to dealings with
bawd brothel-keeper

inoculate our old stock graft on to our nature
relish of it still be tainted with vice
at my / beck waiting to be committed
arrant thorough, complete

HAMLET I humbly thank you, well, well, well.

OPHELIA My lord, I have remembrances of yours
That I have longèd long to re-deliver.
I pray you now receive them.

HAMLET   No, not I,   95
I never gave you aught.

OPHELIA My honoured lord, you know right well you did,
And with them words of so sweet breath composed
As made the things more rich. Their perfume lost,
Take these again, for to the noble mind   100
Rich gifts wax poor when givers prove unkind.
There my lord.

HAMLET Ha, ha, are you honest?

OPHELIA My lord?

HAMLET Are you fair?   105

OPHELIA What means your lordship?

HAMLET That if you be honest and fair, your honesty should admit no
discourse to your beauty.

OPHELIA Could beauty, my lord, have better commerce than with
honesty?   110

HAMLET Ay truly, for the power of beauty will sooner transform
honesty from what it is to a bawd, than the force of honesty can
translate beauty into his likeness. This was sometime a paradox, but
now the time gives it proof. I did love you once.

OPHELIA Indeed my lord you made me believe so.   115

HAMLET You should not have believed me, for virtue cannot so
inoculate our old stock but we shall relish of it. I loved you not.

OPHELIA I was the more deceived.

HAMLET Get thee to a nunnery – why wouldst thou be a breeder of
sinners? I am myself indifferent honest, but yet I could accuse me   120
of such things, that it were better my mother had not borne me.
I am very proud, revengeful, ambitious, with more offences at my
beck than I have thoughts to put them in, imagination to give them
shape, or time to act them in. What should such fellows as I do
crawling between earth and heaven? We are arrant knaves all,   125
believe none of us. Go thy ways to a nunnery. Where's your father?

OPHELIA At home my lord.

HAMLET Let the doors be shut upon him, that he may play the fool
nowhere but in's own house. Farewell.

Hamlet reviles Ophelia, wishing her ill and slandering all women. She sorrows over his fall from excellence into madness. Claudius suspects Hamlet is not mad, and plans to send him to England.

---

1 Experiencing a tongue-lashing (in groups of eight to ten)

This activity helps bring out the devastating power of Hamlet's verbal assault on Ophelia. One person volunteers to take the part of Ophelia. The others surround her as Hamlet. The 'Hamlets' select short extracts from lines 103–43 (e.g. 'are you honest?', 'Get thee to a nunnery', 'marry a fool'). The Hamlets hurl their insults at Ophelia, who tries to get away from them, saying 'What means your lordship?' It can be a very cruel experience for Ophelia – so volunteers only. Afterwards, discuss how it feels to be on the receiving end of such a tongue-lashing, and the state of mind of the person who inflicts it.

2 Renaissance man – or idealised prince?

In lines 145–8, Ophelia paints a picture of the ideal prince. Hamlet exemplified the ideal qualities of the courtier, soldier and scholar. He was the hope and crowning glory ('expectancy and rose') of Denmark. He was the very mirror and model ('glass' and 'mould of form') of behaviour and taste, looked up to as an ideal example ('Th'observed of all observers') by everyone.

But many people agree that Hamlet has shown few, if any, of these qualities in the play so far. Consider each quality in turn and write a sentence saying how far your perception of Hamlet matches, or does not match, that quality.

3 How to play Ophelia?

There is debate about how to play Ophelia: as a meek, passive victim of Hamlet's anger or as a stronger character. Try lines 144–55 in both ways. See also page 262.

---

dowry wedding gift
chaste virginal
calumny malicious lies
paintings make-up
jig dance
make . . . ignorance pretend your immorality comes from innocence

glass mirror
blown blossoming-ripe
hatch outcome
disclose result
tribute Danegeld (protection money paid by England to Denmark)

OPHELIA Oh help him you sweet heavens!   130
HAMLET If thou dost marry, I'll give thee this plague for thy dowry:
be thou as chaste as ice, as pure as snow, thou shalt not escape
calumny. Get thee to a nunnery, go. Farewell. Or if thou wilt needs
marry, marry a fool, for wise men know well enough what monsters
you make of them. To a nunnery go, and quickly too. Farewell.   135
OPHELIA O heavenly powers, restore him!
HAMLET I have heard of your paintings too, well enough. God hath
given you one face and you make yourselves another. You jig, you
amble, and you lisp, you nickname God's creatures, and make your
wantonness your ignorance. Go to, I'll no more on't, it hath made   140
me mad. I say we will have no mo marriages. Those that are married
already, all but one shall live, the rest shall keep as they are. To
a nunnery, go.   *Exit*
OPHELIA Oh what a noble mind is here o'erthrown!
    The courtier's, soldier's, scholar's, eye, tongue, sword,   145
    Th'expectancy and rose of the fair state,
    The glass of fashion and the mould of form,
    Th'observed of all observers, quite, quite down,
    And I of ladies most deject and wretched,
    That sucked the honey of his music vows,   150
    Now see that noble and most sovereign reason,
    Like sweet bells jangled, out of time and harsh;
    That unmatched form and feature of blown youth
    Blasted with ecstasy. Oh woe is me
    T'have seen what I have seen, see what I see.   155

Enter KING *and* POLONIUS

CLAUDIUS Love? His affections do not that way tend;
    Nor what he spake, though it lacked form a little,
    Was not like madness. There's something in his soul
    O'er which his melancholy sits on brood,
    And I do doubt the hatch and the disclose   160
    Will be some danger; which for to prevent,
    I have in quick determination
    Thus set it down: he shall with speed to England
    For the demand of our neglected tribute.

Polonius agrees with Claudius's plan to send Hamlet to England. He proposes to spy on Gertrude's meeting with Hamlet. In Scene 2, Hamlet instructs the players on acting style.

---

1 A loving father? (in small groups)

'How now Ophelia? / You need not tell us what Lord Hamlet said, / We heard it all.' These are the last words spoken by Polonius to his daughter in the play. Just how does he speak them? Remember that she has been on the receiving end of a brutal tongue-lashing from Hamlet. Is Polonius sympathetic, officious, uncaring or . . .? Experiment with styles to see if you can agree on how he should speak the lines to match his character and the occasion.

2 '. . . must not unwatched go'

Once again the theme of surveillance is given verbal expression in Claudius's final line in the scene. Suggest how Ophelia and Polonius react to it, and how they leave the stage.

3 'Out-Herods Herod' (individuals, then groups)

Hamlet uses a noun as a verb to suggest ranting and raving more than Herod himself (Herod and Termagant were noisy, raging characters in medieval Mystery plays). Use the same technique to invent some telling comparisons of your own, for example with the name of a public figure (or someone you know). What would it be to out-Shakespeare Shakespeare? Or out-Polonius Polonius?

Once everyone has made up at least one such phrase, collect them together as a group and then put them in order of effectiveness; or each person could write some of them into a speech of advice to actors.

Haply   perhaps
variable objects   notable sights
From fashion of   at odds with
round   strict, forthright
trippingly   lightly
as lief   rather

robustious   violent, loud-mouthed
periwig-pated   wig-wearing
groundlings   poorest theatre-goers, who stood in the open yard in front of the stage
capable of   understand

Haply the seas, and countries different,   165
With variable objects, shall expel
This something-settled matter in his heart,
Whereon his brains still beating puts him thus
From fashion of himself. What think you on't?
POLONIUS It shall do well. But yet do I believe   170
The origin and commencement of his grief
Sprung from neglected love. How now Ophelia?
You need not tell us what Lord Hamlet said,
We heard it all. My lord, do as you please,
But if you hold it fit, after the play,   175
Let his queen mother all alone entreat him
To show his grief. Let her be round with him,
And I'll be placed, so please you, in the ear
Of all their conference. If she find him not,
To England send him; or confine him where   180
Your wisdom best shall think.
CLAUDIUS   It shall be so.
Madness in great ones must not unwatched go.

Exeunt

Act 3 Scene 2
The Great Hall of Elsinore Castle

Enter HAMLET and two or three of the PLAYERS

HAMLET Speak the speech I pray you as I pronounced it to you,
trippingly on the tongue; but if you mouth it as many of our players
do, I had as lief the town-crier spoke my lines. Nor do not saw the
air too much with your hand thus, but use all gently; for in the
very torrent, tempest, and, as I may say, whirlwind of your passion,   5
you must acquire and beget a temperance that may give it
smoothness. Oh, it offends me to the soul to hear a robustious
periwig-pated fellow tear a passion to totters, to very rags, to split
the ears of the groundlings, who for the most part are capable of
nothing but inexplicable dumb-shows and noise. I would have such   10
a fellow whipped for o'erdoing Termagant – it out-Herods Herod.
Pray you avoid it.

Hamlet urges moderation in acting. He defines theatre as the mirror of nature and society. He criticises bad actors and overambitious clowns. Preparations for the play begin.

1 Hamlet's manual for actors?

Hamlet sets himself up as an authority on acting (see also pp. 252–3). He advises that actors should aim at moderation, not excess. That seems ironic after his unrestrained and violent words to Ophelia shortly before. Hamlet's advice covers four topics:

Acting Don't overact! (lines 1–11, 14–16, 24–9)

The purpose of theatre To mirror and comment critically on the times (lines 17–20)

Clowns Don't ad lib or laugh at your own jokes (lines 31–6)

Audiences A very mixed bunch (lines 21–4, 33–4).

Work out a way of presenting Hamlet's advice to the players in lines 1–36. You might write a 'manual for actors', design a set of cartoons showing 'right' and 'wrong' ways of acting, or have one person narrate the lines as the others act out each section.

2 '. . . some necessary question of the play' = themes

Every play has a set of 'necessary questions' (lines 34–5): central themes or issues. For example, one 'necessary question' of this play is revenge. But there is an irony in Hamlet's advice, because his delay in taking his revenge can be seen as his own continued refusal to consider that 'necessary question'.

What are the 'necessary questions' in *Hamlet*? Make a list of what you consider to be the play's central themes. Compare your list with those of other students and with pages 242–53. Remember that themes may not always be characterised by single words like 'revenge' or 'death', but can be more complex; for example, 'the relationship between physicality and the soul'.

warrant will do so
modesty moderation
come tardy off imperfectly done
censure judgement
profanely blasphemously
gait walk

journeymen unskilled workmen
indifferently to some extent
presently immediately
just well balanced
As e'er . . . coped withal as I've ever met

ɪ PLAYER I warrant your honour.

HAMLET Be not too tame neither, but let your own discretion be your
tutor. Suit the action to the word, the word to the action, with this   15
special observance, that you o'erstep not the modesty of nature. For
anything so o'erdone is from the purpose of playing, whose end both
at the first and now, was and is, to hold as 'twere the mirror up
to nature; to show virtue her own feature, scorn her own image,
and the very age and body of the time his form and pressure. Now   20
this overdone, or come tardy off, though it makes the unskilful
laugh, cannot but make the judicious grieve, the censure of the
which one must in your allowance o'erweigh a whole theatre of
others. Oh, there be players that I have seen play, and heard others
praise and that highly, not to speak it profanely, that neither having   25
th'accent of Christians, nor the gait of Christian, pagan, nor man,
have so strutted and bellowed that I have thought some of nature's
journeymen had made men, and not made them well, they imitated
humanity so abominably.

ɪ PLAYER I hope we have reformed that indifferently with us, sir.   30

HAMLET Oh reform it altogether. And let those that play your clowns
speak no more than is set down for them, for there be of them that
will themselves laugh, to set on some quantity of barren spectators
to laugh too, though in the meantime some necessary question of
the play be then to be considered. That's villainous, and shows   35
a most pitiful ambition in the fool that uses it. Go make you ready.

Exeunt Players

Enter POLONIUS, ROSENCRANTZ *and* GUILDENSTERN

How now my lord, will the king hear this piece of work?

POLONIUS And the queen too, and that presently.

HAMLET Bid the players make haste.

Exit Polonius

Will you two help to hasten them?   40

ROSENCRANTZ Ay my lord.

Exeunt Rosencrantz and Guildenstern

HAMLET What ho, Horatio!

Enter HORATIO

HORATIO Here sweet lord, at your service.

HAMLET Horatio, thou art e'en as just a man
As e'er my conversation coped withal.   45

Hamlet praises Horatio's well-balanced character and criticises obsequious flatterers. He urges Horatio to watch Claudius closely for any guilty reaction during the play.

---

1 Friendship – how might Hamlet perform? (in small groups)

Hamlet expresses his deep friendship for Horatio (lines 46–64). It is genuine friendship, not flattery; Horatio is not wealthy ('no revenue') and so can offer no advantage ('advancement'). Hamlet admires Horatio for bearing suffering without complaint ('suffering all . . . nothing'), and for his equable temperament ('blood and judgement are so well commeddled'): emotions and reason are well mixed.

Divide Hamlet's speech into three or four sections, as a director or actor would in order to perform it on stage. Characterise each of the sections by the way in which you would deliver it – for example, quietly, as if speaking in Horatio's ear; with more public declamation, as if addressing an audience; meditatively, as if to himself.

Now perform the speech to other groups, using different voices to mark where you see the different sections of the speech.

2 Vivid images: flattery and fortune (see pp. 264–6)

Make a drawing of one or both of the images used by Hamlet, using pages 264–6 to help you:

- Lines 50–2 describe the sweet-tongued courtier ('candied tongue') who flatters vain people in high positions ('lick absurd pomp'), and bows and scrapes readily ('crook the pregnant . . . knee') for profit ('thrift').
- Lines 57–8 and 60–1 turn Fortune into a woman, buffeting and rewarding human beings, or treating them like a musical instrument ('pipe') on which she can play any tune she pleases ('sound what stop she please').

---

election choice
Sh'ath sealed she has chosen
tane taken
prithee pray you
afoot in action, presented
very comment keenest watching
occulted hidden

unkennel reveal
Vulcan's stithy god of fire's smithy (workshop)
censure of his seeming judgement of his looks
a steal aught he hides anything
idle unoccupied (or mad)

HORATIO Oh my dear lord.

HAMLET   Nay, do not think I flatter,
For what advancement may I hope from thee,
That no revenue hast but thy good spirits
To feed and clothe thee? Why should the poor be flattered?
No, let the candied tongue lick absurd pomp   50
And crook the pregnant hinges of the knee
Where thrift may follow fawning. Dost thou hear?
Since my dear soul was mistress of her choice,
And could of men distinguish her election,
Sh'ath sealed thee for herself, for thou hast been   55
As one in suffering all that suffers nothing,
A man that Fortune's buffets and rewards
Hast tane with equal thanks. And blest are those
Whose blood and judgement are so well commeddled
That they are not a pipe for Fortune's finger   60
To sound what stop she please. Give me that man
That is not passion's slave, and I will wear him
In my heart's core, ay in my heart of heart,
As I do thee. Something too much of this.
There is a play tonight before the king: 65
One scene of it comes near the circumstance
Which I have told thee of my father's death.
I prithee when thou seest that act afoot,
Even with the very comment of thy soul
Observe my uncle. If his occulted guilt   70
Do not itself unkennel in one speech,
It is a damnèd ghost that we have seen,
And my imaginations are as foul
As Vulcan's stithy. Give him heedful note,
For I mine eyes will rivet to his face,   75
And after we will both our judgements join
In censure of his seeming.

HORATIO   Well my lord.
If a steal aught the whilst this play is playing
And scape detecting, I will pay the theft.
                    Sound a flourish

HAMLET They are coming to the play. I must be idle.   80
Get you a place.

Hamlet revels in wordplay. He puns on what Claudius and Polonius say to him, and subjects Ophelia to much sexual innuendo. He comments bitterly on Gertrude's appearance.

1 Hamlet's wordplay: insulting and obsessive? (in groups of five)

Hamlet has just promised to be 'idle' – to appear mad. His words now are deliberately disconcerting as he seizes on meanings that neither Claudius nor Polonius nor Ophelia intends.

Claudius's line 82 means 'How are you?' But Hamlet interprets 'fares' as meaning 'feeds', so he replies as if Claudius had asked him what he has eaten. He mocks Claudius about his earlier promise (that Hamlet should succeed him), suggesting that it is just empty air.

Hamlet also mocks Polonius, punning on 'Brutus' and 'Capitol' with 'brute' and 'capital', adding the insulting 'calf' (fool). This was also, for Shakespeare's company, a theatrical in-joke, because Shakespeare wrote *Julius Caesar* shortly before *Hamlet*, and the same pair of actors probably played Brutus/Caesar and Hamlet/Polonius.

Hamlet's verbal treatment of Ophelia is much crueller, filled with crude sexual jokes ('country matters' = sexual intercourse, 'nothing' = female genitalia).

a Take parts as Hamlet, Claudius, Polonius, Gertrude and Ophelia. Read the opposite page several times. Stress Hamlet's puns. Then, in role, say how you think each character regards Hamlet at this moment.

b There is a theatrical tradition that when Shakespeare's dialogue is set out as opposite (each speech in a single line) the lines are spoken rapidly, with no pauses between speeches. Experiment with that style of delivery, then speak again, using pauses. Which style seems more effective dramatically?

c Notice that Hamlet ends by returning to his obsession: his mother's sexuality and marriage to Claudius. Explore ways of speaking lines 111–20 to express Hamlet's intense feelings.

---

fares does, eats
cousin (used for any close relative)
chameleon lizard that changes colour (and was thought to eat only air)
capons fattened chickens

Capitol seat of government in ancient Rome
metal a pun on 'mettle' (= spirit)
your only jig-maker I'm the only comedian here

Danish march (trumpets and kettle-drums). Enter KING, QUEEN,
POLONIUS, OPHELIA, ROSENCRANTZ, GUILDENSTERN *and other*
LORDS *attendant, with his* GUARD *carrying torches*

CLAUDIUS How fares our cousin Hamlet?

HAMLET Excellent i'faith, of the chameleon's dish: I eat the air,
promise-crammed. You cannot feed capons so.

CLAUDIUS I have nothing with this answer Hamlet, these words are not   85
mine.

HAMLET No, nor mine now. – My lord, you played once i'th'university,
you say.

POLONIUS That did I my lord, and was accounted a good actor.

HAMLET And what did you enact?   90

POLONIUS I did enact Julius Caesar. I was killed i'th'Capitol. Brutus
killed me.

HAMLET It was a brute part of him to kill so capital a calf there. – Be
the players ready?

ROSENCRANTZ Ay my lord, they stay upon your patience.   95

GERTRUDE Come hither my dear Hamlet, sit by me.

HAMLET No good mother, here's metal more attractive.

POLONIUS Oh ho, do you mark that?

HAMLET Lady, shall I lie in your lap?

OPHELIA No my lord.   100

HAMLET I mean, my head upon your lap?

OPHELIA Ay my lord.

HAMLET Do you think I meant country matters?

OPHELIA I think nothing my lord.

HAMLET That's a fair thought to lie between maids' legs.   105

OPHELIA What is, my lord?

HAMLET Nothing.

OPHELIA You are merry my lord.

HAMLET Who, I?

OPHELIA Ay my lord.   110

HAMLET O God, your only jig-maker. What should a man do but be
merry? for look you how cheerfully my mother looks, and my father
died within's two hours.

OPHELIA Nay, 'tis twice two months my lord.

Hamlet comments bitterly on his mother's hasty second marriage. The dumb-show presents a mirror-image of the murder of Hamlet's father. Hamlet again vents his cynicism on Ophelia.

Hamlet and the court watch the dumb-show (Royal Shakespeare Company, 1992). In Elizabethan drama, a dumb-show (mime) often preceded the play, summarising the action ('imports the argument'). This dumb-show presents a sleeping king being murdered by a man who steals both his crown and queen. It is a mirror-image of what Claudius did to his brother. How will Claudius behave as he sees his own villainy being acted out in front of him? He might ignore it altogether (as he talks lovingly to Gertrude). Or he might gradually realise what it means, reacting in very different ways (with fear, suspicion, anger or in some other way). Or he might watch it imperturbably, utterly calm.

Work out how you think Claudius should behave, and why. Suggest what Claudius does at each point in the dumb-show. Then act it out!

---

sables expensive mourning clothes
byrlady by the Virgin Mary
a must build . . . on he must build churches or be forgotten
hobby-horse prostitute, or character in a morris dance
Hoboys oboes

makes show of protestation shows her love
mutes silent actors
miching mallecho sneaky villainy
naught improper, rude
clemency kindness
posy of a ring a motto engraved on a ring

HAMLET So long? Nay then let the devil wear black, for I'll have a suit   115
of sables. O heavens! die two months ago, and not forgotten yet?
Then there's hope a great man's memory may outlive his life half
a year, but byrlady a must build churches then, or else shall a suffer
not thinking on, with the hobby-horse, whose epitaph is, 'For O,
for O, the hobby-horse is forgot.'   120

Hoboys play. The dumb-show enters

Enter a KING *and a* QUEEN, *very lovingly, the Queen embracing him. She
kneels and makes show of protestation unto him. He takes her up, and declines
his head upon her neck. He lies him down upon a bank of flowers. She, seeing
him asleep, leaves him. Anon comes in another man, takes off his crown, kisses
it, pours poison in the sleeper's ears, and leaves him. The Queen returns,
finds the King dead, and makes passionate action. The poisoner, with some
two or three mutes, comes in again, seeming to condole with her. The dead
body is carried away. The poisoner woos the Queen with gifts. She seems
harsh awhile, but in the end accepts his love.*   *Exeunt*

OPHELIA What means this my lord?
HAMLET Marry this is miching mallecho, it means mischief.
OPHELIA Belike this show imports the argument of the play?

Enter PROLOGUE

HAMLET We shall know by this fellow; the players cannot keep counsel,
they'll tell all.   125
OPHELIA Will a tell us what this show meant?
HAMLET Ay, or any show that you'll show him. Be not you ashamed
to show, he'll not shame to tell you what it means.
OPHELIA You are naught, you are naught. I'll mark the play.

PROLOGUE For us and for our tragedy,   130
Here stooping to your clemency,
We beg your hearing patiently.

HAMLET Is this a prologue, or the posy of a ring?
OPHELIA 'Tis brief my lord.
HAMLET As woman's love.   135

The Player King speaks of thirty years of loving and holy marriage. The Player Queen expresses worries about his health, but vows not to marry again. He replies that vows are often broken.

1 The play: a tale of love (in groups of four)

The players' speeches sound very formal. This is because both players speak in rhymed couplets, use stylised language, and make classical references: for example, Phoebus (Apollo, the sun god), Tellus (goddess of Earth).

a **Ceremony**   Work out an equally stylised and ritualistic style of moving and acting to fit the formality of the language. As two persons speak the lines, the other two play out the words with ceremonious, stylised gestures and movement.

b **Stereotyping**   The Player Queen says that women's fear and love are equal ('hold quantity'), either extreme or barely felt (lines 148–9). One student's reaction to that was 'Rubbish!' But another student argued that it is inappropriate to judge this 'play scene' as if it represents ordinary life. She said, 'It's so obviously artificial – a theatrical convention.' Join in the argument, saying why you agree or disagree with either student.

c **Gertrude's reactions**   One person reads the Player Queen's speeches, pausing after each unit of meaning (usually about two or three lines). In each pause, the others, as Gertrude, suggest what Gertrude thinks as she hears and sees herself portrayed on stage with her first husband.

d **Comparisons**   Place ten lines or so from the players' speeches (e.g. lines 142–53) alongside ten lines of Hamlet's (e.g. Act 2, Scene 2, lines 511–23). Compare the movement of the lines, the flow across line-endings, the feeling(s) expressed and the length of the sentences. Discuss the differences you discover.

Phoebus' cart   the sun
Neptune's salt wash   the sea
Tellus' orbèd ground   Earth
borrowed sheen   reflected light
Hymen   god of marriage
Unite commutual . . . bands   join in marriage

distrust you   worry about you
operant powers . . . do   faculties (eyesight, and so on) are failing
wormwood   bitter
instances   motives
base . . . thrift   thoughts of money

Enter the PLAYER KING *and* QUEEN

PLAYER KING Full thirty times hath Phoebus' cart gone round
    Neptune's salt wash and Tellus' orbèd ground,
    And thirty dozen moons with borrowed sheen
    About the world have times twelve thirties been,
    Since love our hearts, and Hymen did our hands, 140
    Unite commutual in most sacred bands.
PLAYER QUEEN So many journeys may the sun and moon
    Make us again count o'er ere love be done.
    But woe is me, you are so sick of late,
    So far from cheer and from your former state, 145
    That I distrust you. Yet though I distrust,
    Discomfort you my lord it nothing must.
    For women's fear and love hold quantity,
    In neither aught, or in extremity.
    Now what my love is, proof hath made you know; 150
    And as my love is sized, my fear is so.
    [Where love is great, the littlest doubts are fear;
    Where little fears grow great, great love grows there.]
PLAYER KING Faith, I must leave thee love, and shortly too:
    My operant powers their functions leave to do; 155
    And thou shalt live in this fair world behind,
    Honoured, beloved; and haply one as kind
    For husband shalt thou –
PLAYER QUEEN   Oh confound the rest!
    Such love must needs be treason in my breast.
    In second husband let me be accurst: 160
    None wed the second but who killed the first.

HAMLET That's wormwood, wormwood.

PLAYER QUEEN The instances that second marriage move
    Are base respects of thrift, but none of love.
    A second time I kill my husband dead 165
    When second husband kisses me in bed.
PLAYER KING I do believe you think what now you speak,
    But what we do determine oft we break.

The Player King argues that strong intentions don't last, because time makes us forget. Changing social conditions change the emotions. But the Player Queen swears she will never remarry.

---

1 It won't last! (in small groups)

The Player King's speech is a sustained reflection on the theme that strong intentions don't last. In rhyming couplets, he argues repeatedly that time wears away resolutions ('Purpose'), however passionately ('Of violent birth') they were originally declared. This reflects Hamlet's situation. He has sworn passionately to revenge his father's murder, but he procrastinates: time may wear away his resolution.

One person reads lines 167–96, two lines at a time. After each pair of lines, the others say 'Hamlet, your desire for revenge will fade' (or a similar sentence of your own). Afterwards, talk together about whether you agree with the Player King's view that strong intentions won't last (the desire for revenge will fade, the widow will forget her previous vow and remarry, and so on).

2 Money brings you friends? (in pairs)

Lines 181–90 echo the Roman philosopher Cicero. He wrote that friendship ('love', 'favourite') changes with circumstances ('fortune'). When someone has wealth, they also have friends. But when a rich person loses their money, they are deserted by their friends.

Read lines 181–90, two lines at a time. Discuss each pair of lines to test whether they reflect what Cicero claimed.

3 'Our thoughts are ours, their ends none of our own.'

Think through line 194. Write a paragraph explaining its meaning, and how it applies to *Hamlet*.

---

validity   strength, sticking power
enactures   actions
is not for aye   does not last eternally
flies   deserts him
poor advanced   poor man promoted
not needs   is rich
in want   is poor
seasons him   turns him into

devices still   plans always
anchor's cheer   hermit's food and condition (poverty and loneliness)
scope   future
blanks the face of joy   changes a happy face to a sad one
here and hence   in this world and the next

Purpose is but the slave to memory,
Of violent birth but poor validity, 170
Which now like fruit unripe sticks on the tree,
But fall unshaken when they mellow be.
Most necessary 'tis that we forget
To pay ourselves what to ourselves is debt.
What to ourselves in passion we propose, 175
The passion ending, doth the purpose lose.
The violence of either grief or joy
Their own enactures with themselves destroy.
Where joy most revels, grief doth most lament;
Grief joys, joy grieves, on slender accident. 180
This world is not for aye, nor 'tis not strange
That even our loves should with our fortunes change,
For 'tis a question left us yet to prove,
Whether love lead fortune, or else fortune love.
The great man down, you mark his favourite flies; 185
The poor advanced makes friends of enemies,
And hitherto doth love on fortune tend;
For who not needs shall never lack a friend,
And who in want a hollow friend doth try
Directly seasons him his enemy. 190
But orderly to end where I begun,
Our wills and fates do so contrary run
That our devices still are overthrown;
Our thoughts are ours, their ends none of our own.
So think thou wilt no second husband wed, 195
But die thy thoughts when thy first lord is dead.
PLAYER QUEEN Nor earth to me give food, nor heaven light,
Sport and repose lock from me day and night,
[To desperation turn my trust and hope,
An anchor's cheer in prison be my scope,] 200
Each opposite that blanks the face of joy
Meet what I would have well, and it destroy;
Both here and hence pursue me lasting strife,
If once a widow, ever I be wife.

HAMLET If she should break it now! 205

The Player King sleeps. Hamlet hints that he knows Claudius is a murderer. He again subjects Ophelia to bitter sexual innuendo, and curses Lucianus, urging him to speak. Lucianus poisons the Player King.

---

1 Gertrude's reply, Hamlet's jibe (in pairs)

a Gertrude's judgement on the Player Queen has become a famous saying ('The lady doth protest too much methinks': she is over the top [too rash] with her promises of everlasting love.) Talk together about what lies behind Gertrude's comment. She probably suspects that Hamlet intends her to recognise herself in the Player Queen. So how might she speak line 211?

b Hamlet almost reveals his knowledge of Claudius's guilt when he seizes on the king's 'offence' and turns it into poison, traps and murder. But just how does Hamlet speak lines 214–20? Savagely? Off-handedly? Laughingly? Advise the actor.

2 Taunting Ophelia (in small groups)

Ophelia again has to endure Hamlet's bitter sexual language. His first reply is doubly obscene (he could add a commentary, like a puppet-master, to Ophelia and her lover's flirting; or 'puppets' = sexual organs). Then he seizes on her word 'keen', making it explicitly sexual. (To reduce his desire he would make her pregnant and so groan in childbirth.) Finally, he twists 'better and worse', implying that wives mistake (betray) their husbands. Talk together about why you think Hamlet directs so much sexual venom towards Ophelia and what she may think and feel about his words.

3 Lucianus – over the top?

Lucianus speaks the language of melodrama. Judging by Hamlet's admonition ('Pox, leave / thy damnable faces and begin'), he overacts too. Invent movement, expressions and gestures for lines 231–6.

---

fain . . . beguile   I would gladly while away
Tropically   metaphorically
free souls   clear consciences
galled jade   saddle-sore horse
withers   neck joints
unwrung   not hurt

dallying   making love
croaking . . . revenge   (Hamlet misquotes an old play)
Confederate season   good opportunity, perfect time
Hecat   queen of witches
usurp   overthrow, destroy

PLAYER KING 'Tis deeply sworn. Sweet, leave me here awhile;
    My spirits grow dull, and fain I would beguile
    The tedious day with sleep.
              Sleeps
PLAYER QUEEN   Sleep rock thy brain,
    And never come mischance between us twain.   *Exit*

HAMLET Madam, how like you this play?   210
GERTRUDE The lady doth protest too much methinks.
HAMLET Oh but she'll keep her word.
CLAUDIUS Have you heard the argument? Is there no offence in't?
HAMLET No, no, they do but jest, poison in jest, no offence i'th'world.
CLAUDIUS What do you call the play?   215
HAMLET The Mousetrap. Marry how? Tropically. This play is the
    image of a murder done in Vienna. Gonzago is the duke's name,
    his wife Baptista. You shall see anon. 'Tis a knavish piece of work,
    but what o' that? Your majesty, and we that have free souls, it
    touches us not. Let the galled jade winch, our withers are unwrung.   220

                Enter LUCIANUS

    This is one Lucianus, nephew to the king.
OPHELIA You are as good as a chorus my lord.
HAMLET I could interpret between you and your love if I could see the
    puppets dallying.
OPHELIA You are keen my lord, you are keen.   225
HAMLET It would cost you a groaning to take off mine edge.
OPHELIA Still better and worse.
HAMLET So you mistake your husbands. Begin, murderer. Pox, leave
    thy damnable faces and begin. Come, the croaking raven doth
    bellow for revenge.   230

LUCIANUS Thoughts black, hands apt, drugs fit, and time agreeing,
    Confederate season, else no creature seeing.
    Thou mixture rank, of midnight weeds collected,
    With Hecat's ban thrice blasted, thrice infected,
    Thy natural magic and dire property   235
    On wholesome life usurp immediately.
           Pours the poison in his ears

Claudius abruptly leaves the play, calling for light. Hamlet is delighted that his plot succeeded. He believes the Ghost has told the truth and that Claudius has revealed his guilt.

---

1 Claudius's reaction – Panic? Calm? Or . . .?

Just how does Claudius react to Hamlet's words? Some productions show him terrified and agitated, and his confusion is reflected in his courtiers' behaviour. In other productions his exit is calm and dignified. Write, with reasons, how you would stage lines 237–45.

2 A turning point?

The effect of the play on Claudius is often seen as a turning point for Hamlet. When you have read to the end of the play, come back to this point and gauge for yourself whether or not you see this as a turning point. If so, of what kind and significance?

3 Hamlet exults

Hamlet is overjoyed at the success of his plan. He sings an old song: wounded ('strucken') deer were believed to go off on their own to weep, while the unwounded male ('hart ungallèd') played on unconcerned.

Then Hamlet says that even if everything else fails, the success of the play would gain him the exotic dress and footwear ('feathers' and 'razed shoes') of an actor. It would purchase him a whole share in an acting company, like Shakespeare's own, where leading actors were entitled to a percentage ('fellowship/share') of the admission money.

Hamlet sings another old song that parallels the situation in Denmark where the good king ('Jove') is dead ('dismantled') and a villain ('pajock') rules in his place. So the Ghost has told the truth.

Work out Hamlet's movements to match his lines 246–68.

---

for's estate   for his lands and title
is extant   still exists
anon   soon
false fire   blank ammunition
   (make-believe)
turn Turk   get worse

razed   decorated with cuts
Damon   close friend (from the
   legendary friendship of Damon and
   Pythias)
perdy   by God (*par dieu*)
vouchsafe   grant

HAMLET A poisons him i'th'garden for's estate. His name's Gonzago.
The story is extant, and written in very choice Italian. You shall
see anon how the murderer gets the love of Gonzago's wife.

OPHELIA The king rises.   240

HAMLET What, frighted with false fire?

GERTRUDE How fares my lord?

POLONIUS Give o'er the play.

CLAUDIUS Give me some light. Away!

LORDS Lights, lights, lights!   245

Exeunt all but Hamlet and Horatio

HAMLET Why, let the strucken deer go weep,
         The hart ungallèd play,
     For some must watch while some must sleep,
         Thus runs the world away.
     Would not this, sir, and a forest of feathers, if the rest of my fortunes   250
     turn Turk with me, with two provincial roses on my razed shoes,
     get me a fellowship in a cry of players, sir?

HORATIO Half a share.

HAMLET A whole one I.
         For thou dost know, O Damon dear,   255
             This realm dismantled was
         Of Jove himself, and now reigns here
             A very, very – pajock.

HORATIO You might have rhymed.

HAMLET O good Horatio, I'll take the ghost's word for a thousand   260
     pound. Didst perceive?

HORATIO Very well my lord.

HAMLET Upon the talk of the poisoning?

HORATIO I did very well note him.

Enter ROSENCRANTZ *and* GUILDENSTERN

HAMLET Ah ha! – Come, some music! Come, the recorders!   265
         For if the king like not the comedy,
             Why then – belike he likes it not, perdy.
     Come, some music!

GUILDENSTERN Good my lord, vouchsafe me a word with you.

HAMLET Sir, a whole history.   270

GUILDENSTERN The king, sir –

HAMLET Ay sir, what of him?

Hamlet disconcerts Guildenstern by deliberately misunderstanding him. He mocks Rosencrantz too, but agrees to visit Gertrude. Hamlet denies any hope of becoming king.

---

1 Shaking off old friends (in groups of three)

Take parts as Hamlet, Rosencrantz and Guildenstern, and read lines 269–336. Change roles so that everyone has a chance to read Hamlet. Emphasise the words with which Hamlet mocks the two courtiers. Notice particularly that lines 301–2 are the only time in the play that Hamlet uses the royal 'we'. Afterwards, talk together about the ways in which Hamlet clearly shows that their friendship is at an end.

2 Is it a threat? (in pairs)

Does Rosencrantz threaten Hamlet with imprisonment in lines 305–7? Or does he have some other meaning in mind?

Suggest what seems most likely to be Rosencrantz's meaning at this moment, and advise the actor on how to speak the lines.

3 Thoughts of kingship

a 'I lack advancement . . .'   Hamlet says at line 308 that he lacks 'advancement' (has no ambition – or hope – to rule Denmark). But Rosencrantz assures Hamlet that he will succeed Claudius as king. Hamlet responds (line 311) with a proverb: 'But while the grass grows, the starving horse dies.' Think of one or two reasons why Hamlet makes this reply.

b '. . . for your succession in Denmark'   There are few references in the play to Hamlet's rightful role as prince and successor to the throne of Denmark. Collect those that have been made up to this point. Add to your list as you read on. When you reach the end of the play, write about their significance.

---

distempered disturbed
choler anger
purgation cure, cleansing
discourse talk
frame order
breed kind
admiration astonishment

no sequel no consequence
Impart tell me
closet bedroom or private room
pickers and stealers hands (from the *Book of Common Prayer*: 'keep my hands from picking and stealing')

GUILDENSTERN Is in his retirement marvellous distempered.

HAMLET With drink sir?

GUILDENSTERN No my lord, rather with choler.   275

HAMLET Your wisdom should show itself more richer to signify this
  to his doctor, for, for me to put him to his purgation would perhaps
  plunge him into far more choler.

GUILDENSTERN Good my lord, put your discourse into some frame,
  and start not so wildly from my affair.   280

HAMLET I am tame sir, pronounce.

GUILDENSTERN The queen your mother, in most great affliction of
  spirit, hath sent me to you.

HAMLET You are welcome.

GUILDENSTERN Nay good my lord, this courtesy is not of the right   285
  breed. If it shall please you to make me a wholesome answer, I will
  do your mother's commandment. If not, your pardon and my return
  shall be the end of my business.

HAMLET Sir, I cannot.

ROSENCRANTZ What, my lord?   290

HAMLET Make you a wholesome answer; my wit's diseased. But, sir,
  such answer as I can make, you shall command, or rather, as you
  say, my mother. Therefore no more, but to the matter. My mother,
  you say.

ROSENCRANTZ Then thus she says. Your behaviour hath struck her   295
  into amazement and admiration.

HAMLET O wonderful son that can so stonish a mother! But is there
  no sequel at the heels of this mother's admiration? Impart.

ROSENCRANTZ She desires to speak with you in her closet ere you go
  to bed.   300

HAMLET We shall obey, were she ten times our mother. Have you any
  further trade with us?

ROSENCRANTZ My lord, you once did love me.

HAMLET And do still, by these pickers and stealers.

ROSENCRANTZ Good my lord, what is your cause of distemper? You   305
  do surely bar the door upon your own liberty if you deny your griefs
  to your friend.

HAMLET Sir, I lack advancement.

ROSENCRANTZ How can that be, when you have the voice of the king
  himself for your succession in Denmark?   310

HAMLET Ay sir, but while the grass grows – the proverb is something
  musty.

Hamlet bitterly accuses Guildenstern of treating him as a mere musical instrument, to be made to say anything at someone else's wish. He demonstrates that process on Polonius.

---

1 'You would pluck out the heart of my mystery'

What is Hamlet's 'mystery' – his inmost essence? After over four hundred years of performance and criticism, argument continues as to what it might be. Throughout this edition you are invited to explore aspects of Hamlet's character, and pages 254–62 will help your understanding. One aspect to think about at this particular moment is just why he is so incensed by Guildenstern here.

2 Playing on Polonius

To show Rosencrantz and Guildenstern how they are treating him, Hamlet does the same to Polonius. He plays upon him like a recorder, making him say anything that he, Hamlet, chooses. So Polonius is made to say he sees the imaginary shapes Hamlet suggests are in the clouds.

Some directors and critics challenge this view of Polonius as a silly old man humouring someone he thinks is a lunatic. They argue that Polonius replies in a dignified and tolerant manner, showing that he knows that Hamlet is trying to make fun of him. And certain critics have tried to show that 'camel', 'weasel' and 'whale' are symbols for certain themes of the play.

a Direct Polonius as to how he should behave in lines 337–47.

b Work out an explanation of how 'camel', 'weasel' and 'whale' could have significance in the play. You don't have to be too serious about it. You could invent some spoof criticism, if you wish.

---

withdraw   be private
recover the wind of me   direct me (like hunters keeping upwind of their prey)
toil   net
ventages, **stops**   finger holes

mystery   innermost secrets
compass   range
'Sblood   God's blood
fret   irritate, or add a fret on a lute
th'mass   the Roman Catholic Mass
bent   utmost limit (like a stretched bow)

Enter the PLAYERS *with recorders*

Oh, the recorders. Let me see one. To withdraw with you – Why
do you go about to recover the wind of me, as if you would drive
me into a toil?   315
GUILDENSTERN O my lord, if my duty be too bold, my love is too
unmannerly.
HAMLET I do not well understand that. Will you play upon this pipe?
GUILDENSTERN My lord, I cannot.
HAMLET I pray you.   320
GUILDENSTERN Believe me I cannot.
HAMLET I do beseech you.
GUILDENSTERN I know no touch of it my lord.
HAMLET 'Tis as easy as lying. Govern these ventages with your fingers
and thumb, give it breath with your mouth, and it will discourse   325
most eloquent music. Look you, these are the stops.
GUILDENSTERN But these cannot I command to any utterance of
harmony. I have not the skill.
HAMLET Why look you now how unworthy a thing you make of me.
You would play upon me, you would seem to know my stops, you   330
would pluck out the heart of my mystery, you would sound me from
my lowest note to the top of my compass – and there is much music,
excellent voice, in this little organ, yet cannot you make it speak.
'Sblood, do you think I am easier to be played on than a pipe? Call
me what instrument you will, though you can fret me, you cannot   335
play upon me.

Enter POLONIUS

God bless you sir.
POLONIUS My lord, the queen would speak with you, and presently.
HAMLET Do you see yonder cloud that's almost in shape of a camel?
POLONIUS By th'mass, and 'tis like a camel indeed.   340
HAMLET Methinks it is like a weasel.
POLONIUS It is backed like a weasel.
HAMLET Or like a whale?
POLONIUS Very like a whale.
HAMLET Then I will come to my mother by and by. – They fool me   345
to the top of my bent. – I will come by and by.

Hamlet threatens bloody revenge. He decides to visit Gertrude to upbraid but not harm her. Claudius, fearing Hamlet's growing dangerousness, briefs Rosencrantz and Guildenstern to take Hamlet to England.

1 The language of revenge (in pairs)

In lines 349–53, Hamlet uses the language of the traditional revenger in Elizabethan drama (see pp. 246–7). Talk together about whether you think the lines are out of character with Hamlet's personality, reducing him to a stereotype of traditional Revenge Tragedy.

For example, conventional revengers in Elizabethan and Jacobean tragedy – like Hieronimo in *The Spanish Tragedy* and Vindice in *The Revenger's Tragedy* – draw on dark, nightmarish imagery to bolster their causes. Write ten lines in continuation of lines 349–53. You could refer to Macbeth's speech in Act 3 Scene 2, lines 46–55 (in the Cambridge School Shakespeare or New Cambridge Shakespeare), where he invokes darkness, not for revenge, but for murder.

2 'I will speak daggers to her'

Hamlet intends to 'speak daggers' to his mother but not to hurt her physically. He is horrified because she has married Claudius, but does he suspect her of anything else? Make a list of all the things he is likely to accuse her of. Check how accurate your predictions are when you read Scene 4.

3 Work out the scene change

In Shakespeare's Globe Theatre the scenes flowed quickly and smoothly, without long intervals for changing from one to the next. Most modern productions also aim at one scene flowing directly into the next. Work out how you would stage the change from Scene 2 to Scene 3. Might Claudius actually glimpse Hamlet at line 1?

Contagion evil
Soft careful
Nero Roman emperor who murdered his mother
How in my words somever however much in my speech

shent punished, shamed
seals action
commission letters of instruction
The terms of our estate my status as king
provide make preparations

POLONIUS I will say so.   *Exit*

HAMLET By and by is easily said. – Leave me, friends.

Exeunt all but Hamlet

'Tis now the very witching time of night,
When churchyards yawn, and hell itself breathes out   350
Contagion to this world. Now could I drink hot blood,
And do such bitter business as the day
Would quake to look on. Soft, now to my mother.
O heart, lose not thy nature; let not ever
The soul of Nero enter this firm bosom.   355
Let me be cruel, not unnatural:
I will speak daggers to her but use none.
My tongue and soul in this be hypocrites,
How in my words somever she be shent,
To give them seals never my soul consent.   *Exit*   360

Act 3 Scene 3
The king's private chapel

Enter CLAUDIUS, ROSENCRANTZ and GUILDENSTERN

CLAUDIUS I like him not, nor stands it safe with us
To let his madness range. Therefore prepare you:
I your commission will forthwith dispatch,
And he to England shall along with you.
The terms of our estate may not endure   5
Hazard so near us as doth hourly grow
Out of his brows.
GUILDENSTERN   We will ourselves provide.
Most holy and religious fear it is
To keep those many many bodies safe
That live and feed upon your majesty.   10

Rosencrantz contrasts the private individual with a king. Everyone depends upon the ruler: when he dies, everyone suffers. Polonius reports that he will spy on Hamlet and Gertrude.

1 Flattering the king: Rosencrantz

Rosencrantz mouths the flattering belief that all tyrants love to hear: everything and everybody depends on the monarch ('That spirit'). In Tudor England the ruling class made it the official ideology.

Rosencrantz uses two striking images. First, the king's death ('cess'), like a whirlpool ('gulf'), draws everything in to disaster. The second image is that of a huge ('massy') wheel, the king at the centre, everybody else firmly attached ('mortised and adjoined'). When the wheel breaks, every tiny part ('annexment') suffers.

a Choose either the whirlpool or wheel image and illustrate it. Then compare your illustration with others in the class and discuss differences.

b Research 'the Elizabethan World Picture' (belief in a harmonious hierarchical society, depending on the king at the top). Shakespeare presents the belief clearly in *Troilus and Cressida*, Act 1 Scene 3, lines 77–123. But there, as here, a scheming character (Ulysses) speaks, so you need to be wary of taking it as the truth.

c Advise Claudius about how to react to Rosencrantz's flattery, especially when he hears the words 'The cess of majesty'. Does he recall his murder of King Hamlet?

2 More flattery: Polonius

Polonius suggests that the idea of spying on Hamlet and Gertrude was the king's (line 30). In fact, Polonius himself proposed it. Do you think he is flattering the king, protecting himself, or has some other motive?

---

single and peculiar life private individual
noyance harm
weal health
boisterous tumultuous
a general groan the sorrow of everyone

fetters chains
arras hanging tapestry
tax him home criticise him strongly
'Tis meet it's fitting
partial biased
of vantage also

ROSENCRANTZ The single and peculiar life is bound
    With all the strength and armour of the mind
    To keep itself from noyance; but much more
    That spirit upon whose weal depends and rests
    The lives of many. The cess of majesty   15
    Dies not alone, but like a gulf doth draw
    What's near it with it. It is a massy wheel
    Fixed on the summit of the highest mount,
    To whose huge spokes ten thousand lesser things
    Are mortised and adjoined, which when it falls,   20
    Each small annexment, petty consequence,
    Attends the boisterous ruin. Never alone
    Did the king sigh, but with a general groan.
CLAUDIUS Arm you I pray you to this speedy voyage,
    For we will fetters put about this fear   25
    Which now goes too free-footed.
ROSENCRANTZ   We will haste us.
      Exeunt Rosencrantz and Guildenstern

      Enter POLONIUS

POLONIUS My lord, he's going to his mother's closet.
    Behind the arras I'll convey myself
    To hear the process. I'll warrant she'll tax him home,
    And as you said, and wisely was it said,   30
    'Tis meet that some more audience than a mother,
    Since nature makes them partial, should o'erhear
    The speech of vantage. Fare you well my liege,
    I'll call upon you ere you go to bed
    And tell you what I know.
CLAUDIUS   Thanks, dear my lord.   35
          Exit Polonius

Claudius hopes for divine mercy for his brother's murder. But he knows that pardon is impossible while he retains the fruits of his crime, even though villainy can triumph on Earth. He tries to pray.

1 The conscience of the king (in small groups)

Claudius agonises over his dilemma. He has committed murder, yet hopes for heavenly pardon. He knows that although he might escape judgement on Earth, there is no escape for him in heaven, except God's forgiveness through prayer and repentance. Though he is in no state to pray or repent, he calls on angels to help, and kneels to pray.

Each person speaks a section of the soliloquy, then hands on to the next person. Read around the group in different ways:

- a line at a time
- a sentence at a time
- up to any punctuation mark
- saying only one powerful word from each line
- a 'sense unit' of your own choice.

Try to make your reading sound like a developing argument that Claudius is having with himself. Experiment with whispers, fear, puzzlement and anger. Can you find moments of hope in the soliloquy?

After your explorations, decide on the style you prefer and make a presentation of Claudius's lines to the class.

2 Heaven and hell: salvation and sin

Research the Christian iconography of heaven and hell as depicted in medieval and Renaissance times. Present your findings to show what bearing Christian morality (which prohibited revenge) has upon the play as a whole. Pages 249–51 will help you.

---

rank stinking, rotten
primal eldest first and oldest (in the Bible the killing of Abel by Cain)
inclination desire
will determination
visage face
forestallèd prevented
corrupted currents wicked ways
Offence's gilded hand rich criminals

wicked prize profits from crimes
above / There heaven
shuffling deceit
Even . . . evidence to tell our wickedest sins
limèd trapped (like a bird snared by lime)
assay attempt

Oh my offence is rank, it smells to heaven;
It hath the primal eldest curse upon't,
A brother's murder. Pray can I not,
Though inclination be as sharp as will.
My stronger guilt defeats my strong intent,   40
And like a man to double business bound,
I stand in pause where I shall first begin,
And both neglect. What if this cursèd hand
Were thicker than itself with brother's blood,
Is there not rain enough in the sweet heavens   45
To wash it white as snow? Whereto serves mercy
But to confront the visage of offence?
And what's in prayer but this two-fold force,
To be forestallèd ere we come to fall,
Or pardoned being down? Then I'll look up,   50
My fault is past. But oh, what form of prayer
Can serve my turn? 'Forgive me my foul murder'?
That cannot be, since I am still possessed
Of those effects for which I did the murder,
My crown, mine own ambition, and my queen.   55
May one be pardoned and retain th'offence?
In the corrupted currents of this world
Offence's gilded hand may shove by justice,
And oft 'tis seen the wicked prize itself
Buys out the law. But 'tis not so above;   60
There is no shuffling, there the action lies
In his true nature, and we ourselves compelled
Even to the teeth and forehead of our faults
To give in evidence. What then? What rests?
Try what repentance can. What can it not?   65
Yet what can it when one cannot repent?
Oh wretched state! Oh bosom black as death!
Oh limèd soul that struggling to be free
Art more engaged! Help, angels! – Make assay:
Bow stubborn knees, and heart with strings of steel   70
Be soft as sinews of the new-born babe.
All may be well.
                    [*He kneels*]

Hamlet refrains from killing Claudius because the king is praying, and so would go to heaven. Hamlet resolves to kill him at a sinful moment, and thus send him to hell. But Claudius has prayed in vain.

1 Hamlet delays

Hamlet does not kill Claudius because the king is praying. Hamlet's own father suffers after death because Claudius killed him at a moment when he was unprepared for heaven ('grossly, full of bread' = full of sin, no opportunity to fast), not having confessed his sins. Hamlet therefore decides to wait for a moment ('hent' = opportunity) when Claudius is committing a sin. Killing Claudius, then, when he has no thought of heaven in his mind, will surely send Claudius to hell. Or is Hamlet merely finding another excuse for delay?

Experiment with dramatic ways of presenting Hamlet's lines. You will find that intercutting Hamlet's lines with Claudius's soliloquy on page 137 can lead to fascinating discoveries.

pat instantly, neatly
a is a-praying he's praying
would be scanned needs study
hire and salary legal payment (not punishment)
broad blown in full blossom
as flush full of life

audit account with God
in our circumstance . . . thought it is generally believed
purging cleansing
fit and seasoned fully prepared
relish of salvation hope of heaven
physic medicine

Enter HAMLET

HAMLET Now might I do it pat, now a is a-praying,
        And now I'll do't – and so a goes to heaven,
        And so am I revenged. That would be scanned.   75
        A villain kills my father, and for that,
        I his sole son do this same villain send
        To heaven.
        Why, this is hire and salary, not revenge.
        A took my father grossly, full of bread,   80
        With all his crimes broad blown, as flush as May,
        And how his audit stands who knows save heaven?
        But in our circumstance and course of thought
        'Tis heavy with him. And am I then revenged
        To take him in the purging of his soul,   85
        When he is fit and seasoned for his passage?
        No.
        Up sword, and know thou a more horrid hent,
        When he is drunk asleep, or in his rage,
        Or in th'incestuous pleasure of his bed,   90
        At game a-swearing, or about some act
        That has no relish of salvation in't –
        Then trip him that his heels may kick at heaven,
        And that his soul may be as damned and black
        As hell whereto it goes. My mother stays.   95
        This physic but prolongs thy sickly days.   *Exit*
CLAUDIUS My words fly up, my thoughts remain below.
        Words without thoughts never to heaven go.   *Exit*

Polonius advises Gertrude to speak sharply to her son, and then hides. Hamlet is vehemently critical of Gertrude, making her fear for her life. Her alarm makes Polonius call for help – with fatal results.

1 Read through the scene (in groups of three)

To gain a first impression, take parts and read through the whole scene. The same person can read Polonius and the Ghost. Don't pause over unfamiliar words or phrases. The purpose is to gather a sense of how the scene flows.

2 Where is the scene set?

Scene 4 is known as 'the closet scene'. A closet was a private room. But for the last hundred years the stage convention has been to set it in Gertrude's bedroom. This usually has the effect of heightening the impression of Hamlet having an Oedipus complex (a desire to sleep with his mother – see p. 256). Laurence Olivier's film heavily emphasised this Oedipal interpretation.

Imagine you are directing the play and you have a leading Shakespeare scholar as your consultant. They write to you: 'In Shakespeare's day "closet" meant private room, and the Oedipus complex hadn't been thought of, so I advise you not to bring a bed on stage.' Do you take their advice? Why or why not? Write your reply.

3 The killing of Polonius (in pairs)

Hamlet thrusts his sword through the arras, killing Polonius. This is the first killing by Hamlet in the play. Is it an act of premeditated revenge, or an impulsive, excited lunge through the arras? It is clear from the lines which follow that Hamlet thinks it must be Claudius. Discuss how the action provides insights into Hamlet's character. Especially explore whether you feel such a killing is in character, or unlike the Hamlet you have known so far in the play.

---

straight immediately
lay home deal firmly with, talk severely
your grace . . . and him like a firescreen you have shielded Hamlet from criticism
round outspoken, firm

warrant assure, promise
rood holy cross of Christ
I'll set . . . speak I'll fetch others to correct you
glass mirror
ducat gold coin ('I'll bet I've killed him')

Act 3 Scene 4
Gertrude's private room

Enter GERTRUDE *and* POLONIUS

POLONIUS A will come straight. Look you lay home to him.
      Tell him his pranks have been too broad to bear with,
      And that your grace hath screened and stood between
      Much heat and him. I'll silence me e'en here.
      Pray you be round with him.   5
HAMLET (*Within*) Mother, mother, mother!
GERTRUDE I'll warrant you, fear me not. Withdraw, I hear him coming.
      [*Polonius hides himself behind the arras*]

Enter HAMLET

HAMLET Now mother, what's the matter?
GERTRUDE Hamlet, thou hast thy father much offended.
HAMLET Mother, you have my father much offended.   10
GERTRUDE Come, come, you answer with an idle tongue.
HAMLET Go, go, you question with a wicked tongue.
GERTRUDE Why, how now Hamlet?
HAMLET   What's the matter now?
GERTRUDE Have you forgot me?
HAMLET   No by the rood, not so.
      You are the queen, your husband's brother's wife,   15
      And, would it were not so, you are my mother.
GERTRUDE Nay, then I'll set those to you that can speak.
HAMLET Come, come and sit you down, you shall not budge.
      You go not till I set you up a glass
      Where you may see the inmost part of you.   20
GERTRUDE What wilt thou do? thou wilt not murder me?
      Help, help, ho!
POLONIUS (*Behind*) What ho! Help, help, help!
HAMLET (*Draws*) How now, a rat? Dead for a ducat, dead.
                  Kills Polonius
POLONIUS (*Behind*) Oh, I am slain!

Hamlet dismisses the dead Polonius as a meddling fool. He accuses Gertrude of shamefully defiling true love and marriage, making heaven blush with shame.

1 Did she know? (in small groups)

'As kill a king?' echoes Gertrude (line 30). But did she know that Claudius had murdered her first husband? On stage, a clue is often given in the way Gertrude behaves as she speaks these four words. Talk together about whether you think Gertrude knew anything about the murder. Advise her on how to deliver the line.

2 A just epitaph?

Hamlet says, 'wretched, rash, intruding fool'. Would Ophelia or the queen accept this as an appropriate epitaph for Polonius? Write the four words each of them would substitute for Hamlet's callous dismissal. Then write four words of your own to describe Polonius.

3 'What have I done . . .?' (in small groups)

Hamlet does not answer Gertrude's question directly, but embarks on a densely packed diatribe against her. He includes the image of prostitutes being branded ('blister') on the forehead, and says she has torn the heart ('plucks / The very soul') out of the marriage contract ('the body of contraction'), making religion a meaningless jumble ('rhapsody') of words. Her act makes heaven blush ('glow') with shame, and Earth is sad and sickened as if Doomsday had come.

Identify in lines 40–51 the eight consequences of Gertrude's 'act' (some are given in the paragraph above). Present a tableau for each. Compare your tableaux with those of other students. (The eight consequences end with these words: modesty, hypocrite, there, oaths, soul, words, glow, act).

---

thy better   the king
damnèd custom   wicked habits
brazed   hardened (like brass)
proof and bulwark   armoured strongly
sense   feeling
grace and blush   innocence

dicers' oaths   gamblers' promises
solidity and compound mass   the world
tristful visage   sad face
doom   Day of Judgement
index   list of sins

GERTRUDE   Oh me, what hast thou done?   25
HAMLET Nay I know not, is it the king?
GERTRUDE Oh what a rash and bloody deed is this!
HAMLET A bloody deed? Almost as bad, good mother,
　　　　　As kill a king and marry with his brother.
GERTRUDE As kill a king?
HAMLET   Ay lady, 'twas my word.   30
　　　　　[*Lifts up the arras and reveals the body of Polonius*]
　　　　　Thou wretched, rash, intruding fool, farewell.
　　　　　I took thee for thy better. Take thy fortune.
　　　　　Thou find'st to be too busy is some danger. –
　　　　　Leave wringing of your hands. Peace! Sit you down
　　　　　And let me wring your heart, for so I shall   35
　　　　　If it be made of penetrable stuff,
　　　　　If damnèd custom have not brazed it so,
　　　　　That it be proof and bulwark against sense.
GERTRUDE What have I done, that thou dar'st wag thy tongue
　　　　　In noise so rude against me?
HAMLET   Such an act   40
　　　　　That blurs the grace and blush of modesty,
　　　　　Calls virtue hypocrite, takes off the rose
　　　　　From the fair forehead of an innocent love
　　　　　And sets a blister there, makes marriage vows
　　　　　As false as dicers' oaths. Oh such a deed   45
　　　　　As from the body of contraction plucks
　　　　　The very soul, and sweet religion makes
　　　　　A rhapsody of words. Heaven's face doth glow;
　　　　　Yea, this solidity and compound mass,
　　　　　With tristful visage as against the doom,   50
　　　　　Is thought-sick at the act.
GERTRUDE   Ay me, what act,
　　　　　That roars so loud and thunders in the index?

Hamlet compares his father with Claudius: the good man against the bad. He berates Gertrude for not seeing the difference, and deplores her inability to control her sexual desires.

1 Two pictures – what are they?

Hamlet shows Gertrude two portraits ('counterfeit presentment') to compare his father and Claudius. He presents his father as god-like: 'Hyperion' = the sun god; 'Jove' = king of the gods; 'Mars' = Roman god of war; 'Mercury' = winged messenger of the gods.

In many productions Hamlet has his father's picture in a miniature on a chain around his neck. Gertrude wears her husband's picture similarly. But might there be portraits on the wall? Which would be the best form of presentation, in your view?

2 Gertrude's point of view (in pairs)

What does Gertrude feel at being subjected to such a tongue-lashing? Write some lines for Gertrude and interject them at key points in Hamlet's verbal attack on her. Then perform the speech by Hamlet and its interjections by Gertrude, asking your audience to comment critically on how you have depicted Gertrude.

3 Blaming parents (in small groups)

In lines 82–8, Hamlet demands to know how young people can be expected to control their passions, if mothers can't control theirs ('mutine in a matron's bones' = run riot in a mother's body). When middle age ('frost') is highly sexually active ('doth burn') and intellect helps to satisfy desire ('reason panders will'), then there is no shame in anyone's passion. Discuss whether Hamlet's anger at his mother's sexuality is typical of young people today.

---

station   posture
New-lighted   recently landed
mildewed ear   rotten ear of corn
batten   greedily feed
Sense   sexual desire
motion   emotions
apoplexed   paralysed
ecstasy   madness

thralled   enslaved
But it . . . difference   but it could
  choose good from bad
cozened   cheated
hoodman-blind   blind man's buff
sans all   without anything else
so mope   be so stupid

HAMLET Look here upon this picture, and on this,
The counterfeit presentment of two brothers.
See what a grace was seated on this brow;   55
Hyperion's curls, the front of Jove himself,
An eye like Mars, to threaten and command;
A station like the herald Mercury,
New-lighted on a heaven-kissing hill;
A combination and a form indeed,   60
Where every god did seem to set his seal
To give the world assurance of a man.
This was your husband. Look you now what follows.
Here is your husband, like a mildewed ear
Blasting his wholesome brother. Have you eyes?   65
Could you on this fair mountain leave to feed
And batten on this moor? Ha! have you eyes?
You cannot call it love, for at your age
The heyday in the blood is tame, it's humble,
And waits upon the judgement; and what judgement   70
Would step from this to this? [Sense sure you have,
Else could you not have motion, but sure that sense
Is apoplexed, for madness would not err,
Nor sense to ecstasy was ne'er so thralled,
But it reserved some quantity of choice   75
To serve in such a difference.] What devil was't
That thus hath cozened you at hoodman-blind?
[Eyes without feeling, feeling without sight,
Ears without hands or eyes, smelling sans all,
Or but a sickly part of one true sense   80
Could not so mope.]
O shame, where is thy blush? Rebellious hell,
If thou canst mutine in a matron's bones,
To flaming youth let virtue be as wax
And melt in her own fire. Proclaim no shame   85
When the compulsive ardour gives the charge,
Since frost itself as actively doth burn,
And reason panders will.

Hamlet expresses his disgust at Gertrude's sexuality. She pleads with him to stop. He reviles Claudius. The Ghost reminds Hamlet of his mission and urges him to comfort Gertrude. She is amazed by his words.

'*Enter* GHOST': an eighteenth-century staging. The first published version of the play had the stage direction '*Enter the Ghost in his nightgown*'. In one production the Ghost sat alongside Hamlet and put its arm around Hamlet's shoulders, whispering the lines. Work out how you would stage the Ghost's entry, appearance (Nightgown? Armour?), movement and manner of speech.

1 Why does the Ghost return?

Why does the Ghost return? It appears that Hamlet was 'getting through' to Gertrude ('These words like daggers . . .'). Suggest several reasons for the Ghost's reappearance at this critical moment.

---

grainèd   indelibly stained
leave their tinct   lose their stain
tithe   tenth part
vice   clown in medieval morality plays, dressed in multicoloured costume ('A king of shreds and patches')
cutpurse   thief

tardy   slow
whet   sharpen
amazement   bewilderment
Conceit   imagination
bend your eye   look
th'incorporal   bodiless

GERTRUDE   O Hamlet, speak no more.
       Thou turn'st my eyes into my very soul,
       And there I see such black and grainèd spots   90
       As will not leave their tinct.
HAMLET   Nay, but to live
       In the rank sweat of an enseamèd bed,
       Stewed in corruption, honeying and making love
       Over the nasty sty.
GERTRUDE   Oh speak to me no more.
       These words like daggers enter in my ears.   95
       No more sweet Hamlet.
HAMLET   A murderer and a villain,
       A slave that is not twentieth part the tithe
       Of your precedent lord, a vice of kings,
       A cutpurse of the empire and the rule,
       That from a shelf the precious diadem stole   100
       And put it in his pocket.
GERTRUDE   No more!

                    Enter GHOST

HAMLET A king of shreds and patches –
       Save me and hover o'er me with your wings,
       You heavenly guards! – What would your gracious figure?
GERTRUDE Alas he's mad!   105
HAMLET Do you not come your tardy son to chide,
       That lapsed in time and passion lets go by
       Th'important acting of your dread command? Oh say!
GHOST Do not forget. This visitation
       Is but to whet thy almost blunted purpose.   110
       But look, amazement on thy mother sits.
       Oh step between her and her fighting soul:
       Conceit in weakest bodies strongest works.
       Speak to her, Hamlet.
HAMLET   How is it with you lady?
GERTRUDE Alas, how is't with you,   115
       That you do bend your eye on vacancy,
       And with th'incorporal air do hold discourse?
       Forth at your eyes your spirits wildly peep,

Gertrude, unable to see the Ghost, is bewildered by Hamlet's behaviour. Hamlet fears that his impulse to revenge might soften to pity. He says he is not mad, and urges Gertrude to repent.

---

1 The mind's construction in the face? (in groups of three)

Hamlet says the combination of the Ghost's appearance and plea for justice would make even stones feel pity ('form and cause conjoined . . . capable'). Hamlet implores the Ghost to turn his gaze away because it weakens his impulse to revenge (lines 126–9). Enact lines 115–37, concentrating on facial expression and positioning/ movement of the three characters in relation to each other.

2 Why can't Gertrude see the Ghost?

Write two or more paragraphs about whether you think Gertrude's inability to see the Ghost signifies her moral blindness, and what other possible explanations there might be.

3 Images of corruption (in small groups)

Hamlet rejects Gertrude's accusation that he is mad. It's your crime ('trespass'), not my madness that has called up the Ghost, he says. To believe otherwise is just an ointment ('unction') to cover ('skin and film') the corruption deep and growing within her (lines 145–50). He attributes virtue to himself and vice to Gertrude: she is the one who should repent. In these sick ('pursy') times, virtue must ask forgiveness of vice (see also p. 265).

How does Hamlet speak lines 140–56? Does he plead with her, trying to appeal to her reason with rational argument? Or does he speak vehemently and accusingly, stressing intensely all the words to do with madness and corruption? Experiment with ways of speaking the lines to express Hamlet's emotional state at this point in the play.

---

in th'alarm woken by call to battle	**portal** door
bedded smoothed down	**coinage** creation
excrements outgrowths (hair)	**ecstasy / Is very cunning in**
stern effects intention to revenge	madness invents
want true colour lose its real	**gambol** leap, shy away
character	**curb and woo** flatter
habit as he lived everyday clothes	**leave** permission

	And, as the sleeping soldiers in th'alarm,
	Your bedded hair, like life in excrements, 120
	Start up and stand an end. O gentle son,
	Upon the heat and flame of thy distemper
	Sprinkle cool patience. Whereon do you look?
HAMLET	On him, on him! Look you how pale he glares.
	His form and cause conjoined, preaching to stones, 125
	Would make them capable. – Do not look upon me,
	Lest with this piteous action you convert
	My stern effects. Then what I have to do
	Will want true colour: tears perchance for blood.
GERTRUDE	To whom do you speak this? 130
HAMLET	Do you see nothing there?
GERTRUDE	Nothing at all, yet all that is I see.
HAMLET	Nor did you nothing hear?
GERTRUDE	No, nothing but ourselves.
HAMLET	Why, look you there – look how it steals away – 135
	My father in his habit as he lived –
	Look where he goes, even now out at the portal.

Exit Ghost

GERTRUDE	This is the very coinage of your brain.
	This bodiless creation ecstasy
	Is very cunning in.
HAMLET	Ecstasy? 140
	My pulse as yours doth temperately keep time,
	And makes as healthful music. It is not madness
	That I have uttered. Bring me to the test,
	And I the matter will reword, which madness
	Would gambol from. Mother, for love of grace, 145
	Lay not that flattering unction to your soul,
	That not your trespass but my madness speaks;
	It will but skin and film the ulcerous place,
	Whiles rank corruption, mining all within,
	Infects unseen. Confess yourself to heaven, 150
	Repent what's past, avoid what is to come,
	And do not spread the compost on the weeds
	To make them ranker. Forgive me this my virtue,
	For in the fatness of these pursy times
	Virtue itself of vice must pardon beg, 155
	Yea, curb and woo for leave to do him good.

Hamlet pleads with Gertrude not to sleep with Claudius tonight: that abstinence will begin what can become a virtuous habit. He claims to be heaven's agent in killing Polonius.

1 Custom – will Hamlet's advice work? (in small groups)

Hamlet argues (lines 162–71) that 'custom' destroys sensibility, but it also can result in virtue. Good things, as well as bad, can come about through habitual practice. If Gertrude doesn't sleep with Claudius tonight, that will make it easier for her to refrain the next night, and on further nights. Discuss whether you agree with Hamlet's argument, or whether you think abstinence just stores up emotion that leads to a later explosion. Will Gertrude follow Hamlet's advice?

2 What's the missing word?

No one knows what Shakespeare intended to write in line 170. The word is missing in all the earliest printed editions. Which word do you think would fit? Suggestions have been: curb, master, aid, shame, speed, quell, house, lodge and oust.

3 Is Hamlet God's agent? (in pairs)

Traditional revengers do not see themselves as agents for good, but for a kind of rough justice in the world. In lines 174–6, Hamlet appears not so much to *blame* heaven for the death of Polonius, as to see himself as God's agent – but also as being punished for the act of murder. Is that how you see him? Discuss to what extent you see him as a force for good in the play.

4 'I must be cruel only to be kind' (in small groups)

Hamlet's line 179 has become part of everyday language. Give examples from your own experience of when you have used it (or when it has been said to or about you).

---

cleft my heart in twain broken my heart in two
sense finer feelings, sensibility
Of habits devil the evil spirit of all habits
frock or livery clothing or uniform

Refrain don't go to bed with him
wondrous potency amazing power
scourge and minister whip and officer who wields it
bestow dispose of
remains behind lies ahead

GERTRUDE Oh Hamlet, thou hast cleft my heart in twain.
HAMLET Oh throw away the worser part of it
      And live the purer with the other half.
      Good night – but go not to my uncle's bed;   160
      Assume a virtue if you have it not.
      [That monster custom, who all sense doth eat,
      Of habits devil, is angel yet in this,
      That to the use of actions fair and good
      He likewise gives a frock or livery   165
      That aptly is put on.] Refrain tonight,
      And that shall lend a kind of easiness
      To the next abstinence, [the next more easy,
      For use almost can change the stamp of nature,
      And either . . . the devil, or throw him out,   170
      With wondrous potency.] Once more good night,
      And when you are desirous to be blessed,
      I'll blessing beg of you. For this same lord,
      I do repent; but heaven hath pleased it so,
      To punish me with this, and this with me,   175
      That I must be their scourge and minister.
      I will bestow him, and will answer well
      The death I gave him. So again, good night.
      I must be cruel only to be kind;
      Thus bad begins, and worse remains behind.   180
      One word more good lady.
GERTRUDE   What shall I do?

Hamlet urges Gertrude not to reveal his pretended madness to Claudius. He threatens her. She promises to keep silent. Hamlet plans to kill Rosencrantz and Guildenstern, who are involved in a plot against him.

1 Irony or sarcasm?

Lines 183–92 are heavily ironic, even sarcastic. Hamlet seems to order Gertrude to reveal his secrets to Claudius. But line 182 makes his intention clear: she is not to do as he commands. Advise the actor playing Hamlet on how to speak lines 182–92. Your interpretation of these lines will have a bearing on whether you take Hamlet's 'mad in craft' at face value, or as a poor attempt by Hamlet to explain his actions and inaction.

2 Imagery: interpretation – and cuts?

a **'The famous ape'**   Perhaps lines 194–7 mean: an ape took a bird cage onto a roof, released the birds, and seeing them fly, decided to imitate them ('try conclusions') – with disastrous results. Hamlet may be using the fable to threaten his mother: if she reveals his secrets to the king, she too will come to grief ('And break your own neck down'). Invent another interpretation that seems plausible.

b **Mining and countermining**   Attackers besieging a city often dug tunnels (mines) under the walls and packed them with explosives to demolish the defences. The defenders dug countermines underneath ('in one line') to blow up the besiegers' tunnels. Thus the 'engineer' (miner) was 'Hoist with his own petar' (blown up with his own bomb).

c **To cut or not to cut?**   The lines in square brackets (lines 203–11) suggest that Hamlet already has plans to kill Rosencrantz and Guildenstern. As Act 5 Scene 2 shows, that may not be true. Imagine you are directing the play and are urged to cut the lines for that reason. What do you reply?

---

bloat   flabby, bloated
wanton   lustfully
reechy   filthy
ravel   unravel, explain
craft   pretence, cunning
paddock, **gib**   toad, cat

dear concernings   important matters
adders fanged   poisonous snakes
mandate   orders
delve   dig
crafts   plots

HAMLET Not this by no means that I bid you do:
    Let the bloat king tempt you again to bed,
    Pinch wanton on your cheek, call you his mouse,
    And let him for a pair of reechy kisses,   185
    Or paddling in your neck with his damned fingers,
    Make you to ravel all this matter out,
    That I essentially am not in madness,
    But mad in craft. 'Twere good you let him know,
    For who that's but a queen, fair, sober, wise,   190
    Would from a paddock, from a bat, a gib,
    Such dear concernings hide? Who would do so?
    No, in despite of sense and secrecy,
    Unpeg the basket on the house's top,
    Let the birds fly, and like the famous ape,   195
    To try conclusions, in the basket creep
    And break your own neck down.
GERTRUDE Be thou assured, if words be made of breath,
    And breath of life, I have no life to breathe
    What thou hast said to me.   200
HAMLET I must to England, you know that?
GERTRUDE   Alack,
    I had forgot. 'Tis so concluded on.
HAMLET [There's letters sealed, and my two schoolfellows,
    Whom I will trust as I will adders fanged,
    They bear the mandate. They must sweep my way   205
    And marshal me to knavery. Let it work,
    For 'tis the sport to have the engineer
    Hoist with his own petar, an't shall go hard
    But I will delve one yard below their mines
    And blow them at the moon. Oh 'tis most sweet   210
    When in one line two crafts directly meet.]
    This man shall set me packing.
    I'll lug the guts into the neighbour room.
    Mother, good night. Indeed, this counsellor
    Is now most still, most secret, and most grave,   215
    Who was in life a foolish prating knave.
    Come sir, to draw toward an end with you.
    Good night mother.
            Exit Hamlet tugging in Polonius; [Gertrude remains]

Looking back at Act 3
Activities for groups or individuals

1 Hamlet: speech, action and response

Hamlet appears in each of the four scenes in Act 3. To further your understanding of his relationships with other characters, copy the table below onto a large sheet of paper and complete the blank spaces.

Scene	Hamlet speaks to or about	A typical line or lines	Hamlet's mood and intention
1	Ophelia		
2	The players		
	Horatio		
	Claudius		
	Polonius		
	Gertrude		
	Ophelia		
	Rosencrantz and Guildenstern		
3	Claudius		
4	Gertrude		

2 Attitudes to Hamlet

Consider each character listed in the table above. Write a sentence for each of them, expressing their attitude to Hamlet as they encounter him in Act 3, and whether they think he is mad.

3 Appearance versus reality

Use the list above. For each character write a sentence saying how their words or actions in some way express the theme of appearance versus reality (Horatio may prove an exception).

4 Hamlet as playwright

Hamlet asked the First Player (Act 2 Scene 2, lines 493–4) to 'study a / speech of some dozen or sixteen lines' he would write specially for *The Murder of Gonzago* play. No one knows for certain if those lines actually were spoken in Scene 2. Try to identify (giving reasons) which lines were Hamlet's. If you think none of the lines was his, write a dozen lines that you think he would have inserted.

Hamlet and Gertrude. Find lines from Scene 4 that could make suitable captions for each picture. Talk together about what you think the director of each production might have in mind about the mother–son relationship.

Gertrude tells Claudius that Hamlet has killed Polonius. Claudius fears that he himself might have been the victim and that he will be blamed for Polonius's death. He lies about his love for Hamlet.

1 Claudius and Gertrude alone – and lying (in pairs)

This short scene is the only time in the play that Claudius and Gertrude are alone together. The best thing to do is to take parts and read the scene aloud (Rosencrantz and Guildenstern do not speak, so just 'imagine' them). You will find that Claudius expresses no word of regret for the dead Polonius; he thinks only that he himself might have been Hamlet's victim.

It is also significant that both Claudius and Gertrude lie to each other. Claudius says he loves Hamlet, and Gertrude, keeping her promise to her son, tells Claudius at least four times that Hamlet is mad (lines 7, 8, 11 and 25).

In your reading try to bring out Claudius's self-centredness and Gertrude's determination to be loyal to Hamlet. She may be nervous, and so might overemphasise (or pause before) her four mentions of his madness. Also consider how they behave towards each other (e.g. might Claudius attempt to comfort his wife by embracing her?).

2 Director's decisions

At the end of Act 3 the stage direction '*Gertrude remains*' is in square brackets because it does not appear in one of the early editions of the play. As director, advise Gertrude whether she should remain on stage until the arrival of Claudius, Rosencrantz and Guildenstern, or whether she should exit and re-enter with Claudius. Which is the more dramatically convincing? Also decide if you would cut line 4, 'Bestow this place on us a little while' (Why bring on Rosencrantz and Guildenstern only to dismiss them?).

---

profound heaves deep sighs and shudders
translate explain
contend dispute
lawless unruly
brainish apprehension frenzied state of mind
providence foresight

short confined
out of haunt out of the public eye
divulging becoming generally known
pith core, essence
draw apart cut up
ore . . . pure pure metal shining among crude ones

Act 4 Scene 1
Gertrude's private room

Enter CLAUDIUS *with* ROSENCRANTZ *and* GUILDENSTERN

CLAUDIUS There's matter in these sighs, these profound heaves.
　　　　You must translate, 'tis fit we understand them.
　　　　Where is your son?
GERTRUDE [Bestow this place on us a little while.]
　　　　　　　　　　　[*Exeunt Rosencrantz and Guildenstern*]
　　　　Ah mine own lord, what have I seen tonight!　　　　　　5
CLAUDIUS What, Gertrude? How does Hamlet?
GERTRUDE Mad as the sea and wind, when both contend
　　　　Which is the mightier. In his lawless fit,
　　　　Behind the arras hearing something stir,
　　　　Whips out his rapier, cries 'A rat, a rat!',　　　　　　10
　　　　And in this brainish apprehension kills
　　　　The unseen good old man.
CLAUDIUS 　　　　　　　　　　　Oh heavy deed!
　　　　It had been so with us had we been there.
　　　　His liberty is full of threats to all,
　　　　To you yourself, to us, to everyone.　　　　　　　　15
　　　　Alas, how shall this bloody deed be answered?
　　　　It will be laid to us, whose providence
　　　　Should have kept short, restrained, and out of haunt,
　　　　This mad young man. But so much was our love,
　　　　We would not understand what was most fit,　　　　　20
　　　　But like the owner of a foul disease,
　　　　To keep it from divulging, let it feed
　　　　Even on the pith of life. Where is he gone?
GERTRUDE To draw apart the body he hath killed,
　　　　O'er whom his very madness, like some ore　　　　　25
　　　　Among a mineral of metals base,
　　　　Shows itself pure; a weeps for what is done.

Claudius decides to send Hamlet away from Denmark. He orders Rosencrantz and Guildenstern to join with others to find Polonius's body and take it to the chapel. He hopes he can avoid slanderous accusations.

---

1 Character and relationships

Neither Gertrude nor Claudius offers comforting words to the other in Scene 1. Lines 28–45 afford dramatic opportunities for actors to express character and relationships. Write a paragraph on each of the following, saying how you would use each to give the audience insight into character and relationships.

a Claudius three times gives an order to Gertrude: 'come away', 'Come', 'come away'. How might she respond to each?

b Gertrude says nothing during Claudius's final speech. What is she doing throughout?

c Claudius makes a decision to exile Hamlet, but to whom might he speak lines 29–32?

d In lines 41–4 Claudius seems concerned that slanders and rumours must not damage his reputation. He proposes to brief his 'wisest friends' to prevent it happening. What does that suggest about his character?

2 For your information: missing words

The dots at line 40 suggest that two words are missing. Lines 41 to 44 are in square brackets because they do not appear in the First Folio version of the play, printed later than other versions (see p. 269). In performance, actors often speak 'For slander' here (see **d** above).

3 'Oh here they come'

Experiment with ways of speaking 'Oh here they come' (lines 3–4). Give reasons for how you think Hamlet should speak it.

---

countenance condone, accept
join you with . . . aid recruit more help
speak fair humour him
untimely wrongly, inappropriately
o'er the world's diameter to the ends of the world

level accurately
blank target
name reputation
woundless invulnerable
Compounded mixed, blended
kin related

CLAUDIUS Oh Gertrude, come away!
The sun no sooner shall the mountains touch
But we will ship him hence, and this vile deed   30
We must with all our majesty and skill
Both countenance and excuse. Ho, Guildenstern!

Enter Rosencrantz and Guildenstern

Friends both, go join you with some further aid.
Hamlet in madness hath Polonius slain,
And from his mother's closet hath he dragged him.   35
Go seek him out, speak fair, and bring the body
Into the chapel. I pray you haste in this.
                Exeunt Rosencrantz and Guildenstern
Come Gertrude, we'll call up our wisest friends
And let them know both what we mean to do
And what's untimely done   40
[Whose whisper o'er the world's diameter,
As level as the cannon to his blank,
Transports his poisoned shot, may miss our name
And hit the woundless air.] Oh come away,
My soul is full of discord and dismay.   45
                                        Exeunt

Act 4 Scene 2
A corridor in the castle

Enter HAMLET

HAMLET Safely stowed.
GENTLEMEN (*Within*) Hamlet! Lord Hamlet!
HAMLET But soft, what noise? Who calls on Hamlet? Oh here they
come.

Enter ROSENCRANTZ *and* GUILDENSTERN

ROSENCRANTZ What have you done my lord with the dead body?   5
HAMLET Compounded it with dust whereto 'tis kin.

Hamlet's replies bewilder Rosencrantz and Guildenstern. He does not reveal where Polonius's body is hidden. Claudius feels he cannot punish Hamlet severely because Hamlet is popular in Denmark.

---

1 Act out Scene 2 – Hamlet's evasiveness (in groups of three)

The very short Scene 2 offers excellent opportunities for acting out. Hamlet has been presented in many different ways (washing a blood-stained shirt, waking from sleep etc.), and his mocking language invites the actor to all kinds of stage business.

Take parts and act the scene to maximise dramatic effect. It will help your performance if you think about the different strategies Hamlet uses in lines 9–27 to avoid telling Rosencrantz and Guildenstern where Polonius's body is hidden:

- He insults Rosencrantz with the 'sponge' and 'ape' comparisons.
- He brands Rosencrantz as too dull to recognise satire.
- He speaks an enigmatic riddle, 'The body is with the king . . .'.
- 'Hide fox, and all after!' In some productions, Hamlet runs away as he speaks line 27, chased by the two courtiers. But consider other possibilities and work out how the three characters leave the stage. Think about how the hunting image might be applicable to the play as a whole.

2 Invent images for characters

Hamlet uses extended imagery (see pp. 264–5) to sum up Rosen-crantz's nature: he is a sponge, or he is like food to be sucked and swallowed by a king in the same way that an ape eats. Invent an extended image to describe each of the following, then, for one or more of these characters, write a paragraph that justifies your invented image:

Hamlet (e.g. think of a chameleon, or changeable weather)
Guildenstern
Horatio
Claudius
Gertrude.

---

replication reply
countenance favour, goodwill
authorities influence
gleaned gathered, harvested
knavish sarcastic, satirical

the strong law strict restraints
distracted muddled, irrational
like . . . eyes love him for his looks
rather than for sound reasons

ROSENCRANTZ Tell us where 'tis, that we may take it thence and bear
it to the chapel.

HAMLET Do not believe it.

ROSENCRANTZ Believe what?   10

HAMLET That I can keep your counsel and not mine own. Besides, to
be demanded of a sponge, what replication should be made by the
son of a king?

ROSENCRANTZ Take you me for a sponge my lord?

HAMLET Ay sir, that soaks up the king's countenance, his rewards, his   15
authorities. But such officers do the king best service in the end:
he keeps them like an ape in the corner of his jaw, first mouthed
to be last swallowed. When he needs what you have gleaned, it is
but squeezing you, and, sponge, you shall be dry again.

ROSENCRANTZ I understand you not my lord.   20

HAMLET I am glad of it, a knavish speech sleeps in a foolish ear.

ROSENCRANTZ My lord, you must tell us where the body is, and go
with us to the king.

HAMLET The body is with the king, but the king is not with the body.
The king is a thing –   25

GUILDENSTERN A thing my lord?

HAMLET Of nothing. Bring me to him. Hide fox, and all after!

Exeunt

Act 4 Scene 3
A state room

Enter CLAUDIUS, and two or three ATTENDANTS

CLAUDIUS I have sent to seek him, and to find the body.
How dangerous is it that this man goes loose,
Yet must not we put the strong law on him;
He's loved of the distracted multitude,
Who like not in their judgement, but their eyes;   5

Claudius reflects that he must use desperate methods. Hamlet is brought in. He taunts Claudius with images of the corruption of dead bodies, then reveals where Polonius's body is hidden.

The 1970 Royal Shakespeare Company production showed Hamlet stripped and beaten by Rosencrantz and Guildenstern. How would you present the stage direction at line 15?

1 '. . . through the guts of a beggar' (in pairs)

In taunting Claudius, Hamlet stresses corruption ('worms') and the levelling nature of death: a king may go 'a progress' (a royal journey) through the guts of a beggar. Hamlet also puns on the Diet ('convocation') of Worms (a town in Germany), where in 1521 the Protestant Martin Luther defended his anti-papal views. The worms are 'politic' because they infiltrate the body in the same way as Polonius had insinuated his way into state affairs and Hamlet's privacy. Take parts and speak lines 16–49, making Hamlet mockingly ironic and Claudius struggling to control his anger.

---

scourge punishment
weighed noted
Deliberate pause planned
appliance remedies
variable service different dishes in a menu

i'th'other place hell
A will stay till you come he won't move (in the theatre, Hamlet's ironic remark often makes the audience laugh)

And where 'tis so, th'offender's scourge is weighed,
But never the offence. To bear all smooth and even,
This sudden sending him away must seem
Deliberate pause. Diseases desperate grown
By desperate appliance are relieved,   10
Or not at all.

Enter ROSENCRANTZ

How now, what hath befallen?
ROSENCRANTZ Where the dead body is bestowed, my lord,
    We cannot get from him.
CLAUDIUS   But where is he?
ROSENCRANTZ Without, my lord, guarded, to know your pleasure.
CLAUDIUS Bring him before us.
ROSENCRANTZ   Ho! bring in my lord.   15

Enter HAMLET *and* GUILDENSTERN

CLAUDIUS Now Hamlet, where's Polonius?
HAMLET At supper.
CLAUDIUS At supper? Where?
HAMLET Not where he eats, but where a is eaten. A certain convocation
    of politic worms are e'en at him. Your worm is your only emperor   20
    for diet: we fat all creatures else to fat us, and we fat ourselves for
    maggots. Your fat king and your lean beggar is but variable service,
    two dishes, but to one table; that's the end.
CLAUDIUS Alas, alas.
HAMLET A man may fish with the worm that hath eat of a king, and   25
    eat of the fish that hath fed of that worm.
CLAUDIUS What dost thou mean by this?
HAMLET Nothing but to show you how a king may go a progress
    through the guts of a beggar.
CLAUDIUS Where is Polonius?   30
HAMLET In heaven, send thither to see. If your messenger find him not
    there, seek him i'th'other place yourself. But if indeed you find him
    not within this month, you shall nose him as you go up the stairs
    into the lobby.
CLAUDIUS Go seek him there.   35
HAMLET A will stay till you come.

[*Exeunt Attendants*]

Claudius tells Hamlet a ship and attendants wait to take him to England. Hamlet bids Claudius an ironic farewell. Claudius reveals he has written letters ordering Hamlet's immediate execution in England.

1 Two crucial moments – your decisions?

a **Hamlet's suspicions** Who is the 'cherub'? At line 44, Claudius replies to Hamlet's positive acceptance of exile to England with: 'So is it if thou knew'st our purposes.' The words have sinister implications: Claudius is planning to have Hamlet killed. Hamlet responds: 'I see a cherub that sees them' (line 45). At whom (or what) does Hamlet look when he says 'cherub', and why does he use that word? Give reasons for your decisions, and say whether you think Hamlet suspects that Claudius intends to have him killed.

b **Hamlet's obsession** '. . . man and wife / is one flesh'. Throughout the play Hamlet has been obsessed by his mother's sexuality. His lines 48–9 reveal that fixation. But how does he speak the lines (with loathing, humour, calm logic, or with some other feeling or combination of feelings)? Advise the actor, giving reasons.

2 'Do it England': kill Hamlet! (in large groups)

Claudius reveals his plans for Hamlet's death. His soliloquy (lines 54–64) suggests that Denmark has recently won a great victory over England, whose 'cicatrice' (battle-scar) 'looks raw and red'. England voluntarily ('free awe') pays Claudius tribute money, and is unlikely to ignore his royal wishes ('sovereign process').

Half of the group, chorally, reads aloud lines 54–64. The other half says 'England' each time Claudius refers to England (there are eight references). Change roles and repeat, then talk together about how you think Claudius might deliver the soliloquy. For example, what would be the dramatic effect if he addressed a map, clearly visible to the audience? And what if 'England' means 'King of England'?

---

do tender have concern for
bark ship
at foot closely
else leans on is connected with
at aught as having any value
coldly set look at with indifference

imports means, implies
congruing leading, agreeing
present immediate
hectic terrible fever
haps fortunes

CLAUDIUS Hamlet, this deed, for thine especial safety,
    Which we do tender, as we dearly grieve
    For that which thou hast done, must send thee hence
    With fiery quickness. Therefore prepare thyself. 40
    The bark is ready and the wind at help,
    Th'associates tend, and everything is bent
    For England.
HAMLET   For England?
CLAUDIUS   Ay Hamlet.
HAMLET   Good.
CLAUDIUS So is it if thou knew'st our purposes.
HAMLET I see a cherub that sees them. But come, for England! Farewell 45
  dear mother.
CLAUDIUS Thy loving father, Hamlet.
HAMLET My mother. Father and mother is man and wife, man and wife
  is one flesh, and so, my mother. Come, for England.   *Exit*
CLAUDIUS Follow him at foot, tempt him with speed aboard. 50
    Delay it not, I'll have him hence tonight.
    Away, for everything is sealed and done
    That else leans on th'affair. Pray you make haste.
       [*Exeunt Rosencrantz and Guildenstern*]
    And England, if my love thou hold'st at aught,
    As my great power thereof may give thee sense, 55
    Since yet thy cicatrice looks raw and red
    After the Danish sword, and thy free awe
    Pays homage to us – thou mayst not coldly set
    Our sovereign process, which imports at full,
    By letters congruing to that effect, 60
    The present death of Hamlet. Do it England,
    For like the hectic in my blood he rages,
    And thou must cure me. Till I know 'tis done,
    Howe'er my haps, my joys were ne'er begun. *Exit*

Fortinbras sends a captain to ask Claudius for permission to pass through Danish territory. The captain tells Hamlet the army will fight for a tiny, unprofitable part of Poland. Hamlet reflects on a sick society.

Fortinbras and his army. The Russian film director Kozintsev's imaginative re-creation of Scene 4 (see also p. 274).

1 More imagery of corruption

Lines 27–9 express another of the play's images of corruption (see p. 265): the sickness of a healthy society ('th'impostume of much wealth and peace') sends thousands to die for a triviality. But you will find that the sight of Fortinbras's army spurs Hamlet to revenge (turn the page).

would aught   wishes to negotiate
in his eye   face to face
softly   quietly, carefully
How purposed   with what purpose
main   entire country
addition   exaggeration
ducats   gold coins

ranker rate   greater price
in fee   outright
Will not debate . . . straw   will not be enough to resolve this trivial matter
impostume   abscess, inner sore
without   outside
God buy you   God be with you

Act 4 Scene 4
The sea coast near Elsinore

Enter FORTINBRAS *with his army*

FORTINBRAS Go captain, from me greet the Danish king.
    Tell him that by his licence, Fortinbras
    Craves the conveyance of a promised march
    Over his kingdom. You know the rendezvous.
    If that his majesty would aught with us,   5
    We shall express our duty in his eye,
    And let him know so.
CAPTAIN   I will do't, my lord.
FORTINBRAS Go softly on.

                   [Exit Fortinbras, with the army]

      [Enter HAMLET, ROSENCRANTZ, *etc.*

HAMLET Good sir, whose powers are these?
CAPTAIN They are of Norway sir.   10
HAMLET How purposed sir I pray you?
CAPTAIN Against some part of Poland.
HAMLET Who commands them sir?
CAPTAIN The nephew to old Norway, Fortinbras.
HAMLET Goes it against the main of Poland sir,   15
    Or for some frontier?
CAPTAIN Truly to speak, and with no addition,
    We go to gain a little patch of ground
    That hath in it no profit but the name.
    To pay five ducats, five, I would not farm it,   20
    Nor will it yield to Norway or the Pole
    A ranker rate, should it be sold in fee.
HAMLET Why then the Polack never will defend it.
CAPTAIN Yes, it is already garrisoned.
HAMLET Two thousand souls and twenty thousand ducats   25
    Will not debate the question of this straw.
    This is th'impostume of much wealth and peace,
    That inward breaks, and shows no cause without
    Why the man dies. I humbly thank you sir.
CAPTAIN God buy you sir.   *[Exit]*

Hamlet criticises his delay in revenging his father's death. Is it forgetfulness or too much thought that stops him? Prompted by his encounter with Fortinbras's army, he resolves to speed to his revenge.

---

1 Hamlet is spurred on to revenge (in small groups)

Hamlet's soliloquy contains five sections:

Lines 32–3 'How all occasions . . . revenge!': everything I encounter prompts me to revenge.

Lines 33–46 'What is a man . . . To do't': man has great intelligence, but somehow I delay, even though I have good cause.

Lines 46–56 'Examples . . . stake': many examples prompt me, but this sight of Fortinbras's army teaches me that honour must be defended.

Lines 56–65 'How stand I . . . slain': I have great cause, yet do nothing, but I see thousands of men about to die for a trivial cause.

Lines 65–6 'Oh from this time forth . . . nothing worth': from now on, I will pursue only revenge.

Sometimes the soliloquy is cut in performance because it does not appear in the First Folio (see p. 269). Although Hamlet finally determines on revenge, he deludes himself when in line 45 he says he has 'cause, and will, and strength, and means' to do it: he is a prisoner under guard being escorted to exile. Scene 6 will reveal that another chance encounter (this time with pirates) frees him to find the strength and means for revenge.

Explore different ways of speaking the soliloquy: individually; or echoing words and phrases you think especially important; or speaking short sections in turn as a kind of anxious 'conversation', or as if you are trying to persuade someone of the argument you are developing. After your explorations, each person writes notes on how the soliloquy might be delivered on stage.

---

inform against rebuke
good and market profit
large discourse powerful intelligence
fust go stale
Bestial oblivion animal forgetfulness
craven scruple cowardly restraint

mass and charge numbers and cost
Makes . . . event mocks death
stained defiled
Whereon . . . the cause where there is not enough room to fight
continent large enough container

ROSENCRANTZ   Will't please you go my lord?   30
HAMLET   I'll be with you straight; go a little before.

                                        [*Exeunt all but Hamlet*]

How all occasions do inform against me,
And spur my dull revenge! What is a man
If his chief good and market of his time
Be but to sleep and feed? A beast, no more.   35
Sure he that made us with such large discourse,
Looking before and after, gave us not
That capability and god-like reason
To fust in us unused. Now whether it be
Bestial oblivion, or some craven scruple   40
Of thinking too precisely on th'event –
A thought which quartered hath but one part wisdom
And ever three parts coward – I do not know
Why yet I live to say this thing's to do,
Sith I have cause, and will, and strength, and means   45
To do't. Examples gross as earth exhort me.
Witness this army of such mass and charge,
Led by a delicate and tender prince,
Whose spirit with divine ambition puffed
Makes mouths at the invisible event,   50
Exposing what is mortal and unsure
To all that fortune, death and danger dare,
Even for an egg-shell. Rightly to be great
Is not to stir without great argument,
But greatly to find quarrel in a straw   55
When honour's at the stake. How stand I then,
That have a father killed, a mother stained,
Excitements of my reason and my blood,
And let all sleep, while to my shame I see
The imminent death of twenty thousand men,   60
That for a fantasy and trick of fame
Go to their graves like beds, fight for a plot
Whereon the numbers cannot try the cause,
Which is not tomb enough and continent
To hide the slain. Oh from this time forth,   65
My thoughts be bloody or be nothing worth.   *Exit*]

Gertrude refuses to see Ophelia, but is told that Ophelia is mad and needs pity. Gertrude agrees to admit Ophelia, but expresses guilt and misgivings about the future.

---

1 A graphic picture of mental illness (in pairs)

The Gentleman gives a moving account of an extremely disturbed young woman. Ophelia's thoughts are full of her father, she thinks the world to be corrupt ('There's tricks i'th'world'), beats her breast, flies into a temper at the slightest thing, and so on. Take turns to speak lines 4–13, trying to express Ophelia's pitiable state.

2 Does Gertrude share Claudius's secret? (in pairs)

Gertrude's lines 17–20 display a guilty conscience. She speaks of her 'sick soul', and says that guilty people give themselves away because they cannot hide their fear of being found out. Some critics argue that these lines show she shares, or suspects, Claudius's secret, and is complicit in her first husband's murder.

What is your view? Look back at Gertrude's appearances (Act 1 Scene 2; Act 2 Scene 2; Act 3 Scenes 1, 2 and 4; Act 4 Scene 1). One person looks for evidence to support the view that Gertrude does not know that Claudius killed King Hamlet. The other person's task is to find evidence that Gertrude does know about Claudius's crime. Present your conflicting arguments as powerfully as possible.

3 Ophelia enters – '*playing on a lute*'?

In the First Quarto (see p. 269) the stage direction at line 20 is '*Enter Ophelia playing on a lute, and her hair down singing*'. In Shakespeare's time it was customary for madness in women to be marked by a long wig of loose hair. How would you stage her entrance? The picture caption on page 172 and the picture on page 180 will help.

---

importunate persistent
distract mad
What would she have? What does she want?
hems clears her throat
Spurns . . . straws gets angry at little things

to collection to work out a meaning
yawn guess
conjectures suppositions, ideas
ill-breeding suspicious, trouble-makers'
toy trifle
amiss misfortune

Act 4 Scene 5
The Great Hall of Elsinore Castle

Enter HORATIO, GERTRUDE *and a* GENTLEMAN

GERTRUDE I will not speak with her.

GENTLEMAN She is importunate, indeed distract;
    Her mood will needs be pitied.

GERTRUDE   What would she have?

GENTLEMAN She speaks much of her father, says she hears
    There's tricks i'th'world, and hems, and beats her heart,   5
    Spurns enviously at straws, speaks things in doubt
    That carry but half sense. Her speech is nothing,
    Yet the unshapèd use of it doth move
    The hearers to collection. They yawn at it,
    And botch the words up fit to their own thoughts,   10
    Which, as her winks and nods and gestures yield them,
    Indeed would make one think there might be thought,
    Though nothing sure, yet much unhappily.

HORATIO 'Twere good she were spoken with, for she may strew
    Dangerous conjectures in ill-breeding minds.   15

GERTRUDE Let her come in.

                       [*Exit Gentleman*]

    (*Aside*) To my sick soul, as sin's true nature is,
    Each toy seems prologue to some great amiss.
    So full of artless jealousy is guilt,
    It spills itself in fearing to be spilt.   20

Enter OPHELIA *distracted*

OPHELIA Where is the beauteous majesty of Denmark?

Ophelia's first song recalls the death of her father. She replies enigmatically to Claudius, declares that the future is uncertain, then sings a song about the loss of virginity.

Hamlet © 1990 World Icon N.V. Licensed by Warner Bros. Entertainment Inc. All Rights Reserved.

In some modern stage productions Ophelia wears articles of Polonius's clothing, adding poignancy to the fragments of ballads she sings. Her mental and emotional derangement has been acted in many ways: dreamily trance-like, frantically angry, sexually obsessed and so on. Her remark 'They say the owl was a baker's daughter' may be from a traditional tale. The picture shows how Ophelia appeared in Zeffirelli's 1990 film. How closely does she match your image of Ophelia driven into madness? See also page 263.

cockle hat a hat with a shell emblem, worn by pilgrims
shoon shoes
imports means
shrowd death sheet, shroud
Larded decorated

good dild God reward
owl symbol of death?
baker's daughter symbol of lust?
Conceit wild thoughts
betime early
dupped undid

GERTRUDE How now Ophelia?

OPHELIA   *She sings*
　　　　　　How should I your true love know
　　　　　　From another one?
　　　　　　By his cockle hat and staff   25
　　　　　　And his sandal shoon.

GERTRUDE Alas sweet lady, what imports this song?

OPHELIA Say you? Nay, pray you mark.
　　　　　　He is dead and gone lady,   *Song*
　　　　　　He is dead and gone;   30
　　　　　　At his head a grass-green turf,
　　　　　　At his heels a stone.

　　Oho!

GERTRUDE Nay but Ophelia –

OPHELIA Pray you mark.   35
　　　　　　White his shrowd as the mountain snow –   *Song*

　　　　　Enter CLAUDIUS

GERTRUDE Alas, look here my lord.

OPHELIA   Larded all with sweet flowers,
　　　　　　Which bewept to the grave did not go
　　　　　　With true-love showers.   40

CLAUDIUS How do you, pretty lady?

OPHELIA Well good dild you. They say the owl was a baker's daughter.
　　Lord, we know what we are, but know not what we may be. God
　　be at your table.

CLAUDIUS Conceit upon her father.   45

OPHELIA Pray let's have no words of this, but when they ask you what
　　it means, say you this –

　　　　　　Tomorrow is Saint Valentine's day,   *Song*
　　　　　　All in the morning betime,
　　　　　　And I a maid at your window,   50
　　　　　　To be your Valentine.

　　　　　　Then up he rose and donned his clothes
　　　　　　And dupped the chamber door;
　　　　　　Let in the maid that out a maid
　　　　　　Never departed more.   55

CLAUDIUS Pretty Ophelia!

Ophelia sings of betrayed love. She talks distractedly. Claudius reflects that sorrows never come alone: Polonius killed, the citizens restless, Ophelia mad and Laertes a prey to rumour among the people.

1 Act out Ophelia's troubled state (in groups of three)

Ophelia's song tells of young men's sexual appetite, and how they refuse to marry women with whom they have slept. The song has been interpreted both as Ophelia's seduction by Hamlet, and as Gertrude's seduction by Claudius. Ophelia's songs, her sorrow for her father, her threat that 'My brother shall know of it', and her strange farewell 'Good night ladies . . .' both enthrall and disturb audiences in the theatre.

To experience the emotional and dramatic power of the episode of Ophelia's first 'mad' appearance, take parts as Gertrude, Claudius and Ophelia, and act out lines 21–72. It will help you to know that:

'Indeed la!' may be an ironic response to Claudius
'Gis' = Jesus
'tumbled' = had sex with.

2 Show the 'sorrows' that besiege Claudius (in small groups)

In lines 74–95, Claudius reflects that sorrows never come alone, but all together ('not single spies, / But in battalions'). He lists the troubles that beset him: Polonius's death, Hamlet's exile, suspicious citizens, the secret burial of Polonius, Ophelia's madness, and the returned Laertes surrounded by rumour-mongers ('wants not buzzers') who stop at nothing ('nothing stick') to invent lies.

One person reads lines 74–95; the others mime each 'sorrow'.

Afterwards, talk together about how each of these 'sorrows' has both 'personal' and 'political' significance in the play.

---

remove banishment
muddied agitated
greenly naively, foolishly
In hugger-mugger in secret
as much containing as serious
Feeds . . . clouds imagines all kinds of things

infect his ear poison his mind
necessity, of matter beggared they are obliged, lacking facts
our . . . arraign to accuse me
murdering piece small cannon
superfluous death multiple deaths

OPHELIA Indeed la! Without an oath I'll make an end on't.

> By Gis and by Saint Charity,
>> Alack and fie for shame,
> Young men will do't if they come to't –   60
>> By Cock, they are to blame.

> Quoth she, 'Before you tumbled me,
>> You promised me to wed.'

He answers –

> So would I ha' done, by yonder sun,   65
>> And thou hadst not come to my bed.

CLAUDIUS How long hath she been thus?

OPHELIA I hope all will be well. We must be patient, but I cannot
choose but weep to think they would lay him i'th' cold ground. My
brother shall know of it, and so I thank you for your good counsel.   70
Come, my coach. Good night ladies, good night sweet ladies, good
night, good night.   *Exit*

CLAUDIUS Follow her close, give her good watch I pray you.

                                        [*Exit Horatio*]

> Oh this is the poison of deep grief, it springs
> All from her father's death, [and now behold –]   75
> Oh Gertrude, Gertrude,
> When sorrows come, they come not single spies,
> But in battalions. First, her father slain;
> Next, your son gone, and he most violent author
> Of his own just remove; the people muddied,   80
> Thick and unwholesome in their thoughts and whispers
> For good Polonius' death – and we have done but greenly
> In hugger-mugger to inter him; poor Ophelia
> Divided from herself and her fair judgement,
> Without the which we are pictures, or mere beasts;   85
> Last, and as much containing as all these,
> Her brother is in secret come from France,
> Feeds on his wonder, keeps himself in clouds,
> And wants not buzzers to infect his ear
> With pestilent speeches of his father's death,   90
> Wherein necessity, of matter beggared,
> Will nothing stick our person to arraign
> In ear and ear. O my dear Gertrude, this,
> Like to a murdering piece, in many places
> Gives me superfluous death.   95

A Messenger tells Claudius that Laertes and an angry mob are coming, and that some of the rioters shout that Laertes should be king. Laertes bursts in and demands to know what happened to his father.

1 A political crisis (in pairs)

After so much attention to 'family matters' in the play, politics makes a full-blooded appearance. Laertes, leading a 'rabble' of citizens, has swept aside Claudius's bodyguards. The citizens wish to overthrow Claudius's regime and place Laertes on the throne. The Messenger gives a graphic account of the insurrection, comparing the violent approach of the citizens to the ocean's tide rushing over the shore.

a Take turns to speak the Messenger's lines 98–108. Bring out the urgency (and fear?) he feels as he sees the potential collapse of Claudius's government.

b Talk together about how you would stage the episode between lines 110 and 116, in which the ordinary people of Denmark are briefly glimpsed and heard.

2 'You false Danish dogs!'

The actor playing Gertrude says: 'I just don't believe Gertrude would say lines 109–10. There's nothing in the play up to this point that suggests she could speak like that. It's quite out of character.' Write a paragraph giving your response to this comment. (It may help you to know that Gertrude uses an image from hunting: dogs follow a trail of scent, but if they run 'counter', they follow the trail in the wrong direction.)

3 Three vivid images

Laertes uses an image (see pp. 264–5) of branding a prostitute's forehead. Identify two other images in lines 118–21 which express his feelings.

Attend! Attention!
Swissers Swiss guards
overpeering of his list breaking its boundary
flats shore
impitious impetuous, without pity

head advance party
ratifiers and props supporters
counter wrong-headed, improper
That drop . . . calm cool feelings
cuckold deceived husband

A noise within

GERTRUDE Alack, what noise is this?

CLAUDIUS Attend! Where are my Swissers? Let them guard the door.

Enter a MESSENGER

What is the matter?

MESSENGER   Save yourself my lord.
    The ocean, overpeering of his list,
    Eats not the flats with more impitious haste   100
    Than young Laertes in a riotous head
    O'erbears your officers. The rabble call him lord,
    And, as the world were now but to begin,
    Antiquity forgot, custom not known,
    The ratifiers and props of every word,   105
    They cry 'Choose we! Laertes shall be king.'
    Caps, hands and tongues applaud it to the clouds,
    'Laertes shall be king, Laertes king!'

GERTRUDE How cheerfully on the false trail they cry!
    Oh this is counter, you false Danish dogs!   110

A noise within

CLAUDIUS The doors are broke.

Enter LAERTES *with others*

LAERTES Where is this king? – Sirs, stand you all without.

ALL No, let's come in.

LAERTES I pray you give me leave.

ALL We will, we will.   115

LAERTES I thank you. Keep the door.

[Exeunt followers]

               O thou vile king,
    Give me my father.

GERTRUDE   Calmly, good Laertes.

LAERTES That drop of blood that's calm proclaims me bastard,
    Cries cuckold to my father, brands the harlot
    Even here, between the chaste unsmirchèd brow   120
    Of my true mother.

Claudius is unafraid to face the wrath of Laertes. Claudius claims to be protected by the divine aura of kingship. He urges Laertes to distinguish between friends and foes, and says he is innocent of Polonius's death.

---

1 Claudius: the hypocrite (in groups of three)

Claudius is unperturbed by Laertes's anger. He asserts that God himself prevents a monarch coming to harm ('There's such divinity doth hedge a king . . .'). Claudius sounds completely confident, but his words betray his utter hypocrisy: God did not protect old Hamlet from being murdered by his own brother.

Take parts and speak all the lines on the opposite page. Bring out Claudius's devious self-assurance, Gertrude's protectiveness, and Laertes's enraged desire for revenge.

2 Four revengers

Laertes swears to avenge his father's death. He becomes the fourth revenger in the play. The others are Hamlet (revenge for his father's death); Fortinbras (campaigns to win back his father's lost land); Pyrrhus (slaughters Priam to avenge his own father's death).

In lines 130–6 Laertes uses the exaggerated language of the traditional hero of Revenge Tragedy (see p. 247). Speak the lines as bombastically as you can. Then identify lines earlier in the play where Hamlet's language is similar in tone to Laertes's.

3 Imagery: gambling and the mythical pelican

In lines 139–43, Claudius asks Laertes if in his revenge he will kill the innocent and guilty alike, like reckless gamblers sweeping up all the stakes ('soopstake'), whether they have won or lost. Laertes replies he will kill only Polonius's murderers and treat his friends kindly, like the pelican that was believed to pierce its breast to feed its young with its own blood. See pages 264–5 for more on imagery.

---

hedge surround
Acts little of his will cannot do what it would like to
vows promises of loyalty
both the worlds I give to negligence I care not for heaven or hell

husband manage
Repast feed
most sensibly in grief grieving deeply
level well aimed

CLAUDIUS   What is the cause, Laertes,
          That thy rebellion looks so giant-like? –
          Let him go, Gertrude, do not fear our person.
          There's such divinity doth hedge a king
          That treason can but peep to what it would,   125
          Acts little of his will. – Tell me Laertes,
          Why thou art thus incensed. – Let him go Gertrude. –
          Speak man.
LAERTES   Where is my father?
CLAUDIUS   Dead.
GERTRUDE   But not by him.
CLAUDIUS Let him demand his fill.
LAERTES How came he dead? I'll not be juggled with.   130
          To hell allegiance, vows to the blackest devil,
          Conscience and grace to the profoundest pit!
          I dare damnation. To this point I stand,
          That both the worlds I give to negligence,
          Let come what comes, only I'll be revenged   135
          Most throughly for my father.
CLAUDIUS   Who shall stay you?
LAERTES My will, not all the world.
          And for my means, I'll husband them so well,
          They shall go far with little.
CLAUDIUS   Good Laertes,
          If you desire to know the certainty   140
          Of your dear father, is't writ in your revenge
          That, soopstake, you will draw both friend and foe,
          Winner and loser?
LAERTES   None but his enemies.
CLAUDIUS Will you know them then?
LAERTES To his good friends thus wide I'll ope my arms,   145
          And like the kind life-rendering pelican,
          Repast them with my blood.
CLAUDIUS   Why now you speak
          Like a good child and a true gentleman.
          That I am guiltless of your father's death,
          And am most sensibly in grief for it,   150
          It shall as level to your judgement pierce
          As day does to your eye.

Laertes is appalled by Ophelia's madness. It moves him even more strongly to revenge. Ophelia sings again of death. She distributes herbs and flowers.

After her song, to which characters does Ophelia give the flowers and herbs in lines 174–81? Think of the symbolic significance of each of the herbs and flowers, and write notes suggesting which she gives to whom. The herbs and flowers include fennel (flattery), columbines (ingratitude and infidelity), rue (sorrow), daisy (springtime, love) and violets (sweetness).

1 '. . . the wheel', 'the false steward' – your suggestions

In line 171, 'wheel' might mean 'refrain', 'spinning-wheel' or the wheel of Fortune, which brought either good fortune (when you were on the top of the wheel) or bad fortune (when you were at the bottom); 'the false steward' may be from a traditional ballad – no one knows. Justify your own preferred meanings for each.

sense and virtue power and effectiveness
our scale turn the beam revenge tilts the scales our way
fine refined
instance part
bier funeral carriage

a-down with lower tone (also a refrain)
nothing's nonsense is
matter sense
document lesson
thoughts melancholy
favour good end

A noise within: 'Let her come in'

LAERTES How now, what noise is that?

Enter OPHELIA

O heat dry up my brains, tears seven times salt
Burn out the sense and virtue of mine eye!   155
By heaven, thy madness shall be paid with weight
Till our scale turn the beam. O rose of May,
Dear maid, kind sister, sweet Ophelia –
O heavens, is't possible a young maid's wits
Should be as mortal as an old man's life?   160
Nature is fine in love, and where 'tis fine,
It sends some precious instance of itself
After the thing it loves.

OPHELIA   They bore him bare-faced on the bier   *Song*
                 Hey non nonny, nonny, hey nonny,   165
                 And in his grave rained many a tear –
Fare you well my dove.

LAERTES Hadst thou thy wits, and didst persuade revenge,
It could not move thus.

OPHELIA You must sing a–down a–down, and you call him a–down-a.   170
Oh how the wheel becomes it. It is the false steward that stole his
master's daughter.

LAERTES This nothing's more than matter.

OPHELIA There's rosemary, that's for remembrance – pray you, love,
remember – and there is pansies, that's for thoughts.   175

LAERTES A document in madness, thoughts and remembrance fitted.

OPHELIA There's fennel for you, and columbines. There's rue for you,
and here's some for me; we may call it herb of grace a Sundays.
Oh you must wear your rue with a difference. There's a daisy. I
would give you some violets, but they withered all when my father   180
died. They say a made a good end.
                        [*Sings*]
                 For bonny sweet Robin is all my joy.

LAERTES Thought and affliction, passion, hell itself,
She turns to favour and to prettiness.

Ophelia again sings about her father's death. Claudius sympathises with Laertes's grief, and makes an offer: if Claudius proves to blame, Laertes can be king. If not, Claudius will help Laertes find justice and revenge.

---

1 Ophelia – a case study

Either answer this question: 'Ophelia's songs show that her true nature is quite different from that she has shown up to Act 4. She is by no means as innocent or naive as she appears.' Consider each song in turn and (using evidence from the script) write about whether you agree with this student's view of Ophelia.

Or imagine you are the doctor at the court of Elsinore. Write your case notes on Ophelia.

2 Claudius seizes his opportunity (in pairs)

Claudius has been trying to control and direct Laertes's anger. Now, the entrance of Ophelia and her effect on Laertes give him an opportunity to exploit the situation to his own advantage.

Take parts and read lines 196–214 several times. Make Claudius as persuasive as you can, and consider Laertes's confused feelings as he watches his sister's bizarre behaviour. Express his anger about his father being buried without ceremony. Also, think especially about whether you should leave a long pause before Laertes says 'Let this be so' in line 207.

After your readings talk together about how Claudius manages to turn Laertes's passion for revenge to his own ends.

3 The silent Gertrude – what is she thinking?

Gertrude does not speak in this scene after line 128. Write several paragraphs suggesting what she might be feeling and how she would react as she listens to Claudius talking with Laertes throughout lines 129–214.

All flaxen was his poll   his hair was white
God buy you   God be with you
commune with   share
of whom   of whichever
collateral   indirect
touched   guilty

lend   grant
labour   work
hatchment   coat of arms
ostentation   display of mourning
where th'offence . . . axe fall   let the guilty be punished

OPHELIA   And will a not come again?   *Song*   185
                 And will a not come again?
                   No, no, he is dead,
                   Go to thy death-bed,
                 He never will come again.
                 His beard was as white as snow,   190
                 All flaxen was his poll,
                   He is gone, he is gone,
                   And we cast away moan,
                 God-a-mercy on his soul.

           And of all Christian souls, I pray God. God buy you.   *Exit*   195
LAERTES Do you see this, O God?
CLAUDIUS Laertes, I must commune with your grief,
                 Or you deny me right. Go but apart,
                 Make choice of whom your wisest friends you will,
                 And they shall hear and judge 'twixt you and me.   200
                 If by direct or by collateral hand
                 They find us touched, we will our kingdom give,
                 Our crown, our life, and all that we call ours,
                 To you in satisfaction. But if not,
                 Be you content to lend your patience to us,   205
                 And we shall jointly labour with your soul
                 To give it due content.
LAERTES   Let this be so.
                 His means of death, his obscure funeral,
                 No trophy, sword, nor hatchment o'er his bones,
                 No noble rite, nor formal ostentation,   210
                 Cry to be heard, as 'twere from heaven to earth,
                 That I must call't in question.
CLAUDIUS   So you shall.
                 And where th'offence is, let the great axe fall.
                 I pray you go with me.
                                                              Exeunt

Hamlet's letter reveals that he has been captured in a sea battle. By doing a deal with the pirates, he has returned to Denmark. He has sent letters to the king, and urgently wishes to meet Horatio.

---

1 Hamlet and the pirates (in groups of four or more)

One production solved the problem of why Horatio reads the letter aloud by having the sailor hold the letter up in front of him. Horatio gently turned the letter upside down (showing that the sailors cannot read). He began to read it silently. The sailors then threatened him, obviously wanting to know how the letter affected them, having done a deal with Hamlet. So Horatio was forced to read it aloud. Choose from the following activities:

a **Act it out**   Occasionally, a production has acted out the letter's contents at the back of the stage, as Horatio reads the action. Follow that example. As one person speaks as Horatio, the others enact what is described in lines 13–18.

b **Improvise**   Imagine the scene where Hamlet has boarded the pirate ship. They would be puzzled to find out who he was, where he was going and why he needed to return to Denmark. Some of them may wish to kill him. Others see him as a valuable prisoner whom they can exchange for a large ransom. Improvise the scene where Hamlet persuades the pirates to spare him and to help him return to Denmark. Start with his being threatened by them. What is the deal that he strikes with the pirates?

c **Write a film script**   Work in pairs. You are the joint directors of a film of *Hamlet*. Films have different opportunities from stage productions: settings can be changed instantly, a character's thoughts can be presented visually, 'realistic' settings can be used. Work out how you will film Scene 6. For example, Horatio's reading might be done as a voice-over, while the film shows the action described. Your task is to rewrite Scene 6 as a film script.

---

and please him   if it pleases God
Ere   before
of very warlike / appointment   heavily armed
put on a compelled valour   were obliged to be brave and fight

thieves of mercy   thieves with compassion
repair thou   return, come
for the bore / of the matter   for the weight of their meaning

Act 4 Scene 6
A room in the castle

Enter HORATIO *with an* ATTENDANT

HORATIO What are they that would speak with me?
ATTENDANT Seafaring men sir, they say they have letters for you.
HORATIO Let them come in.

> [*Exit Attendant*]

I do not know from what part of the world
I should be greeted, if not from Lord Hamlet.   5

Enter SAILORS

1 SAILOR God bless you sir.
HORATIO Let him bless thee too.
1 SAILOR A shall sir, and please him. There's a letter for you sir, it came
   from th'ambassador that was bound for England, if your name be
   Horatio, as I am let to know it is.   10
HORATIO (*Reads the letter*) 'Horatio, when thou shalt have overlooked
   this, give these fellows some means to the king; they have letters
   for him. Ere we were two days old at sea, a pirate of very warlike
   appointment gave us chase. Finding ourselves too slow of sail, we
   put on a compelled valour, and in the grapple I boarded them. On   15
   the instant they got clear of our ship, so I alone became their
   prisoner. They have dealt with me like thieves of mercy, but they
   knew what they did: I am to do a good turn for them. Let the king
   have the letters I have sent, and repair thou to me with as much
   speed as thou wouldst fly death. I have words to speak in thine   20
   ear will make thee dumb, yet are they much too light for the bore
   of the matter. These good fellows will bring thee where I am.
   Rosencrantz and Guildenstern hold their course for England. Of
   them I have much to tell thee. Farewell.

>   He that thou knowest thine,   25
>   Hamlet.'

Come, I will give you way for these your letters,
And do't the speedier that you may direct me
To him from whom you brought them.

> *Exeunt*

Claudius claims that Hamlet not only killed Polonius, but was intent on killing him, too. He explains that he did not punish Hamlet for two reasons: love of Gertrude, and Hamlet's popularity with the people.

1 Why doesn't he mention Hamlet's madness?

The previous 'letter' scene has given Claudius time to tell Laertes how Polonius was killed. Now he gives two reasons why he took no action against Hamlet (see above). He does not mention Hamlet's madness. Suggest a reason for Claudius's omission.

Claudius begins to plot with Laertes against Hamlet. From the Royal Shakespeare Company's modern-dress production, 1988.

my acquittance seal confirm my innocence	**but by her** move without her
Sith since	**count** account
knowing understanding	**general gender** populace
feats deeds	**spring** lime-rich water
capital deserving of death	**gyves** chains (vices)
mainly mightily, greatly	**Too slightly timbered** not strong enough
unsinewed weak	**Stood challenger . . . perfections** was more perfect than all other women
conjunctive closely joined	
sphere orbit	

Act 4 Scene 7
A state room in the castle

CLAUDIUS Now must your conscience my acquittance seal,
      And you must put me in your heart for friend,
      Sith you have heard, and with a knowing ear,
      That he which hath your noble father slain
      Pursued my life.
LAERTES   It well appears. But tell me   5
      Why you proceeded not against these feats,
      So crimeful and so capital in nature,
      As by your safety, wisdom, all things else,
      You mainly were stirred up.
CLAUDIUS   Oh for two special reasons,
      Which may to you perhaps seem much unsinewed,   10
      But yet to me they're strong. The queen his mother
      Lives almost by his looks, and for myself,
      My virtue or my plague, be it either which,
      She's so conjunctive to my life and soul,
      That as the star moves not but in his sphere,   15
      I could not but by her. The other motive,
      Why to a public count I might not go,
      Is the great love the general gender bear him,
      Who, dipping all his faults in their affection,
      Work like the spring that turneth wood to stone,   20
      Convert his gyves to graces, so that my arrows,
      Too slightly timbered for so loud a wind,
      Would have reverted to my bow again,
      And not where I had aimed them.
LAERTES And so have I a noble father lost,   25
      A sister driven into desperate terms,
      Whose worth, if praises may go back again,
      Stood challenger on mount of all the age
      For her perfections. But my revenge will come.

Claudius assures Laertes that he will not let Hamlet's actions go unpunished. A Messenger brings letters from Hamlet, telling of his return to Denmark. Laertes welcomes the chance to be revenged on Hamlet.

---

1 Claudius's pleasure is abruptly ended (in pairs)

Claudius makes it clear that he intends to punish Hamlet. He uses an image familiar to Elizabethans: don't let anyone think they can pull my beard and get away with it (lines 32–3). Indeed, at this moment Claudius thinks that on his orders Hamlet will shortly be executed in England. Very soon, he hopes to tell Laertes of Hamlet's death. The letter from Hamlet denies him that pleasure.

a **Reading between the lines**   Imagine you are Hamlet writing his letter (lines 43–6) to Claudius. One person reads up to a punctuation mark, then pauses. In each pause, the partner speaks Hamlet's thoughts on what he has just written.

b **Naked**   Claudius is puzzled by Hamlet describing himself as 'set naked on your / kingdom'. This probably doesn't mean that Hamlet is literally without clothes – but what can it mean? Suggest several explanations for the word that seem to you to be appropriate to the play.

2 Point out who's who (in groups of eight)

One person slowly reads the whole page opposite, emphasising each pronoun or name ('your', 'you', 'Hamlet', 'Claudio' and so on). The others point emphatically to the character (or characters) mentioned each time (cast the parts as you read).

Pointing out words in this way can help increase your understanding. This process of identifying who's who is technically known as **deixis** (usually pronounced 'dyke-sis'). It pinpoints who is taking part in a discussion, and who is being referred to.

---

flat   unfeeling
pastime   trivial
abuse   trick
no such thing   no such thing has happened
hand   handwriting

character   style (or handwriting)
devise   help
warms   inflames, does good
o'errule me to a peace   force me to be friendly

CLAUDIUS Break not your sleeps for that. You must not think 30
    That we are made of stuff so flat and dull
    That we can let our beard be shook with danger
    And think it pastime. You shortly shall hear more.
    I loved your father, and we love ourself,
    And that I hope will teach you to imagine – 35

      Enter a MESSENGER *with letters*

    How now? What news?
MESSENGER   Letters my lord from Hamlet.
    This to your majesty, this to the queen.
CLAUDIUS From Hamlet? Who brought them?
MESSENGER Sailors my lord they say, I saw them not;
    They were given me by Claudio – he received them 40
    Of him that brought them.
CLAUDIUS   Laertes, you shall hear them.
    Leave us.

                    Exit Messenger

[*Reads*] 'High and mighty, you shall know I am set naked on your
kingdom. Tomorrow shall I beg leave to see your kingly eyes, when
I shall, first asking your pardon thereunto, recount th'occasion of 45
my sudden and more strange return.

                              Hamlet.'
    What should this mean? Are all the rest come back?
    Or is it some abuse, and no such thing?
LAERTES Know you the hand?
CLAUDIUS   'Tis Hamlet's character. Naked? 50
    And in a postscript here he says alone.
    Can you devise me?
LAERTES I'm lost in it my lord. But let him come –
    It warms the very sickness in my heart
    That I shall live and tell him to his teeth 55
    'Thus didest thou!'
CLAUDIUS   If it be so, Laertes –
    As how should it be so? – how otherwise? –
    Will you be ruled by me?
LAERTES   Ay my lord,
    So you will not o'errule me to a peace.

Claudius begins to hatch a new plot to kill Hamlet. He says that Hamlet envies Laertes, but delays naming the reason for that envy. Instead, Claudius talks of Lamord, an accomplished French soldier.

1 The 'temptation' scene – whisper it! (in pairs)

Claudius realises his plan to have Hamlet killed in England has failed. Now he sees he can use Laertes's desire for revenge to achieve his aim. Claudius's plot against Hamlet will 'work him / To an exploit . . . Under the which he shall not choose but fall'.

Claudius does not immediately tell Laertes of his plan. Instead he talks of 'a quality' of Laertes. When Laertes asks him what that quality is (line 75), Claudius again does not reply directly, but calls the unnamed quality 'A very riband in the cap of youth' (mere ribbon, a decoration on a cap). Yet this quality is 'needful' (or necessary), because it suits youth in the same way that 'health and graveness' suit older people. Claudius then talks about a Frenchman, Lamord.

Lines 60–161 are often called the 'temptation' scene because Claudius tempts Laertes into a murderous plot. To gain a sense of the conspiracy, sit closely together and quietly speak the lines to each other. Then work on some activities on the following pages.

2 Lamord – part of Claudius's plotting

Claudius makes Lamord sound a remarkable character. He is a 'gallant' (fine young man), 'incorpsed and demi-natured' (part of the same body) with his horse. He 'topped' (surpassed) Claudius's imagination ('thought', 'forgery') of any feat of horsemanship ('shapes and tricks'). Shakespeare may have included him because Lamord sounds like the French *la mort* – death. But as you read on, you will discover that Claudius uses Lamord to draw Laertes further into his plot.

---

checking at abandoning
an exploit a plot
ripe in my device ready in my scheming
uncharge the practice not suspect trickery
The rather the better

organ agent
falls right falls into place
unworthiest siege least account
sables dark clothes
weeds sober garments
can well are skilful
brooch jewel in the crown

CLAUDIUS To thine own peace. If he be now returned,   60
　　　　　As checking at his voyage, and that he means
　　　　　No more to undertake it, I will work him
　　　　　To an exploit, now ripe in my device,
　　　　　Under the which he shall not choose but fall,
　　　　　And for his death no wind of blame shall breathe,   65
　　　　　But even his mother shall uncharge the practice
　　　　　And call it accident.
[LAERTES　　　　　　　　　My lord, I will be ruled,
　　　　　The rather if you could devise it so
　　　　　That I might be the organ.
CLAUDIUS　　　　　　　　　　　It falls right.
　　　　　You have been talked of since your travel much,   70
　　　　　And that in Hamlet's hearing, for a quality
　　　　　Wherein they say you shine. Your sum of parts
　　　　　Did not together pluck such envy from him
　　　　　As did that one, and that in my regard
　　　　　Of the unworthiest siege.
LAERTES　　　　　　　　　　What part is that my lord?   75
CLAUDIUS A very riband in the cap of youth,
　　　　　Yet needful too, for youth no less becomes
　　　　　The light and careless livery that it wears
　　　　　Than settled age his sables and his weeds
　　　　　Importing health and graveness.] Two months since   80
　　　　　Here was a gentleman of Normandy.
　　　　　I've seen myself, and served against, the French,
　　　　　And they can well on horseback, but this gallant
　　　　　Had witchcraft in't. He grew unto his seat,
　　　　　And to such wondrous doing brought his horse   85
　　　　　As had he been incorpsed and demi-natured
　　　　　With the brave beast. So far he topped my thought,
　　　　　That I in forgery of shapes and tricks
　　　　　Come short of what he did.
LAERTES　　　　　　　　　　A Norman was't?
CLAUDIUS A Norman.   90
LAERTES Upon my life Lamord.
CLAUDIUS　　　　　　　　The very same.
LAERTES I know him well, he is the brooch indeed
　　　　　And gem of all the nation.

Claudius relates Lamord's praise of Laertes's swordsmanship. Laertes asks what the point of Claudius's words is. Claudius talks of how love fades with time. His words prompt Laertes to seek bloody revenge.

1 Intensifying Laertes's fury (in pairs)

Claudius's two long speeches opposite are intended to work on Laertes's already inflamed emotions. The first speech reports that Lamord and the best swordsmen in France thought that Laertes was a superior swordsman, outclassing them all. In his long second speech, Claudius reflects on how time kills love, goodness dies of its own excess, and intentions fade away if not quickly carried out.

Only when Claudius asks a direct question, 'Laertes, was your father dear to you?' (line 106), does he seem to address what is uppermost in Laertes's thoughts and feelings.

Claudius is deliberately spinning out his story to increase Laertes's resentment against Hamlet: first, by saying that Hamlet envies Laertes's swordsmanship, and wishes to duel with him; second, to imply that Laertes's desire for revenge will fade over time, like love. Claudius wants to work Laertes up into a fury so that he will seize quickly any opportunity to be revenged on Hamlet.

a Experiment with different ways of speaking Claudius's lines opposite. For example, try Claudius always maintaining eye contact with Laertes. Then have Claudius mainly avoiding eye contact, and in his second long speech drifting off into an internal meditation about how love fades with time. Find the style you think is most appropriate.

b Lines 99–101 and 113–22 are in square brackets. They did not appear in the First Folio version of the play (see p. 269). Imagine you are about to put on the play. Will you include these lines or cut them? One of you argues for, the other against, cutting the lines. The person arguing to include them might stress how the second bracketed passage echoes the theme of delay.

---

made confession told the truth
art and exercise . . . defence skill and
  mastery in swordplay
escrimers master swordsmen
play sword fence
passages of proof events that bear
  me out

qualifies moderates, dulls
abate extinguish
is at a like goodness still remains
  good always
plurisy (disease resulting from)
  excess
quick heart

CLAUDIUS He made confession of you,
        And gave you such a masterly report   95
        For art and exercise in your defence,
        And for your rapier most especial,
        That he cried out 'twould be a sight indeed
        If one could match you. [Th'escrimers of their nation
        He swore had neither motion, guard, nor eye,   100
        If you opposed them.] Sir, this report of his
        Did Hamlet so envenom with his envy
        That he could nothing do but wish and beg
        Your sudden coming o'er to play with you.
        Now out of this –
LAERTES   What out of this, my lord?   105
CLAUDIUS Laertes, was your father dear to you?
        Or are you like the painting of a sorrow,
        A face without a heart?
LAERTES   Why ask you this?
CLAUDIUS Not that I think you did not love your father,
        But that I know love is begun by time,   110
        And that I see, in passages of proof,
        Time qualifies the spark and fire of it.
        [There lives within the very flame of love
        A kind of wick or snuff that will abate it,
        And nothing is at a like goodness still,   115
        For goodness, growing to a plurisy,
        Dies in his own too much. That we would do,
        We should do when we would, for this 'would' changes,
        And hath abatements and delays as many
        As there are tongues, are hands, are accidents;   120
        And then this 'should' is like a spendthrift sigh,
        That hurts by easing. But to the quick of th'ulcer –]
        Hamlet comes back; what would you undertake
        To show yourself in deed your father's son
        More than in words?
LAERTES   To cut his throat i'th'church.   125

Claudius plans a duel in which one of the swords will not be blunted. Laertes offers to poison the sharpened foil. To make Hamlet's death certain, Claudius proposes to poison Hamlet's drink.

---

1 'No place indeed should murder sanctuarize'

Line 126 might mean 'no church should give protection [sanctuary] to a murderer like Hamlet' or 'no better place to do the murder of Hamlet'. Which meaning do you think Claudius intends? Why?

2 Insights into character (in pairs)

After careful preparation, Claudius has raised Laertes's hatred of Hamlet to fever pitch. Laertes now plots with Claudius a devious and seemingly foolproof murder of Hamlet. The two men build upon each other's wickedness in devising ways of ensuring Hamlet's death in a duel. The plot to kill Hamlet involves a duelling sword, sharp ('unbated') and poisoned. With it, Laertes will strike Hamlet in a deceitful thrust ('pass of practice'). A poisoned drink will kill Hamlet if Laertes fails to kill him with his sword.

Take parts and read the script opposite. Then talk together to discover how far you agree with the following statements:

- It is surprising that Laertes has brought a poison ('unction') with him.
- Hamlet is accurately described by Claudius as 'remiss, / Most generous, and free from all contriving' ('remiss' = unsuspecting, 'contriving' = deviousness).
- Claudius has all the details of his plot already in his mind, and only pretends to think up the 'back or second' (the poisoned cup).

3 Does Claudius wish for Laertes's death?

Might Claudius hope Laertes dies in the duel? Why? Or why not?

---

sanctuarize protect
keep close stay
in fine finally
peruse the foils inspect the swords
mountebank quack doctor
cataplasm dressing, antidote
simples medicinal herbs

shape plot, design
drift aim
assayed tried
blast in proof fail
preferred offered
nonce occasion

CLAUDIUS No place indeed should murder sanctuarize;
        Revenge should have no bounds. But, good Laertes,
        Will you do this, keep close within your chamber;
        Hamlet, returned, shall know you are come home;
        We'll put on those shall praise your excellence,   130
        And set a double varnish on the fame
        The Frenchman gave you; bring you in fine together,
        And wager on your heads. He being remiss,
        Most generous, and free from all contriving,
        Will not peruse the foils, so that with ease,   135
        Or with a little shuffling, you may choose
        A sword unbated, and in a pass of practice
        Requite him for your father.
LAERTES   I will do't,
        And for that purpose I'll anoint my sword.
        I bought an unction of a mountebank,   140
        So mortal that but dip a knife in it,
        Where it draws blood no cataplasm so rare,
        Collected from all simples that have virtue
        Under the moon, can save the thing from death
        That is but scratched withal. I'll touch my point   145
        With this contagion, that if I gall him slightly,
        It may be death.
CLAUDIUS   Let's further think of this,
        Weigh what convenience both of time and means
        May fit us to our shape. If this should fail,
        And that our drift look through our bad performance,   150
        'Twere better not assayed. Therefore this project
        Should have a back or second, that might hold
        If this did blast in proof. Soft, let me see.
        We'll make a solemn wager on your cunnings –
        I ha't!   155
        When in your motion you are hot and dry,
        As make your bouts more violent to that end,
        And that he calls for drink, I'll have preferred him
        A chalice for the nonce, whereon but sipping,
        If he by chance escape your venomed stuck,   160
        Our purpose may hold there. But stay, what noise?

              Enter GERTRUDE

How, sweet queen!

Gertrude tells how Ophelia drowned: she fell from a willow as she tried to hang flowers on it, and was pulled under by her clothes. Laertes unsuccessfully fights back tears. Claudius lies about calming Laertes.

Ophelia by the Victorian painter Millais.

1 'There is a willow . . .' (individually or in groups)

Lines 166–83 are much admired for their imaginative and poetic quality. The images of nature reflect Shakespeare's use of flowers in the play. Ophelia's innocence and chanting of 'old lauds' (religious hymns) contrast with Laertes's fall from grace. But Laertes, moments ago a pitiless revenger, is moved to tears.

Explore different ways of speaking the lines: individually, chorally, echoing, sharing them between you and so on.

2 True to character – Claudius and Gertrude

Claudius, ever devious, lies to his wife, saying he has attempted to calm Laertes. Will she obey his two commands to 'follow'?

askant   leaning over
hoar   grey
liberal   free-speaking
pendant   hanging
cronet   coronet, garland
sliver   branch
incapable of   uncomprehending

indued   adapted
lay   song
trick   way
The woman will be out   I'll have finished crying
douts   douses, extinguishes

GERTRUDE One woe doth tread upon another's heel,
　　　　　So fast they follow. Your sister's drowned, Laertes.
LAERTES Drowned! Oh where?   165
GERTRUDE There is a willow grows askant a brook,
　　　　　That shows his hoar leaves in the glassy stream.
　　　　　Therewith fantastic garlands did she make,
　　　　　Of crow-flowers, nettles, daisies, and long purples,
　　　　　That liberal shepherds give a grosser name,   170
　　　　　But our cold maids do dead men's fingers call them.
　　　　　There on the pendant boughs her cronet weeds
　　　　　Clamb'ring to hang, an envious sliver broke,
　　　　　When down her weedy trophies and herself
　　　　　Fell in the weeping brook. Her clothes spread wide,   175
　　　　　And mermaid-like awhile they bore her up,
　　　　　Which time she chanted snatches of old lauds
　　　　　As one incapable of her own distress,
　　　　　Or like a creature native and indued
　　　　　Unto that element. But long it could not be   180
　　　　　Till that her garments, heavy with their drink,
　　　　　Pulled the poor wretch from her melodious lay
　　　　　To muddy death.
LAERTES   Alas, then she is drowned?
GERTRUDE Drowned, drowned.
LAERTES Too much of water hast thou, poor Ophelia,   185
　　　　　And therefore I forbid my tears. But yet
　　　　　It is our trick; nature her custom holds,
　　　　　Let shame say what it will. When these are gone,
　　　　　The woman will be out. Adieu my lord,
　　　　　I have a speech of fire that fain would blaze,   190
　　　　　But that this folly douts it.   *Exit*
CLAUDIUS   Let's follow, Gertrude.
　　　　　How much I had to do to calm his rage!
　　　　　Now fear I this will give it start again.
　　　　　Therefore let's follow.
　　　　　　　　　　　　　　　　　　　　　　　　　Exeunt

Looking back at Act 4
Activities for groups or individuals

1 Appearance versus reality

All Shakespeare's plays in some way explore the theme of reality versus appearance. Identify an example in each scene of Act 4 where things are not as they seem. Present your examples in an assignment on 'Reality versus appearance in Act 4 of *Hamlet*'.

2 Political matters, family matters: a citizen's view

Act 4 gives reminders of the play's political context. The audience learn in Scene 3 that England, recently defeated by Claudius, is now Denmark's client state. In Scene 4 Hamlet encounters the Norwegian army marching against Poland. In Scene 7 Claudius reveals he has fought against the French. Insurrection briefly threatens Claudius's rule when in Scene 5 the citizens of Denmark ('the rabble') sweep aside the palace guards and call for Laertes to be king.

You are a life-long Danish citizen, have served in Denmark's army, heard gossip about court happenings, and seen Laertes's return.

Either write your account of what you know.

Or join a group of other 'citizens' and improvise a discussion about events in Act 4.

3 Claudius: a complex character

Act 4 begins and ends with Claudius lying to Gertrude. In Scene 1 he claims to love Hamlet, in Scene 7 he says he tried to calm Laertes's rage. Claudius lies to Hamlet in Scene 3, telling him he is being sent to England 'for thine especial safety'. But Claudius is not simply a liar. He displays other aspects of his character in Act 4. Check through each scene in which he appears and compile a list of the various qualities he shows. Use your findings to write a character analysis of Claudius.

4 Honour and revenge

In Act 4, Hamlet, Fortinbras and Laertes are all concerned with 'honour' and 'revenge'. Find a way of showing the similarities and differences in their conceptions of 'honour' and 'revenge' (e.g. lists, notes, an essay, or designs for coats of arms).

Father, lover, brother. Throughout the play Ophelia is dominated by her
father, her lover and her brother. Her father makes her reveal her secrets
(Act 1) and uses her so that he can spy on Hamlet (Act 2). Her brother
counsels her against Hamlet (Act 1) but is driven to tears by her madness
(Act 4). Hamlet denies he loves her and subjects her to a cruel tongue–lashing
(Act 3). Use the pictures as a basis for an extended essay analysing Ophelia's
relationship with the men in the play.

Two gravediggers discuss Ophelia's death. They think she committed suicide, but is being allowed a Christian burial because of her high rank.

1 Two gravediggers – alternative perspectives (in pairs)

After the sombre atmosphere of the previous scene, the mood of the play switches abruptly to comedy – in a graveyard. But Shakespeare is not simply providing comic relief. He is doing here what he does so often: using comedy and ordinary people to provide alternative perspectives on major issues and themes.

There are comic characters in other Shakespeare plays who similarly mangle the language and yet give insights into central concerns of the play. Here, the first gravedigger mistakes 'salvation' for damnation; '*se offendendo*' for *se defendendo* (self-defence); and 'Argal' for *Ergo* (therefore).

To gain a first impression of the humour, take parts as the two gravediggers (Clown and Other) and read lines 1–50. Afterwards, work out how you would set this scene, and decide how the gravediggers are dressed (see pp. 202 and 240).

2 Suicide – what actions does the gravedigger use?

Lines 8–17 echo a famous Elizabethan law case: the suicide of Sir James Hales in 1554. Suicides were traditionally denied a Christian burial and forfeited their lands, but Sir James's widow took the case to court. In the court case there was much talk of the three parts of an act (lines 9–10) and whether Sir James went to the water or the water came to him.

Invent stage business (actions) to accompany lines 13–17 as the Clown makes clear his meaning.

---

straight   immediately, properly (as appropriate to a Christian burial)
crowner . . . her   coroner has held an inquest
goodman delver   gravedigger
will he, nill he   willy-nilly (whether he wants to or not)

quest law   law of inquest
countenance   permission
even-Christen   ordinary fellow Christians
Adam   the first man
confess thyself –   confess thyself and be hanged (a proverb)

Act 5 Scene 1
A graveyard near the castle

Enter two CLOWNS (gravediggers)

CLOWN Is she to be buried in Christian burial, when she wilfully seeks
her own salvation?

OTHER I tell thee she is, therefore make her grave straight. The crowner
hath sat on her, and finds it Christian burial.

CLOWN How can that be, unless she drowned herself in her own 5
defence?

OTHER Why, 'tis found so.

CLOWN It must be *se offendendo*, it cannot be else. For here lies the
point: if I drown myself wittingly, it argues an act, and an act hath
three branches – it is to act, to do, to perform. Argal, she drowned 10
herself wittingly.

OTHER Nay, but hear you goodman delver –

CLOWN Give me leave. Here lies the water – good. Here stands the
man – good. If the man go to this water and drown himself, it is
will he, nill he, he goes – mark you that. But if the water come to 15
him, and drown him, he drowns not himself. Argal, he that is not
guilty of his own death shortens not his own life.

OTHER But is this law?

CLOWN Ay marry is't, crowner's quest law.

OTHER Will you ha' the truth on't? If this had not been a gentlewoman, 20
she should have been buried out o' Christian burial.

CLOWN Why, there thou sayst – and the more pity that great folk
should have countenance in this world to drown or hang themselves
more than their even-Christen. Come, my spade; there is no ancient
gentlemen but gardeners, ditchers, and gravemakers; they hold up 25
Adam's profession.

OTHER Was he a gentleman?

CLOWN A was the first that ever bore arms.

OTHER Why, he had none.

CLOWN What, art a heathen? How dost thou understand the scripture? 30
The scripture says Adam digged. Could he dig without arms? I'll
put another question to thee. If thou answerest me not to the
purpose, confess thyself –

The gravedigger's question puzzles his mate; the answer praises gravediggers. The gravedigger sings about becoming old. Hamlet speculates on whose skull has been thrown out of the grave.

The gravediggers, Royal National Theatre, 1987.

1 Two puzzles

a Who (or what or where) is Yaughan (line 50)? No one knows. Invent a plausible suggestion ('stoup' = tankard).

b '. . . the hand of little employment hath the daintier sense'. Do you think lines 58–9 mean that people who don't work have finer feelings than those who do? Or that the less often you do something, the more emotional impact it's likely to have on you? Or is Hamlet echoing the Player King's sentiments that custom deadens the senses (as the previous line suggests: 'property of easiness' = a job that causes him no worry)?

Go to!   Get on with it!
frame   structure (gallows)
unyoke   stop work
Mass   by the Mass
mend his pace   go faster
behove   enjoyment, advantage
meet   better

jowls   hurls
Cain   Cain killed his brother Abel with a donkey's jawbone – a subtle reminder of Claudius?
pate   head
o'erreaches   outwits
circumvent   outwit

OTHER Go to!

CLOWN What is he that builds stronger than either the mason, the   35
　　shipwright, or the carpenter?

OTHER The gallows-maker, for that frame outlives a thousand tenants.

CLOWN I like thy wit well in good faith. The gallows does well, but
　　how does it well? It does well to those that do ill. Now, thou dost
　　ill to say the gallows is built stronger than the church; argal, the   40
　　gallows may do well to thee. To't again, come.

OTHER Who builds stronger than a mason, a shipwright, or a carpenter?

CLOWN Ay, tell me that, and unyoke.

OTHER Marry, now I can tell.

CLOWN To't.   45

OTHER Mass, I cannot tell.

Enter HAMLET *and* HORATIO *afar off*

CLOWN Cudgel thy brains no more about it, for your dull ass will not
　　mend his pace with beating; and when you are asked this question
　　next, say a grave-maker. The houses he makes lasts till doomsday.
　　Go, get thee to Yaughan, fetch me a stoup of liquor.   50

　　　　　　　　　　　　　　　　[Exit Second Clown]

　　　　In youth when I did love, did love,　　*Song*
　　　　　Methought it was very sweet
　　　　To contract-o the time for-a my behove,
　　　　　Oh methought there-a was nothing-a meet.

HAMLET Has this fellow no feeling of his business? A sings in   55
　　grave-making.

HORATIO Custom hath made it in him a property of easiness.

HAMLET 'Tis e'en so, the hand of little employment hath the daintier
　　sense.

CLOWN　　　　But age with his stealing steps　　*Song*　60
　　　　　Hath clawed me in his clutch,
　　　　And hath shipped me intil the land,
　　　　　As if I had never been such.
　　　　　　　[Throws up a skull]

HAMLET That skull had a tongue in it, and could sing once. How the
　　knave jowls it to th' ground, as if 'twere Cain's jawbone, that did   65
　　the first murder. This might be the pate of a politician which this
　　ass now o'erreaches, one that would circumvent God, might it not?

HORATIO It might my lord.

The two skulls thrown out by the gravedigger provoke Hamlet to muse on mortality. He reflects that, in spite of all a lawyer's legal documents entitling him to land, death is the only end.

1 Thoughts on a landowning lawyer's fate (in pairs)

As always, an action or a remark sets Hamlet thinking. The gravedigger's casual throwing out of skulls prompts Hamlet to meditate upon death. The flattering courtier (lines 69–72), for all his breeding, finishes up with his bones used as mere skittles (line 77). A landowning lawyer, for all his legal skills and documents, ends up in the grave. Hamlet uses many legal expressions in lines 83–94; most relate to legal documents (deeds) about buying land:

'quiddities', 'quillets' = small distinctions of meaning
'tenures' = renting property or land
'action of battery' = suing for assault
'statutes' = legal documents acknowledging debts
'recognizances' = kinds of statutes
'fines' = legal documents for freehold of land
'vouchers' = persons who warranted (vouched for) titles to land
'recoveries' = legal process of holding fines
'indentures' = joint agreements (each person kept half the deed)
'conveyances' = deeds of land purchase.

a Hamlet uses so much legal language to make a point: for all the complicated disputes about land ownership, all anyone ends up with is two metres of a grave. One person speaks lines 83–94, pausing after each question. In the pause, the other speaks a response: a single word (e.g. 'Death') or a more detailed thought.

b The sentence in lines 89–90 contains four puns on the word 'fine'. Work out the meaning of each.

---

my Lady Worm's dead (belonging to worms)
chopless without jaws
mazard head
revolution change of fortune
trick wit
breeding bringing up

loggets skittles (in the Elizabethan game, sticks were thrown at a post)
shrowding sheet funeral shroud
sconce head
They are sheep . . . in that people who trust in legal documents are stupid

HAMLET Or of a courtier, which could say 'Good morrow sweet lord,
how dost thou sweet lord?' This might be my Lord Such-a-one,   70
that praised my Lord Such-a-one's horse when a meant to beg it,
might it not?

HORATIO Ay my lord.

HAMLET Why, e'en so, and now my Lady Worm's, chopless, and
knocked about the mazard with a sexton's spade. Here's fine   75
revolution, and we had the trick to see't. Did these bones cost no
more the breeding but to play at loggets with 'em? Mine ache to
think on't.

CLOWN   A pickaxe and a spade, a spade,   *Song*
                          For and a shrowding sheet,   80
                       Oh a pit of clay for to be made,
                          For such a guest is meet.
                    [*Throws up another skull*]

HAMLET There's another. Why may not that be the skull of a lawyer?
Where be his quiddities now, his quillets, his cases, his tenures, and
his tricks? Why does he suffer this rude knave now to knock him   85
about the sconce with a dirty shovel, and will not tell him of his
action of battery? Hum, this fellow might be in's time a great buyer
of land, with his statutes, his recognizances, his fines, his double
vouchers, his recoveries. Is this the fine of his fines and the recovery
of his recoveries, to have his fine pate full of fine dirt? Will his   90
vouchers vouch him no more of his purchases, and double ones too,
than the length and breadth of a pair of indentures? The very
conveyances of his lands will scarcely lie in this box, and must
th'inheritor himself have no more, ha?

HORATIO Not a jot more my lord.   95

HAMLET Is not parchment made of sheepskins?

HORATIO Ay my lord, and of calves' skins too.

HAMLET They are sheep and calves which seek out assurance in that.
I will speak to this fellow. Whose grave's this sirrah?

CLOWN Mine sir.   100

                       (Sings)
              Oh a pit of clay for to be made
                 For such a guest is meet.

HAMLET I think it be thine indeed, for thou liest in't.

CLOWN You lie out on't sir, and therefore 'tis not yours. For my part,
I do not lie in't, yet it is mine.   105

The gravedigger's punning and playing with language prompt Hamlet to reflect on the way peasants imitate courtiers. The gravedigger's remarks reveal that Hamlet is about 30 years old.

1 Important matters then – and now

The writings of every dramatist and author reflect something of the age in which they live. Shakespeare is no exception. His plays contain much evidence of matters which preoccupied the thoughts and feelings of people who lived in Elizabethan and Jacobean England. Several lines opposite would have been recognised by Shakespeare's audiences as wry or critical comments on their own society.

Lines 116–18   Low-status persons ('peasant') are more and more ('this three years') imitating courtiers in language and behaviour.

Lines 123–31   All Englishmen are mad (a passage of dialogue that still makes an English audience laugh).

Lines 140–2   Syphilis, a sexually transmitted disease, was an increasing feature of Elizabethan/Jacobean life. Many were killed by the pox ('pocky / corses').

Rewrite each of these references to Shakespeare's England in your own words. To each one add a sentence explaining how it still has significance today. You could also add cuttings from newspapers and magazines, or downloads from the Internet as present-day examples.

2 How old is Hamlet?

Identify the two lines spoken by the gravedigger that suggest Hamlet is about 30. Then think about whether you imagine Hamlet as 30, or older or younger. In what senses might he seem adolescent? How old do you imagine Gertrude to be? Claudius? Horatio? (See also p. 271.)

---

quick living
absolute precise, literal
by the card accurately (like a sailor with a compass card)
equivocation deliberate ambiguity, double meaning
picked overrefined

galls his kibe scuffs his chilblain (treads on his heels)
sexton gravedigger, church caretaker
laying in burial
tanner workman who turns animal skins to leather

HAMLET Thou dost lie in't, to be in't and say 'tis thine. 'Tis for the dead, not for the quick, therefore thou liest.

CLOWN 'Tis a quick lie sir, 'twill away again from me to you.

HAMLET What man dost thou dig it for?

CLOWN For no man sir.   110

HAMLET What woman then?

CLOWN For none neither.

HAMLET Who is to be buried in't?

CLOWN One that was a woman sir, but rest her soul she's dead.

HAMLET How absolute the knave is! We must speak by the card, or   115
equivocation will undo us. By the lord, Horatio, this three years
I have took note of it: the age is grown so picked, that the toe of
the peasant comes so near the heel of the courtier, he galls his kibe.
How long hast thou been grave-maker?

CLOWN Of all the days i'th'year, I came to't that day that our last King   120
Hamlet o'ercame Fortinbras.

HAMLET How long is that since?

CLOWN Cannot you tell that? Every fool can tell that. It was the very
day that young Hamlet was born, he that is mad and sent into
England.   125

HAMLET Ay marry, why was he sent into England?

CLOWN Why, because a was mad. A shall recover his wits there, or if
a do not, 'tis no great matter there.

HAMLET Why?

CLOWN 'Twill not be seen in him there. There the men are as mad as   130
he.

HAMLET How came he mad?

CLOWN Very strangely they say.

HAMLET How, strangely?

CLOWN Faith, e'en with losing his wits.   135

HAMLET Upon what ground?

CLOWN Why, here in Denmark. I have been sexton here man and boy
thirty years.

HAMLET How long will a man lie i'th'earth ere he rot?

CLOWN Faith, if a be not rotten before a die, as we have many pocky   140
corses nowadays that will scarce hold the laying in, a will last you
some eight year, or nine year. A tanner will last you nine year.

HAMLET Why he more than another?

Hamlet expresses disgust at the thought that Yorick, once so full of tricks and laughter, is now merely a skull. The physical corruption brings his mother (or women in general) bitterly to his mind.

'Alas poor Yorick!' In lines 156–65 Hamlet recalls the much-loved companion of his childhood, whose wit and vitality entertained the whole court. The skull prompts him to think of the deceitfulness of women.

hide skin
whoreson poxy (expressing contemptuous familiarity)
lien you lain
Rhenish Rhine wine
My gorge rises I am sickened
gibes jokes
were wont . . . roar made everyone at dinner laugh uproariously

chop-fallen miserable (down in the mouth)
favour appearance
Alexander Alexander the Great, 356–323 BC, conqueror who ruled a vast empire
base uses trivial purposes
return be recycled
too curiously overcomplicatedly

CLOWN Why sir, his hide is so tanned with his trade, that a will keep
out water a great while, and your water is a sore decayer of your   145
whoreson dead body. Here's a skull now: this skull hath lien you
i'th'earth three and twenty years.

HAMLET Whose was it?

CLOWN A whoreson mad fellow's it was. Whose do you think it was?

HAMLET Nay I know not.   150

CLOWN A pestilence on him for a mad rogue, a poured a flagon of
Rhenish on my head once. This same skull sir, was Yorick's skull,
the king's jester.

HAMLET This?

CLOWN E'en that.   155

HAMLET Let me see. [*Takes the skull.*] Alas poor Yorick! I knew him
Horatio, a fellow of infinite jest, of most excellent fancy, he hath
borne me on his back a thousand times – and now how abhorred
in my imagination it is! My gorge rises at it. Here hung those lips
that I have kissed I know not how oft. Where be your gibes now?   160
your gambols, your songs, your flashes of merriment that were wont
to set the table on a roar? Not one now, to mock your own grinning?
Quite chop-fallen? Now get you to my lady's chamber, and tell her,
let her paint an inch thick, to this favour she must come. Make her
laugh at that. – Prithee Horatio, tell me one thing.   165

HORATIO What's that my lord?

HAMLET Dost thou think Alexander looked o' this fashion i'th'earth?

HORATIO E'en so.

HAMLET And smelt so? Pah!   [*Puts down the skull*]

HORATIO E'en so my lord.   170

HAMLET To what base uses we may return, Horatio! Why may not
imagination trace the noble dust of Alexander, till a find it stopping
a bunghole?

HORATIO 'Twere to consider too curiously to consider so.

Hamlet reasons that death transforms great kings into trivial objects. A Priest tells Laertes that Claudius's command has granted Ophelia a Christian funeral. As a suicide, the Church would deny her burial.

---

1 Glory comes to dust – make up your own verse

Write another four-line verse for Hamlet that expresses the sentiments of lines 175–83 ('with modesty / enough' = without exaggeration; 'loam' = mortar; 't'expel' = to keep out; 'flaw' = wind).

2 Funeral procession (individually or in large groups)

Work out how to stage the funeral procession and how each character expresses their feelings. Page 275 shows how Ophelia's funeral was presented in film and stage versions of *Hamlet*.

3 The Priest: harsh or sympathetic?

This is the Priest's only appearance, and he has a mere thirteen lines. Imagine the actor asks you for advice.

Either write a response, taking him through his lines, explaining why he replies as he does to Laertes's angrily repeated question about why Ophelia is not receiving a full Christian burial.

Or work with a partner and improvise a scene in which the Priest talks with Horatio.

For either activity, think about whether the Priest firmly believes in the Church's view of suicides (that they were damned to suffer eternally in hell, were not allowed to be buried on consecrated ground, and were denied the ritual of the Christian burial service). Consider whether the Priest might try to soften that harsh ruling, and speak comfortingly to Laertes. Use the information on pages 250–1 to help you.

---

maimèd rites   incomplete ritual
Fordo   destroy
estate   high rank
Couch   hide
obsequies   funeral rites
warranty   authority
ground unsanctified   unconsecrated ground

last trumpet   Doomsday
Shards   pottery fragments
crants   wreaths of flowers, garlands
strewments   flowers strewn on the grave
sage requiem   solemn music for the dead

HAMLET No faith, not a jot, but to follow him thither with modesty   175
enough, and likelihood to lead it, as thus: Alexander died, Alexander
was buried, Alexander returneth to dust, the dust is earth, of earth
we make loam, and why of that loam whereto he was converted
might they not stop a beer-barrel?

          Imperious Caesar, dead and turned to clay,   180
          Might stop a hole, to keep the wind away.
          Oh that that earth which kept the world in awe
          Should patch a wall t'expel the winter's flaw!
     But soft, but soft! Aside – here comes the king,
     The queen, the courtiers.

Enter CLAUDIUS, GERTRUDE, LAERTES, *and a coffin,* [*with* PRIEST]
and LORDS *attendant*

                Who is this they follow?   185
    And with such maimèd rites? This doth betoken
    The corse they follow did with desperate hand
    Fordo it own life. 'Twas of some estate.
    Couch we awhile and mark.   [*Retiring with Horatio*]
LAERTES What ceremony else?   190
HAMLET That is Laertes, a very noble youth. Mark.
LAERTES What ceremony else?
PRIEST Her obsequies have been as far enlarged
    As we have warranty. Her death was doubtful,
    And but that great command o'ersways the order,   195
    She should in ground unsanctified have lodged
    Till the last trumpet. For charitable prayers,
    Shards, flints, and pebbles should be thrown on her.
    Yet here she is allowed her virgin crants,
    Her maiden strewments, and the bringing home   200
    Of bell and burial.
LAERTES Must there no more be done?
PRIEST   No more be done.
    We should profane the service of the dead
    To sing sage requiem and such rest to her
    As to peace-parted souls.

Laertes insults the Priest. Gertrude mourns Ophelia. Laertes curses Hamlet and leaps into the grave. Hamlet comes forward, and Laertes tries to strangle him. The attendants stop the fight.

1 Gertrude's wish (in pairs)

Talk together about how lines 210–13 add to your knowledge of Gertrude. Begin by telling each other whether her wish for Hamlet and Ophelia to marry came as a surprise to you.

2 Where do they fight – in or out of the grave?

In some productions, Hamlet leaps into the grave and Laertes struggles with him there. The directors of these productions argue that the fight in the grave is dramatically symbolic. Other directors feel strongly that Laertes should climb out of the grave to attack Hamlet.

What is your view? Draw up a list of the advantages and disadvantages of each practice. Use the list to state your own preference.

3 Language matters (in pairs)

a **Brotherly love**   Consider in turn each of the six sentences Laertes speaks opposite. For each, write two words expressing the emotional tone of the sentence (the first might be 'tender, loving').

b **'This is I, / Hamlet the Dane'**   Hamlet seems to be claiming the throne of Denmark: 'the Dane' usually means 'king of Denmark'. Suggest how he speaks the first half of line 225 and how each main character (Claudius, Gertrude, Laertes, Horatio) should react.

c **Revenge Tragedy**   In lines 213–25 both Laertes and Hamlet use the hyperbolic language of the traditional hero of Revenge Tragedy (see pp. 246–7). Take parts and give them full volume.

---

churlish ignorant
liest howling   suffer in hell
decked decorated
thy most ingenious . . . thee of drove you into madness
quick living

Pelion, Olympus   mountains in Greece
Conjures the wandering stars bewitches the planets
splenitive hot tempered

LAERTES   Lay her i'th'earth,   205
          And from her fair and unpolluted flesh
          May violets spring. I tell thee, churlish priest,
          A ministering angel shall my sister be
          When thou liest howling.
HAMLET   What, the fair Ophelia!
GERTRUDE Sweets to the sweet, farewell.   [*Scattering flowers*]   210
          I hoped thou shouldst have been my Hamlet's wife.
          I thought thy bride-bed to have decked, sweet maid,
          And not t'have strewed thy grave.
LAERTES   Oh treble woe
          Fall ten times treble on that cursèd head
          Whose wicked deed thy most ingenious sense   215
          Deprived thee of. Hold off the earth awhile
          Till I have caught her once more in mine arms.
                    Leaps in the grave
          Now pile your dust upon the quick and dead
          Till of this flat a mountain you have made
          T'o'ertop old Pelion or the skyish head   220
          Of blue Olympus.
HAMLET [*Advancing*]   What is he whose grief
          Bears such an emphasis? whose phrase of sorrow
          Conjures the wandering stars, and makes them stand
          Like wonder-wounded hearers? This is I,
          Hamlet the Dane.
                    [*Laertes climbs out of the grave*]
LAERTES   The devil take thy soul. [*Grappling with him*]   225
HAMLET Thou pray'st not well.
          I prithee take thy fingers from my throat,
          For though I am not splenitive and rash,
          Yet have I in me something dangerous
          Which let thy wisdom fear. Hold off thy hand.   230
CLAUDIUS Pluck them asunder.
GERTRUDE   Hamlet, Hamlet!
ALL   Gentlemen!
HORATIO Good my lord, be quiet.
                    [*The Attendants part them*].
HAMLET Why, I will fight with him upon this theme
          Until my eyelids will no longer wag.

Hamlet rants that his love for Ophelia was infinitely greater than Laertes's, and that he can match any action, however improbable. He leaves with an enigmatic remark. Claudius takes control.

---

1 'I'll rant as well as thou' (in pairs)

On page 212, Activity 3c, you were invited to speak in the exaggerated style of the traditional revenger. Hamlet continues in that bombastic manner. In lines 236–51 he rants furiously against Laertes's love for his sister. Speak the lines to each other several times in an over-the-top way, using gestures. Then talk together about the motivation Hamlet has for using such extravagant language. (Is it to convince Claudius he is mad?) Also discuss what his final lines 258–9 might mean (no one can be totally sure).

2 'The female dove . . .' – a strange image?

In lines 253–5, Gertrude says Hamlet will become as meek as a dove whose yellow-feathered chicks have just hatched ('golden couplets are disclosed'). He will become silent and quiet, as if his mission is complete. Invent another image that expresses the same idea.

3 What is Claudius actually thinking? (in pairs)

One person speaks Claudius's five sentences in lines 260–6. After each sentence the other person voices what Claudius has in mind (and notice he says '*your* son', not '*our* son' or '*my* son' as earlier).

4 '*Exeunt*' – everyone leaves the stage (in small groups)

Invent a piece of business (an action) for each character as they exit. Perhaps some actions take place over Ophelia's grave. Each character's wordless action expresses their feelings about what has happened in the scene. Don't forget the gravedigger and the Priest.

---

theme issue
forbear him leave him alone
'Swounds by God's wounds
Woo't would you (wilt thou)
eisel vinegar
outface outdo
prate rant, bluster

our ground . . . zone the earth under our feet touches the sun
Ossa mountain in Greece
Hercules Greek hero with huge strength and boastful manner
the present push immediate action
living lasting

GERTRUDE O my son, what theme?   235

HAMLET I loved Ophelia; forty thousand brothers
        Could not with all their quantity of love
        Make up my sum. What wilt thou do for her?

CLAUDIUS Oh he is mad Laertes.

GERTRUDE For love of God forbear him.   240

HAMLET 'Swounds, show me what thou't do.
        Woo't weep, woo't fight, woo't fast, woo't tear thyself?
        Woo't drink up eisel, eat a crocodile?
        I'll do't. Dost thou come here to whine,
        To outface me with leaping in her grave?   245
        Be buried quick with her, and so will I.
        And if thou prate of mountains, let them throw
        Millions of acres on us, till our ground,
        Singeing his pate against the burning zone,
        Make Ossa like a wart. Nay, and thou'lt mouth,   250
        I'll rant as well as thou.

GERTRUDE   This is mere madness,
        And thus awhile the fit will work on him;
        Anon, as patient as the female dove
        When that her golden couplets are disclosed,
        His silence will sit drooping.

HAMLET   Hear you sir,   255
        What is the reason that you use me thus?
        I loved you ever – but it is no matter.
        Let Hercules himself do what he may,
        The cat will mew, and dog will have his day.   *Exit*

CLAUDIUS I pray thee good Horatio wait upon him.   260

                                                        Exit Horatio

        (*To Laertes*) Strengthen your patience in our last night's
            speech;
        We'll put the matter to the present push. –
        Good Gertrude, set some watch over your son. –
        This grave shall have a living monument.
        An hour of quiet shortly shall we see,   265
        Till then in patience our proceeding be.

                                                        Exeunt

Hamlet tells Horatio how he could not sleep on the ship. He searched in Rosencrantz and Guildenstern's cabin for the letter from Claudius. It ordered that he should be executed immediately on arrival in England.

---

1 Hamlet's tale – first impression (in pairs)

In the first eighty lines of this final scene, Hamlet tells the story of his discovery of Claudius's order to have him executed; how he substituted Rosencrantz and Guildenstern as the victims; and how a chance encounter with pirates ensured his return to Denmark.

To gain a first impression of Hamlet's tale, take parts and read lines 1–80 (Horatio is little more than a 'feed'). Afterwards, work on some of the activities provided.

2 'There's a divinity that shapes our ends'

'Divinity' is the will of God, a kind of Christian plan that determines people's lives. Hamlet says that important matters are decided by a divine force, however much humans try to plan their lives. An individual has little power over what they will become. With lines 10–11 in mind, write a paragraph on each of the following:

a Is Hamlet's fate in the play shaped by a 'divinity' or by other factors (his character, chance, other people's actions and so on)?

b Do *you* believe 'There's a divinity that shapes our ends, / Rough-hew them how we will'? (However you plan and act, what will happen to you is not in your power to determine.)

c How do these two lines signify a development in Hamlet's character?

3 'Here's the commission'

Write the letter from Claudius ordering the immediate execution of Hamlet. Use lines 19–25 as your inspiration.

---

mutines in the bilboes mutineers in their chains
indiscretion instinct, intuition
pall go stale
Rough-hew roughly shape or plan
Fingered their packet stole their documents

in fine in conclusion
Larded decorated
Importing concerning
bugs and goblins . . . life horrors that would follow if I lived
supervise first reading
no leisure bated no time spared

Act 5 Scene 2
The Great Hall of Elsinore Castle

Enter HAMLET *and* HORATIO

HAMLET So much for this sir, now shall you see the other.
       You do remember all the circumstance?
HORATIO Remember it my lord!
HAMLET Sir, in my heart there was a kind of fighting
       That would not let me sleep. Methought I lay   5
       Worse than the mutines in the bilboes. Rashly,
       And praised be rashness for it – let us know,
       Our indiscretion sometime serves us well
       When our deep plots do pall, and that should learn us
       There's a divinity that shapes our ends,   10
       Rough-hew them how we will –
HORATIO   That is most certain.
HAMLET Up from my cabin,
       My sea-gown scarfed about me, in the dark
       Groped I to find out them, had my desire,
       Fingered their packet, and in fine withdrew   15
       To mine own room again, making so bold,
       My fears forgetting manners, to unseal
       Their grand commission; where I found, Horatio –
       O royal knavery! – an exact command,
       Larded with many several sorts of reasons,   20
       Importing Denmark's health, and England's too,
       With ho! such bugs and goblins in my life,
       That on the supervise, no leisure bated,
       No, not to stay the grinding of the axe,
       My head should be struck off.
HORATIO   Is't possible?   25
HAMLET Here's the commission, read it at more leisure.
       But wilt thou hear now how I did proceed?
HORATIO I beseech you.

Hamlet tells how he wrote a substitute letter commanding the execution of Rosencrantz and Guildenstern. He feels no remorse for their death, dismissing them as mere instruments of Claudius.

---

1 Activities on Hamlet's story (in small groups)

Hamlet describes the letter. It is an 'earnest conjuration' (serious plea) from Claudius to the king of England as his faithful subject ('tributary') to execute Rosencrantz and Guildenstern. In line 40 'palm' is the palm tree whose leaves symbolise peace; 'a comma 'tween their amities' (line 42) suggests that there is only a short break in the friendship of Denmark and England.

a **Individually**   Write the letter 'fair' (neatly) with lines 31–47 as a guide. Seal it with wax and the imprint of a ring, or design your own seal.

b **In small groups**   Hamlet sends Rosencrantz and Guildenstern to their death without a qualm of conscience (line 58). Talk together about whether the two courtiers deserve their fate. What does the decision to send his two 'friends' to their death and yet feel no remorse suggest about Hamlet's character?

c **In small groups**   Tom Stoppard's play, *Rosencrantz and Guildenstern Are Dead*, acts out lines 4–55, in which Hamlet describes the theft, the forging, his escape, and how Rosencrantz and Guildenstern sail on to England and death. The 1991 Zeffirelli film also shows the sequence (and the beheading of the two courtiers in England). Take parts as narrator, Hamlet, Rosencrantz and Guildenstern. Create your own narrated mime to show the action described.

---

benetted round   trapped and surrounded
Or . . . to my brains   before I could alert my mind
statists   politicians
yeoman   loyal attendant
debatement   consideration
shriving time   opportunity to confess their sins

ordinant   directing, ordaining
Subscribed   signed
gave't th'impression   sealed it
was sequent   followed on
insinuation   devious intervention
baser nature   inferior people
pass   thrust
fell incensèd points   deadly sword points

HAMLET Being thus benetted round with villainies,
          Or I could make a prologue to my brains,   30
          They had begun the play. I sat me down,
          Devised a new commission, wrote it fair.
          I once did hold it, as our statists do,
          A baseness to write fair, and laboured much
          How to forget that learning; but sir, now   35
          It did me yeoman's service. Wilt thou know
          Th'effect of what I wrote?
HORATIO   Ay good my lord.
HAMLET An earnest conjuration from the king,
          As England was his faithful tributary,
          As love between them like the palm might flourish,   40
          As peace should still her wheaten garland wear,
          And stand a comma 'tween their amities,
          And many suchlike as-es of great charge,
          That on the view and knowing of these contents,
          Without debatement further, more, or less,   45
          He should those bearers put to sudden death,
          Not shriving time allowed.
HORATIO   How was this sealed?
HAMLET Why, even in that was heaven ordinant.
          I had my father's signet in my purse,
          Which was the model of that Danish seal;   50
          Folded the writ up in the form of th'other,
          Subscribed it, gave't th'impression, placed it safely,
          The changeling never known. Now, the next day
          Was our sea-fight, and what to this was sequent
          Thou know'st already.   55
HORATIO So Guildenstern and Rosencrantz go to't.
HAMLET Why man, they did make love to this employment.
          They are not near my conscience. Their defeat
          Does by their own insinuation grow.
          'Tis dangerous when the baser nature comes   60
          Between the pass and fell incensèd points
          Of mighty opposites.
HORATIO   Why, what a king is this!

Hamlet argues that he is well justified in killing Claudius. He regrets his behaviour towards Laertes, seeing him as a fellow revenger. Hamlet comments dismissively on Osric, and mocks him. Osric tells of a wager.

---

1 Four reasons for revenge

Hamlet lists four reasons for revenge in lines 63–6: Claudius has killed his father ('my king'), slept with his mother, pushed in front of Hamlet's own claim to the throne ('Popped in between th'election and my hopes'), and plotted Hamlet's death.

Write the four reasons in order of their importance to Hamlet. Add a paragraph explaining why you have chosen that order.

2 Explanatory language versus dramatic language (in pairs)

In lines 73–80, Hamlet acknowledges that he has only a short time to kill Claudius. But he thinks the advantage is briefly with him because Claudius has not yet learned the news from England. Hamlet expresses regret that he overreacted to Laertes's grief, and recognises that they have a similar motive for revenge. He wishes to make peace with Laertes, and says Laertes's exaggerated grief caused his own outburst.

Match each sentence in the preceding paragraph with the appropriate lines, then talk together about the ways in which Shakespeare's language is so much more dramatic and suited to performance than the bare description given above.

3 Osric, 'this water-fly' (flickering lightweight)

Lines 81–98 give an impression of Osric as a fop, a rich dandy. Hamlet clearly despises him: 'let a beast . . . king's mess' means that, however unworthy a man is, if he has wealth he will be given a place ('crib') at the king's banqueting table ('mess'). You will find more on Osric in the following pages.

Does it . . . stand me now upon don't you think I now must
angle fishing hook (plotted)
cozenage deceit, trickery
perfect conscience morally justified
canker of our nature disease of humanity

come / In further evil grow in more villainy
issue outcome
to say 'one' a brief moment
chough jackdaw

HAMLET Does it not, think thee, stand me now upon –
        He that hath killed my king, and whored my mother,
        Popped in between th'election and my hopes,   65
        Thrown out his angle for my proper life,
        And with such cozenage – is't not perfect conscience
        To quit him with this arm? And is't not to be damned
        To let this canker of our nature come
        In further evil?   70
HORATIO It must be shortly known to him from England
        What is the issue of the business there.
HAMLET It will be short. The interim's mine,
        And a man's life's no more than to say 'one'.
        But I am very sorry, good Horatio,   75
        That to Laertes I forgot myself,
        For by the image of my cause, I see
        The portraiture of his. I'll court his favours.
        But sure the bravery of his grief did put me
        Into a towering passion.
HORATIO   Peace, who comes here?   80

                    Enter young OSRIC

OSRIC Your lordship is right welcome back to Denmark.
HAMLET I humbly thank you sir. – Dost know this water-fly?
HORATIO No my good lord.
HAMLET Thy state is the more gracious, for 'tis a vice to know him.
        He hath much land and fertile; let a beast be lord of beasts, and   85
        his crib shall stand at the king's mess. 'Tis a chough, but as I say,
        spacious in the possession of dirt.
OSRIC Sweet lord, if your lordship were at leisure, I should impart a
        thing to you from his majesty.
HAMLET I will receive it sir with all diligence of spirit. Put your bonnet   90
        to his right use, 'tis for the head.
OSRIC I thank your lordship, it is very hot.
HAMLET No believe me, 'tis very cold, the wind is northerly.
OSRIC It is indifferent cold my lord, indeed.
HAMLET But yet methinks it is very sultry and hot for my complexion.   95
OSRIC Exceedingly my lord, it is very sultry, as 'twere – I cannot tell
        how. But my lord, his majesty bade me signify to you that a has
        laid a great wager on your head. Sir, this is the matter –

Osric praises Laertes as an outstanding model of a gentleman. He uses such affected language that Hamlet makes fun of him by responding in a style that is even more elaborate and obscure.

1 Mocking Osric – without drawing breath

Hamlet obviously detests Osric's affected manner and language. In lines 106–12, Hamlet makes up words ('definement' = definition, 'inventorially' = as an inventory/list); uses pompous phrases ('the verity / of extolment' = the truth of praising); and mocks Osric's praise of Laertes.

In the 1993 Royal Shakespeare Company production, Kenneth Branagh as Hamlet spoke the lines very quickly and utterly clearly, in a single breath. Try it yourself!

Osric, pretentious and superficial, delivers news of Laertes. Royal Shakespeare Company, 1984.

---

excellent differences gifted accomplishments
soft society good manners
card or calendar guide or handbook
the continent . . . would see every attribute a gentleman seeks

perdition loss
yaw zig-zag
infusion qualities
dearth uniqueness
semblable only likeness
umbrage shadow
meed merit, achievements

HAMLET I beseech you remember.

[*Hamlet moves him to put on his hat*]

OSRIC Nay good my lord, for my ease in good faith. Sir, [here is newly   100
come to court Laertes; believe me an absolute gentleman, full of
most excellent differences, of very soft society and great showing.
Indeed, to speak feelingly of him, he is the card or calendar of
gentry, for you shall find in him the continent of what part a
gentleman would see.   105

HAMLET Sir, his definement suffers no perdition in you, though I know
to divide him inventorially would dozy th'arithmetic of memory,
and yet but yaw neither in respect of his quick sail. But in the verity
of extolment, I take him to be a soul of great article, and his infusion
of such dearth and rareness as, to make true diction of him, his   110
semblable is his mirror, and who else would trace him, his umbrage,
nothing more.

OSRIC Your lordship speaks most infallibly of him.

HAMLET The concernancy, sir? Why do we wrap the gentleman in our
more rawer breath?   115

OSRIC Sir?

HORATIO Is't not possible to understand in another tongue? You will
to't sir, really.

HAMLET What imports the nomination of this gentleman?

OSRIC Of Laertes?   120

HORATIO His purse is empty already, all's golden words are spent.

HAMLET Of him sir.

OSRIC I know you are not ignorant –

HAMLET I would you did sir, yet in faith if you did, it would not much
approve me. Well sir?]   125

OSRIC You are not ignorant of what excellence Laertes is.

[HAMLET I dare not confess that, lest I should compare with him in
excellence, but to know a man well were to know himself.

OSRIC I mean sir for his weapon; but in the imputation laid on him
by them, in his meed he's unfellowed.]   130

HAMLET What's his weapon?

OSRIC Rapier and dagger.

HAMLET That's two of his weapons, but well.

Osric tells of Claudius's wager: in a twelve-bout duel between Hamlet and Laertes, Laertes will not win three more bouts than Hamlet. Osric leaves, and Hamlet and Horatio exchange amused comments about him.

---

1 'How if I answer no?'

Experiment with different ways of speaking line 151: 'How if I answer no?' For example, try it as if Hamlet does not want to fight the duel, or as if Hamlet doesn't care what happens, or with defiance. Try leaving a long pause between 'answer' and 'no' to experience the dramatic effect it makes.

Decide which style of speaking you think is most appropriate.

2 Osric's character – and is he in on the plot?

Horatio sees Osric as a precocious (very forward) juvenile: 'This lapwing runs away with the shell on his head.' A lapwing chick leaves its nest very shortly after hatching, often with parts of its shell still sticking to its head.

Hamlet suggests that no one else is likely to praise Osric ('there are no tongues else for's / turn') so he does well 'to commend it [his duty] himself'. He compares him to a baby that 'did comply with his dug' (made a deal with his mother's breast). Hamlet goes on to say that Osric is typical of the flock ('bevy') of frothy, superficial people fashionable in these frivolous ('drossy') times. They burst like bubbles when they face some real test. The 'fanned and winnowed opinions' are the wise, carefully considered opinions that people like Osric simply ignore.

a List Osric's character traits, finding lines to support your ideas. Try to think of someone in public life today who is like Osric.

b Imagine Osric knows of Claudius's murderous plan. How would that affect his performance? How likely is it that he knows?

Barbary Arab
impawned wagered
six French rapiers . . . and so equipment wagered by Laertes
liberal conceit fanciful decoration
edified by the margent enlightened by an explanation (as in the margin of a book)

germane relevant
hangers straps to hold swords to belts
vouchsafe the answer accept the challenge
the breathing exercise
yesty collection yeasty (frothy) brew, trivial people

OSRIC The king sir hath wagered with him six Barbary horses, against
the which he has impawned, as I take it, six French rapiers and   135
poniards, with their assigns, as girdle, hangers, and so. Three of
the carriages in faith are very dear to fancy, very responsive to the
hilts, most delicate carriages, and of very liberal conceit.

HAMLET What call you the carriages?

HORATIO I knew you must be edified by the margent ere you had done.   140

OSRIC The carriages sir are the hangers.

HAMLET The phrase would be more germane to the matter if we could
carry a cannon by our sides; I would it might be hangers till then.
But on, six Barbary horses against six French swords, their assigns,
and three liberal-conceited carriages – that's the French bet against   145
the Danish. Why is this impawned, as you call it?

OSRIC The king sir, hath laid sir, that in a dozen passes between yourself
and him, he shall not exceed you three hits. He hath laid on twelve
for nine. And it would come to immediate trial, if your lordship
would vouchsafe the answer.   150

HAMLET How if I answer no?

OSRIC I mean my lord, the opposition of your person in trial.

HAMLET Sir, I will walk here in the hall. If it please his majesty, it is
the breathing time of day with me. Let the foils be brought, the
gentleman willing, and the king hold his purpose, I will win for   155
him and I can. If not, I will gain nothing but my shame and the
odd hits.

OSRIC Shall I redeliver you e'en so?

HAMLET To this effect sir, after what flourish your nature will.

OSRIC I commend my duty to your lordship.   160

HAMLET Yours, yours.

                                                            [*Exit Osric*]

He does well to commend it himself, there are no tongues else for's
turn.

HORATIO This lapwing runs away with the shell on his head.

HAMLET A did comply with his dug before a sucked it. Thus has he,   165
and many more of the same bevy that I know the drossy age dotes
on, only got the tune of the time and outward habit of encounter,
a kind of yesty collection, which carries them through and through
the most fanned and winnowed opinions; and do but blow them
to their trial, the bubbles are out.   170

                        [*Enter a* LORD

A lord asks if Hamlet will duel with Laertes now or later. Hamlet is ready. Horatio warns that he will lose, and offers to give his apologies, but Hamlet feels the time is ripe. He asks Laertes to pardon him.

1 From 'To be, or not to be' to 'Let be' (in pairs)

Hamlet has journeyed a vast emotional distance from the anxiety of 'To be, or not to be' to the simple acceptance of 'Let be.' He does not think he will lose the duel, but feels foreboding ('how ill all's here about my heart'). But he is resolute, and sees 'special providence in / the fall of a sparrow' (an image from St Matthew's Gospel).

Hamlet seems ready to accept whatever fate has in store for him. Whether death comes sooner or later, it will come. What matters is the frame of mind to meet death: 'the / readiness is all'. Since no one really knows the meaning of life, what does it matter to die early ('betimes')? Concentrate on lines 192–6:

a Talk together about how Hamlet's mood now contrasts with that earlier in the play.

b Experiment with ways of speaking the lines. How might Hamlet vary his tone from thought to thought?

c After the first two sentences, Hamlet uses almost only monosyllables ('If it be now . . . Let be.'). Speak the lines, making each monosyllable sharp and clear. Discuss the dramatic effect of such simple words.

2 A grand entry – potential witnesses to a murder?

The entry of the court is often performed with much ceremony, implying that Claudius wishes to have many witnesses of Hamlet's 'accidental' death. Write notes and draw diagrams to show how you would perform the stage direction between lines 196 and 197.

---

commended him sent his compliments
attend await
play sword fence, duel
In happy time just at the right time (spoken ironically?)
gentle entertainment courteous greetings
at the odds according to the wager
gaingiving misgiving (gainsaying)
repair hither coming here
augury predictions of the future
betimes early
This presence everybody here
exception grievance, wish for revenge

LORD My lord, his majesty commended him to you by young Osric,
who brings back to him that you attend him in the hall. He sends
to know if your pleasure hold to play with Laertes, or that you will
take longer time.

HAMLET I am constant to my purposes, they follow the king's pleasure.   175
If his fitness speaks, mine is ready; now or whensoever, provided
I be so able as now.

LORD The king and queen, and all, are coming down.

HAMLET In happy time.

LORD The queen desires you to use some gentle entertainment to   180
Laertes, before you fall to play.

HAMLET She well instructs me.]

[Exit Lord]

HORATIO You will lose, my lord.

HAMLET I do not think so. Since he went into France, I have been in
continual practice; I shall win at the odds. But thou wouldst not   185
think how ill all's here about my heart – but it is no matter.

HORATIO Nay good my lord –

HAMLET It is but foolery, but it is such a kind of gaingiving as would
perhaps trouble a woman.

HORATIO If your mind dislike anything, obey it. I will forestall their   190
repair hither, and say you are not fit.

HAMLET Not a whit, we defy augury. There is special providence in
the fall of a sparrow. If it be now, 'tis not to come; if it be not to
come, it will be now; if it be not now, yet it will come – the
readiness is all. Since no man of aught he leaves knows, what is't   195
to leave betimes? Let be.

A table prepared, with flagons of wine on it. Trumpets, Drums and Officers
with cushions. Enter CLAUDIUS, GERTRUDE, LAERTES *and* LORDS, *with*
other Attendants with foils, daggers and gauntlets

CLAUDIUS Come Hamlet, come and take this hand from me.

[Hamlet takes Laertes by the hand]

HAMLET Give me your pardon sir, I've done you wrong;
But pardon't as you are a gentleman.
This presence knows,   200
And you must needs have heard, how I am punished
With a sore distraction. What I have done,
That might your nature, honour and exception
Roughly awake, I here proclaim was madness.

Hamlet claims that his madness, rather than he himself, was to blame for the death of Polonius. Laertes, with reservations, accepts Hamlet's apology. Hamlet praises Laertes's fencing skills. They choose rapiers.

1 True or false? Hamlet's apology (in pairs)

Hamlet apologises to Laertes (lines 198–216), fulfilling his mother's request to 'use some gentle entertainment to Laertes' before the duel. Talk together about your views on each of the following statements:

- Hamlet's apology to Laertes is genuine and sincere.
- His explanation for his killing of Polonius ('madness') is false.
- His claim to have suffered from a 'sore distraction' is untrue.
- He seems to have forgotten the death of Ophelia.
- He claims that chance and accident are to blame.

2 True or false? Laertes's reply (in pairs)

Laertes intends, secretly and treacherously, to kill Hamlet. But in lines 216–24, he says he is satisfied as far as natural feelings go ('in nature') but must obey a higher moral code (that of vengeance, his 'terms of honour') to keep his reputation pure ('name ungored'). He promises not to wrong Hamlet's love.

One person reads lines 216–24, pausing at each punctuation mark. In each pause, the other person, as Laertes, says either 'true' or 'false', and explains what his secret thoughts really are at that moment.

3 The choosing of foils – how is it performed?

Write notes for the actors on lines 226–38 to make the choosing of the foils as dramatically effective as possible. Remember: Laertes knows one has an unblunted blade, so how does he ensure he gets the right rapier? Is Osric in on the plot to kill Hamlet (see p. 224)?

---

tane taken
faction party
That I have shot . . . brother I have hurt you accidentally
some elder . . . honour qualified experts

voice . . . peace judgement in favour of reconciliation
Stick fiery off stand out brilliantly
bettered improved
likes me pleases me
all a length all the same length

Was't Hamlet wronged Laertes? Never Hamlet. 205
If Hamlet from himself be tane away,
And when he's not himself does wrong Laertes,
Then Hamlet does it not, Hamlet denies it.
Who does it then? His madness. If't be so,
Hamlet is of the faction that is wronged, 210
His madness is poor Hamlet's enemy.
Sir, in this audience,
Let my disclaiming from a purposed evil
Free me so far in your most generous thoughts,
That I have shot my arrow o'er the house 215
And hurt my brother.

LAERTES   I am satisfied in nature,
Whose motive in this case should stir me most
To my revenge; but in my terms of honour
I stand aloof, and will no reconcilement
Till by some elder masters of known honour 220
I have a voice and precedent of peace
To keep my name ungored. But till that time
I do receive your offered love like love,
And will not wrong it.

HAMLET   I embrace it freely,
And will this brother's wager frankly play. 225
Give us the foils, come on.

LAERTES   Come, one for me.

HAMLET I'll be your foil Laertes. In mine ignorance
Your skill shall like a star i'th'darkest night
Stick fiery off indeed.

LAERTES   You mock me sir.

HAMLET No, by this hand. 230

CLAUDIUS Give them the foils, young Osric. Cousin Hamlet,
You know the wager?

HAMLET   Very well my lord.
Your grace has laid the odds a'th'weaker side.

CLAUDIUS I do not fear it, I have seen you both.
But since he is bettered, we have therefore odds. 235

LAERTES This is too heavy, let me see another.

HAMLET This likes me well. These foils have all a length?

Claudius orders wine and celebrations if Hamlet is successful. He will drink a toast if Hamlet wins, and put a pearl in the wine. Hamlet makes two hits. Claudius offers the poisoned cup, but Hamlet declines to drink.

1 The poisoned cup

Imagine you are directing a rehearsal of the play. You are asked two questions by the actors:

- Is Hamlet suspicious about the drink at line 260?
- How should Claudius say 'Gertrude, do not drink!' at line 268?

Make your replies.

The duel. Choose a line from page 231 or 233 as a suitable caption for this moment.

stoups flagons, large jars (see stage direction after line 196)
quit win
ordnance cannons
an union a pearl
kettle kettle-drum
without outside

wary watchful
palpable tangible, definite
Stay wait
fat unfit, sweaty (Gertrude often shows affection for Hamlet here)
carouses drinks (Is she suspicious? See p. 232.)

OSRIC Ay my good lord.
                         Prepare to play
CLAUDIUS Set me the stoups of wine upon that table.
          If Hamlet give the first or second hit,   240
          Or quit in answer of the third exchange,
          Let all the battlements their ordnance fire.
          The king shall drink to Hamlet's better breath,
          And in the cup an union shall he throw
          Richer than that which four successive kings   245
          In Denmark's crown have worn. Give me the cups,
          And let the kettle to the trumpet speak,
          The trumpet to the cannoneer without,
          The cannons to the heavens, the heaven to earth,
          'Now the king drinks to Hamlet!' Come, begin,   250
          And you the judges bear a wary eye.
                         Trumpets the while
HAMLET Come on sir.
LAERTES Come my lord.
                         They play
HAMLET One.
LAERTES No.   255
HAMLET Judgement.
OSRIC A hit, a very palpable hit.
LAERTES Well, again.
CLAUDIUS Stay, give me drink. Hamlet, this pearl is thine.
          Here's to thy health.
                  Drum, trumpets sound, and shot goes off
                         Give him the cup.   260
HAMLET I'll play this bout first, set it by awhile.
          Come.
                         [*They play*]
                  Another hit. What say you?
LAERTES A touch, a touch, I do confess't.
CLAUDIUS Our son shall win.
GERTRUDE   He's fat and scant of breath.
          Here Hamlet, take my napkin, rub thy brows.   265
          The queen carouses to thy fortune, Hamlet.
HAMLET Good madam.
CLAUDIUS Gertrude, do not drink!

Gertrude drinks from the poisoned cup. Laertes wounds Hamlet. In a scuffle, they exchange rapiers and Hamlet wounds Laertes. The queen falls and dies. Laertes reveals the treacherous plot.

---

1 Staging the duel (in pairs)

The duel and its bloody outcome last only around sixty lines. But Shakespeare provides opportunities to create thrilling stage action. In many productions Laertes wounds Hamlet deceitfully at line 280, a moment that Hamlet thinks is an interval.

Decide whether you think Laertes acts dishonourably. To make your decision clear to an audience, work out how you would stage the wounding of Hamlet by Laertes, the scuffle that follows, the exchange of rapiers, and the wounding of Laertes.

2 The death of Gertrude: accident or suicide? (in pairs)

The queen dies by drinking from the poisoned cup that Claudius intended for her son. Every actor playing Gertrude thinks hard about whether she knows the cup is poisoned and whether her death is an accident or suicide (see line 269). If she decides that Gertrude suspects the cup is poisoned, to be theatrically convincing she should be seen distancing herself from Claudius in earlier scenes (she may point to Claudius as she speaks her final words).

One partner argues for Gertrude committing suicide. The other argues for Gertrude not knowing the drink is poisoned.

3 Accusations: Claudius's reaction (in groups of four or more)

Laertes and Gertrude reveal that treachery is at work. Gertrude says she has been poisoned. Laertes says he has wounded Hamlet with a poisoned rapier and the king is to blame. How does Claudius react to the accusations? Take parts and act out lines 288–300, but with Claudius speaking aloud his thoughts.

---

do but dally   waste time
pass   thrust
make a wanton of me   treat me as a spoilt child
incensed   inflamed, mad, out of control

as a woodcock to mine own springe like a foolish bird, caught in my own trap
sounds   swoons
Unbated and envenomed   sharp and poisonous

GERTRUDE I will my lord, I pray you pardon me.
                                    [Drinks]
CLAUDIUS *[Aside]* It is the poisoned cup. It is too late.   270
HAMLET I dare not drink yet madam, by and by.
GERTRUDE Come, let me wipe thy face.
LAERTES My lord, I'll hit him now.
CLAUDIUS   I do not think't.
LAERTES And yet it is almost against my conscience.
HAMLET Come, for the third, Laertes. You do but dally.   275
          I pray you pass with your best violence.
          I am afeard you make a wanton of me.
LAERTES Say you so? Come on.
                                    Play
OSRIC Nothing neither way.
LAERTES Have at you now!   *[Wounds Hamlet]* 280
          In scuffling they change rapiers
CLAUDIUS Part them. They are incensed.
HAMLET Nay, come again.   *[Wounds Laertes]*
                            [Gertrude falls]
OSRIC Look to the queen there, ho!
HORATIO They bleed on both sides. How is it my lord?
OSRIC How is't Laertes?   285
LAERTES Why, as a woodcock to mine own springe, Osric.
          I am justly killed with mine own treachery.
HAMLET How does the queen?
CLAUDIUS   She sounds to see them bleed.
GERTRUDE No, no, the drink, the drink – O my dear Hamlet –
          The drink, the drink – I am poisoned.   *[Dies]* 290
HAMLET Oh villainy! – Ho, let the door be locked!
          Treachery! Seek it out!
                            [Laertes falls]
LAERTES It is here Hamlet. Hamlet, thou art slain,
          No medicine in the world can do thee good,
          In thee there is not half an hour of life –   295
          The treacherous instrument is in thy hand,
          Unbated and envenomed. The foul practice
          Hath turned itself on me; lo, here I lie,
          Never to rise again. Thy mother's poisoned –
          I can no more – the king, the king's to blame.   300

Hamlet wounds Claudius and forces him to drink from the poisoned cup. Claudius dies. Laertes forgives Hamlet, then dies. Hamlet prevents Horatio from suicide, and asks him to report his (Hamlet's) story.

1 Key moments (individually or in pairs)

a **Staging the death of Claudius**   The killing of Claudius is often a savage affair. Hamlet runs him through with his sword, then, without pity, forces him to drink poison. The courtiers cry 'Treason, treason!', but do nothing. Some productions have Hamlet chasing a terrified Claudius, who tries to hide behind the courtiers. Others have portrayed him facing death with calm dignity.

How would you stage lines 301–6? Write notes on how Hamlet, Claudius and the courtiers behave (in line with your view of Hamlet's and Claudius's characters).

b **'Wretched queen adieu'**   Hamlet's three-word farewell to his mother is often turned into a poignant moment in performance. In one production, Hamlet crawled across to her and kissed her as he spoke. Write notes on how you would turn those three words into a memorable theatrical episode.

c **'Exchange forgiveness with me'**   Laertes turns against Claudius, asking Hamlet for mutual forgiveness. Discuss whether Laertes's last speech is in character, and how it relates to *Hamlet* as Revenge Tragedy.

d **'A wounded name'**   Hamlet forbids Horatio to take the poison and commit suicide, because he wants Horatio to 'report me and my cause aright / To the unsatisfied' (those who do not know the full story). He wants to ensure that his 'name' (reputation) is remembered.

List six words you think Hamlet would wish to be included in Horatio's description of him. Then list six words of your own to describe how *you* see Hamlet. Do the two lists match?

union   precious pearl
is justly served   has received what he deserves
tempered   mixed
chance   mischance
mutes   silent watchers
fell   cruel

antique Roman   ancient Roman (who would commit suicide rather than live dishonourably)
ha't   have it
Absent thee from felicity   leave happiness behind

HAMLET The point envenomed too! Then, venom, to thy work!
                    Hurts the king
ALL Treason, treason!
CLAUDIUS Oh yet defend me friends, I am but hurt.
HAMLET Here, thou incestuous, murderous, damnèd Dane,
    Drink off this potion. Is thy union here?   305
    Follow my mother.   *King dies*
LAERTES   He is justly served,
    It is a poison tempered by himself.
    Exchange forgiveness with me, noble Hamlet.
    Mine and my father's death come not upon thee,
    Nor thine on me.   *Dies* 310
HAMLET Heaven make thee free of it! I follow thee.
    I am dead, Horatio. Wretched queen adieu.
    You that look pale, and tremble at this chance,
    That are but mutes or audience to this act,
    Had I but time, as this fell sergeant death   315
    Is strict in his arrest, oh I could tell you –
    But let it be. Horatio, I am dead,
    Thou livest; report me and my cause aright
    To the unsatisfied.
HORATIO   Never believe it.
    I am more an antique Roman than a Dane.   320
    Here's yet some liquor left.
HAMLET   As th'art a man,
    Give me the cup. Let go, by heaven I'll ha't.
    O God, Horatio, what a wounded name,
    Things standing thus unknown, shall live behind me!
    If thou didst ever hold me in thy heart,   325
    Absent thee from felicity awhile,
    And in this harsh world draw thy breath in pain
    To tell my story.
       March afar off, and shot within
       What warlike noise is this?

Before dying, Hamlet declares Fortinbras is his choice as king of Denmark. Fortinbras wonders at the sight of so many dead bodies. The English ambassador reports that Rosencrantz and Guildenstern are dead.

Hamlet © 1990 World Icon N.V. Licensed by Warner Bros. Entertainment Inc. All Rights Reserved.

In the 1990 Zeffirelli film, Hamlet dies beside his mother. How would you stage Hamlet's death?

1 'Family matters' = 'political matters'

After the 'family' deaths and Horatio's personal, religious farewell ('Good night sweet prince, / And flights of angels sing thee to thy rest') the political world bursts in. *Hamlet* entwines the 'personal' and 'political'. See Activity 2 on page 238, and pages 243–5.

warlike volley gunfire salute
o'ercrows triumphs over
prophesy . . . Fortinbras predict Fortinbras will be chosen as king of Denmark
voice vote
occurrents more and less all the events

solicited brought about (my vote); Hamlet does not complete his sentence
aught anything
quarry heap of dead bodies
cries on suggests
toward being prepared
senseless without sense or feeling

OSRIC Young Fortinbras, with conquest come from Poland,
   To the ambassadors of England gives   330
   This warlike volley.
HAMLET   Oh I die, Horatio,
   The potent poison quite o'ercrows my spirit.
   I cannot live to hear the news from England.
   But I do prophesy th'election lights
   On Fortinbras; he has my dying voice.   335
   So tell him, with th'occurrents more and less
   Which have solicited – the rest is silence.   *Dies*
HORATIO Now cracks a noble heart. Good night sweet prince,
   And flights of angels sing thee to thy rest. –
   Why does the drum come hither?   340

Enter FORTINBRAS *and* ENGLISH AMBASSADORS, *with drum, colours
and Attendants*

FORTINBRAS Where is this sight?
HORATIO   What is it you would see?
   If aught of woe or wonder, cease your search.
FORTINBRAS This quarry cries on havoc. O proud death,
   What feast is toward in thine eternal cell
   That thou so many princes at a shot   345
   So bloodily hast struck?
I AMBASSADOR   The sight is dismal,
   And our affairs from England come too late.
   The ears are senseless that should give us hearing,
   To tell him his commandment is fulfilled,
   That Rosencrantz and Guildenstern are dead.   350
   Where should we have our thanks?

Horatio asks for the bodies to be placed on view, and says he will tell how the carnage came about. Fortinbras claims the throne of Denmark. He commands that Hamlet be carried with due ceremony to the platform.

---

1 Show – or tell – Horatio's story (in small groups)

In lines 359–64 Horatio lists seven incidents he proposes to relate:

Either act out each incident – first, show the actual events in the play; second, let your imagination run freely.

Or write the story Horatio intends to tell.

2 Political matters – personal matters (individuals or groups)

This final episode shows that the private and public aspects of the play are utterly interlocked. Hamlet's obsession with his father's death and his mother's sexuality has caused instability in the state ('men's minds are wild') and brought about regime change.

a **'Proved most royal'** Fortinbras orders that Hamlet be displayed 'like a soldier', and claims that Hamlet possessed the qualities to become a great king. Write a list of what you think are Hamlet's characteristics. How far does your list show that Hamlet possessed soldierly and kingly qualities?

b **Denmark under Fortinbras** One production of *Hamlet* ended with the final line as an instruction for Horatio to be taken off and shot. Fortinbras was obviously going to rule Denmark as a tyrant. Work out how Fortinbras speaks his final nine lines to show what kind of king you think he will be.

c **A final image** The ending can be performed to suggest optimism or dejection, harmony and peace ahead or future troubles. What is the final image an audience would see at the end of your production of *Hamlet*? Write notes, or sketch, or create a tableau of the last image the audience sees as the lights fade.

---

jump upon timely on	**vantage** good fortune
judgements punishments	**presently** immediately
put on (line 362) brought about	**wild** disturbed, uncertain
forced cause distorted truths	**put on** (line 376) made king
purposes mistook bungled plots	**passage** funeral march
inventors conspirators	**rite** rituals
rights of memory claims	***peal of ordnance*** gun salute

HORATIO   Not from his mouth,
    Had it th'ability of life to thank you;
    He never gave commandment for their death.
    But since, so jump upon this bloody question,
    You from the Polack wars, and you from England,   355
    Are here arrived, give order that these bodies
    High on a stage be placèd to the view,
    And let me speak to th'yet unknowing world
    How these things came about. So shall you hear
    Of carnal, bloody, and unnatural acts,   360
    Of accidental judgements, casual slaughters,
    Of deaths put on by cunning and forced cause,
    And in this upshot, purposes mistook
    Fallen on th'inventors' heads. All this can I
    Truly deliver.   365
FORTINBRAS   Let us haste to hear it,
    And call the noblest to the audience.
    For me, with sorrow I embrace my fortune.
    I have some rights of memory in this kingdom,
    Which now to claim my vantage doth invite me.
HORATIO Of that I shall have also cause to speak,   370
    And from his mouth whose voice will draw on more.
    But let this same be presently performed,
    Even while men's minds are wild, lest more mischance
    On plots and errors happen.
FORTINBRAS   Let four captains
    Bear Hamlet like a soldier to the stage,   375
    For he was likely, had he been put on,
    To have proved most royal; and for his passage,
    The soldier's music and the rite of war
    Speak loudly for him.
    Take up the bodies. Such a sight as this   380
    Becomes the field, but here shows much amiss.
    Go bid the soldiers shoot.
      Exeunt marching, after the which a peal of ordnance are shot off

Looking back at the play

Write an analysis of your response to both pictures, suggesting what moment in the graveyard scene each portrays and the dramatic effect you think the actors wished to achieve.

1 The gravedigger's tale

The graveyard scene adds comedy to tragedy. The play's concern with death and corruption is given comic expression by the gravedigger as he refuses to give Hamlet a straight answer, and by Hamlet's sardonic comments about dead politicians, courtiers and lawyers. The gravedigger treats Hamlet as an equal, giving him a dose of his own medicine as he plays with words. His is the voice of the ordinary people. Step into role as the gravedigger and write your story of all you know about the happenings in Denmark from the time you became sexton ('the very / day that young Hamlet was born') to Fortinbras becoming king.

2 Love in *Hamlet*

'. . . forty thousand brothers / Could not with all their quantity of love / Make up my sum' cries Hamlet as he rages against Laertes beside Ophelia's grave. In all the writing about *Hamlet* 'love' is less discussed than 'revenge' or 'madness'. Yet it plays a vitally important part in the tragedy in many ways. Consider each major character and identify who (or what – Polonius loves the sound of his own voice) they love, and if that love is returned or changes. Use your findings to write an extended essay: 'The importance of love in *Hamlet*'.

3 What caused the tragedy?

Write at least a paragraph on each of the following, analysing how it contributes to the tragedy of *Hamlet*:

- the personality of Hamlet (perhaps a fatal flaw; see pp. 254–8)
- the personality of Claudius (see p. 260)
- fate: the inevitable working out of destiny
- the supernatural: ghostly intervention
- Denmark (a corrupt society is perhaps the major cause of the tragedy)
- chance and accident (e.g. the encounter with the pirate ship).

4 'The rest is silence' – an 'early' ending

Some productions have ended at Act 5 Scene 2, line 337: Hamlet's 'the rest is silence.' Give your view on that practice, identifying what is lost or gained dramatically by ending the play at that line.

5 Modern relevance

Write down all the things you would say to include in an argument that *Hamlet* is relevant to today's world.

What is the play about?

Millions of words in thousands of books and articles have been written on *Hamlet*. They stand in ironic contrast to Hamlet's final words 'the rest is silence.' The character of Hamlet himself has attracted most critical commentary. In the nineteenth century he appealed to the romantic melancholic mood and was interpreted as the noble doomed hero. From the second half of the twentieth century more attention has been given to his contradictions and unpleasantness: a man who can speak great poetry yet revile a young woman, stab her father in a sudden violent moment, and send two old friends to their death without a twinge of conscience.

There is something sponge-like about *Hamlet*. It absorbs the interests and anxieties of any culture and any age. When 'squeezed out' in performance and criticism, it renders back those interests and preoccupations as abstracts and brief chronicles of the time. Just as Hamlet described the purpose of playing as to show 'the very age and body of the time his form and pressure', so every society reproduces *Hamlet* to mirror itself. Thus a German production in the 1970s presented Ophelia as a Bader–Meinhof terrorist. A Romanian production in the late 1980s portrayed Denmark as a totalitarian police state in Eastern Europe. And in 2004 London's Old Vic Theatre presented Hamlet as a contemporary disturbed, neurotic adolescent.

One way of answering the question 'What is *Hamlet* about?' is to think of it as the dramatisation of a story. Denmark is under threat of invasion by Fortinbras of Norway. Young Hamlet, prince of Denmark, is deeply depressed. His father the king has recently died in mysterious circumstances. His mother Gertrude has quickly married his uncle Claudius, whom Hamlet detests. Claudius, not Hamlet, has become king. Hamlet's father returns as a Ghost and tells Hamlet that Claudius is responsible for his murder. Hamlet desires revenge and pretends to be mad to achieve that end. But he is uncertain whether the Ghost is honest, or is an agent of the devil, tempting him to do evil. He delays taking revenge. The visit of a group of travelling actors gives him an idea: he will have them perform a murder before Claudius. If Claudius reacts guiltily, it will prove the Ghost has spoken the truth. And that is what happens.

But Hamlet's assumed madness has disastrous consequences. He violently insults Ophelia, the young woman he had loved. Then, confronting his mother, he kills Polonius, Ophelia's father, thinking him to be Claudius. The result is that Ophelia is actually driven mad, and Hamlet is sentenced to be exiled to England, where Claudius plans he shall be executed. But a chance encounter with a pirate ship enables Hamlet to return to Denmark, where he learns that Ophelia has drowned. Her brother Laertes plots with Claudius to kill Hamlet deceitfully in a duel using a poisoned sword and drink. Their plan backfires, and Gertrude drinks the poison and dies. Laertes, fatally wounded, reveals the truth. Hamlet, wounded by the poisoned sword, kills Claudius, and then he too dies. Fortinbras arrives, to become king of Denmark.

Such a brief telling of the story, however, is inadequate to answer the question 'What is *Hamlet* about?' It has become customary to attempt answers by discussing the themes of the play. Themes are ideas or concepts (such as 'delay' or 'surveillance') which recur throughout the play. They suggest that Shakespeare was preoccupied by such ideas as he wrote, and sought to explore them through drama that would entertain his audiences – and make them think. You have been invited to work on the theme of appearance versus reality throughout the play. Other major themes now follow: politics and society, revenge, madness and melancholia, sin and salvation, acting and theatre.

Politics and society – 'Denmark's a prison'

The play is set in a politically and culturally interconnected Europe: Denmark, Norway, Poland, France, Germany, England. Elsinore is not a remote backwater, but a vital strategic place in European political and social life. Its young aristocrats are educated at Wittenberg University, and it claims England as one of its dependent states, subdued by bloody combat (Act 4 Scene 3, lines 54–60).

But Claudius's Denmark is insecure. When the play opens, it is a country feverishly preparing for war. The nervous anxiety of that preparation is evident in the very first words spoken: 'Who's there?' Barnardo, the relieving sentry, mistakenly challenges Francisco, when military discipline requires Francisco to challenge the newcomer. When the Ghost appears, it may be a visitor from the supernatural world, but its meaning is political: it 'bodes some strange eruption to our state' (Act 1 Scene 1, line 69).

There are echoes of an older, feudal world of the dead fathers (old Hamlet and old Fortinbras) who settled disputes by personal combat guided by a chivalric code ('law and heraldy'). But that older society of honour is giving way to the new world of Claudius. He is a smooth negotiator, an efficient unscrupulous schemer who prepares for war but settles territorial quarrels by dispatch of ambassadors and formal treaties. He is truly a 'politician' of the type Hamlet reviles in the graveyard: 'one that would circumvent [outwit] God' (Act 5 Scene 1, line 67).

The people of Denmark barely appear in the play, but Claudius increasingly sees them as a threat to his rule. They are 'the distracted multitude', 'the rabble', 'false Danish dogs' who favour Hamlet, or who call for Laertes to be king. All such unreliable people must be closely watched, even more so those like Hamlet, who are a direct threat to Claudius's rule. It would be dangerous to allow Hamlet to return to Wittenberg, so Claudius refuses permission. He keeps Hamlet under surveillance at home, with the devious words: 'Here in the cheer and comfort of our eye' (Act 1 Scene 2, line 116). That comforting eye will shortly employ two of Hamlet's close friends to spy on him. When Hamlet tells Rosencrantz and Guildenstern 'Denmark's a prison' (Act 2 Scene 2, line 234), he is not simply speaking metaphorically.

The chief minister of state, Polonius, is a willing instrument of Claudius's desire to keep his subjects under surveillance. In the England of Queen Elizabeth I, Polonius's equivalent was Lord Burghley, who also believed in close surveillance to maintain order.

Just as Burghley maintained an extensive network of spies, so Polonius is infected by the desire to overhear in secret, to keep all potential dissidents under surveillance. He spies on Hamlet, using his own daughter as bait. Even his own family must be watched. Though Polonius utters conventional decencies to Laertes ('these few precepts'), he sets a spy on his own son. It is hardly surprising that rumours circulate in Denmark. After the death of Polonius there is no shortage of 'buzzers' (rumour-mongers) to infect Laertes's ears.

For all the ordered formalities of Claudius's court and the seemingly close domesticity of Polonius's family, a sense of corruption grows throughout the play. 'Something is rotten in the state of Denmark' says Marcellus (Act 1 Scene 4, line 90), and the stench of decay at the heart of personal and social life increasingly infects the language. The madness that Hamlet assumes and into which Ophelia descends is the individual symptom of a deeper social malaise. Hamlet projects his disgust onto a variety of targets: Claudius, his mother's or Ophelia's sexuality, death itself. But his words mirror the deeper social corruption that pervades Denmark: 'foul deeds', 'maggots', 'carrion', 'offal', 'rank corruption, mining all within', 'the ulcerous place', 'an unweeded garden'. However civilised outward appearances are, the routine oppressions of a police state prevent truly human growth.

The two women in the play are little more than pawns in a patriarchal world of sexual exploitation. Gertrude has been 'taken to wife' by Claudius. Just as he has seized Denmark, so too he appropriates her body. She has no real power, but is a possession to be fought over by king and prince, husband and son. Ophelia is even more of an object manipulated by men. Her brother lectures her, seeking to control her sexuality. Her father uses her as bait in a spy trap, like a farmyard animal: 'I'll loose my daughter to him' (Act 2 Scene 2, line 160). Hamlet takes out on her all his misogyny (hatred of women). The masculine brutalities of Denmark quite literally drive her mad.

Hamlet, with his reflective self-questioning, is as much a modern man as a Renaissance prince. His preoccupation with notions of sin and salvation (see pp. 249–51) shows he is the product of a feudal world where religion is used as an instrument of control. But his style of thought marks him out as a true individual. He is trapped in this changing world and subject to its contradictions. Hamlet can both reflect 'What a piece of work is a man!' (Act 2 Scene 2, line 286) and casually dismiss Rosencrantz and Guildenstern to their deaths.

His personal vendetta against Claudius is in reality a struggle for political power, just as Claudius's murder of old Hamlet was a political assassination. Such political struggles mirrored the anxieties of Shakespeare's England. Elizabeth's reign might have seemed on the surface to be stable and secure, but it was always subject to dangerous threats of overthrow by a powerful faction of the nobility. At the end of the play, Fortinbras and his army take over. This is not the harmonious end of a domestic tragedy, with order restored by a benevolent ruler. Rather, it is the brutal *Realpolitik* of a society that, at base, rests on the dominance of a state by a small but militarily powerful minority. The voice of the people will be as stifled under Fortinbras as it was under Claudius.

The *quietus* (peace) that Hamlet finally achieves in death might represent private fulfilment, but it is politically empty and futile. Such a way of coming to terms with death is an ideological mystification that masks the harsh realities of political and social life in Hamlet's Denmark.

◆ Use the information given above as the basis of an extended essay on 'How might a production of *Hamlet* explore the political and social implications of the play?'

Revenge – and Revenge Tragedy – 'Oh, vengeance!'

Today, many people consider revenge immoral because it takes the law into its own hands. It is seen as a profoundly unsocial act. But it seems to be a very human impulse: to exact retribution from someone who has done wrong to you or your family. Revenge follows the Old Testament maxim 'an eye for an eye, a tooth for a tooth'. Revenge is still central to some criminal codes of honour (e.g. the vendetta among the Sicilian mafia).

In Shakespeare's time, revenge was a crime in law, and was also an irreligious act. For the Church of the late sixteenth century, revenge was considered a sin. The revenger's soul was damned, condemned to suffer everlasting torment in hell. That thought preoccupies Hamlet for much of the play.

Francis Bacon, a contemporary of Shakespeare, called revenge 'a kind of wild justice'. He wrote in 1625 in an essay on revenge:

> The most tolerable sort of revenge is for those wrongs which there is no law to remedy, but then let a man take heed the revenge be such as there is no law to punish; else a man's enemy is still beforehand, and it is two for one. Some, when they take revenge, are desirous the party should know whence it cometh. This is the more generous. For the delight seemeth to be not so much in doing the hurt as in making the party repent . . . This is certain, that a man that studieth revenge keeps his own wounds green, which otherwise would heal and do well. Public revenges are for the most part fortunate, as that for the death of Caesar. But in private revenges it is not so. Nay rather, vindictive persons live the life of witches, who, as they are mischievous, so end they infortunate.

Either write a reply to Bacon. Begin 'In Hamlet's case . . .', and argue the points Bacon makes in his essay. Alternatively, write a reply that argues with Bacon's position from your own point of view.

Or write a brief outline of a modern revenge story or play. Then write the opening chapter of the story, or the first scene of the play.

Or write a paragraph responding to each of the following statements:

- Revenge is always wrong.
- *Hamlet* is not so much a revenge play as a play about revenge.
- The play suggests that revenge does not pay.
- *Hamlet* is more a tragedy than a revenge play: its focus is on the fall of a hero rather than on the execution of a pledge to revenge.

- The revenge plot of *Hamlet* is one of the least important elements in the play.

Revenge Tragedy was hugely popular when Shakespeare began his play-writing career. The central feature of each revenge play was a hero (or villain) who sought to avenge a wrong. Elizabethan playwrights served up a rich diet of madness, melancholy and revenge. In the ten years before *Hamlet* was performed, enthusiastic crowds flocked to see Thomas Kyd's *The Spanish Tragedy*, Marlowe's *Jew of Malta*, and Shakespeare's *Titus Andronicus*.

Shakespeare also knew a twelfth-century revenge story about Amleth, prince of Denmark. In the tale a brother murders the king and marries his wife. The son, Amleth, pretends to be mad to pursue revenge. He slays one of his uncle's spies, forges a letter to have the king's two accomplices executed in England, and finally kills his uncle and becomes king.

Elizabethan Revenge Tragedy contained typical ingredients: a melancholy hero/avenger; a hesitating avenger (without hesitation the play would be over too quickly); a villain who was to be killed in revenge; complex plotting; murders (usually from sexual motives) and other physical horrors; a play-within-a-play; sexual obsession and lust related to the passion for revenge; a ghost who calls for revenge; real or feigned madness; the death of the revenger. The plays were usually set in Italy or Spain, but the Elizabethans seemed able to relate the wider themes of each play to their own world.

The typical structure of a Revenge Tragedy had five parts:

- *exposition* usually by a ghost (providing motivation for revenge)
- *anticipation* in which detailed planning of the revenge takes place
- *confrontation* between avenger and intended victim
- *delay* as the revenger hesitates to perform the killing
- *completion* of the revenge (often with the death of the revenger).

Hamlet has four revenge plots. Hamlet vows to revenge his father's death at the hands of Claudius. Laertes swears to avenge *his* father's death at the hands of Hamlet. Fortinbras seeks to avenge *his* father's death at the hands of King Hamlet. Another son seeking revenge is Pyrrhus: he slaughters Priam, whose son had killed Pyrrhus's father.

Hamlet has many elements of Elizabethan Revenge Tragedy. Merely telling the story makes it sound very sensational: eight deaths, a mad woman, a fight in a grave, and so on. But *Hamlet* has outlived most other revenge plays and is still immensely popular. Why?

◆ Use the information given above to identify in what ways *Hamlet* can be regarded as an Elizabethan Revenge Tragedy. Then suggest reasons why *Hamlet* continues to hold great appeal after four hundred years.

Madness and melancholia – 'This is mere madness'

Today, doctors and psychiatrists rarely use the words 'mad' or 'lunacy'. Instead, they use such expressions as 'manic-depression' (violent mood swings), 'schizophrenia' (deranged perceptions and emotions), 'suffering from a nervous breakdown', 'psychotic' (suffering from delusions, dangerously out of contact with reality), 'emotionally disturbed' and 'mentally ill'. Shakespeare's Elizabethan and Jacobean audiences had few qualms about using the term 'mad'. Often, when people were considered mad they were thought to be possessed by devils, and were confined to asylums. Visiting such places to watch the behaviour of 'mad' men and women was considered a source of amusement.

Madness was one of the conventions of Revenge Tragedy (see pp. 246–7). Following that convention, Hamlet proposes to 'put an antic disposition on' (Act 1 Scene 5, line 172). From then on, the question of whether he is merely feigning madness, or has indeed descended into real mental derangement, has divided critics and audiences alike. Every new production of the play raises the issue afresh.

Some of his behaviour, particularly his virulent verbal assault on Ophelia in Act 3 Scene 1 ('To a nunnery, go'), is extreme. Her lament 'Oh what a noble mind is here o'erthrown!' seems a well-judged comment on what she has experienced, and she thinks him 'Blasted with ecstasy.' But her earlier description of his behaviour 'Pale as his shirt, his knees knocking each other' (Act 2 Scene 1, line 79) may make him sound rather like a man putting on an act. Yet Hamlet himself, as he prepares for the duel with Laertes, offers an apology – apparently sincere – that claims he was indeed mad: 'His madness is poor Hamlet's enemy' (Act 5 Scene 2, line 211).

The one person in the play who is without doubt driven to mental breakdown is Ophelia. Her two 'mad scenes' (in Act 4 Scene 5) are both poignant and bizarre, 'A document in madness'. The terrible blow of her father's death has tipped her over the edge, and her songs display a curious mixture of innocence and sexuality, sense and nonsense. Her evident dementia stands in contrast to the constant puzzle that attends all instances of Hamlet's 'madness': is he just 'putting it on'?

- Step into role in turn as Claudius, Gertrude, Polonius, Ophelia, Horatio, Rosencrantz and Guildenstern. Give each character's response, with reasons, to the question 'Is Hamlet mad?' Then speak Hamlet's own answer to that question.
- An Elizabethan medical text described the symptoms of melancholy: 'sad and fearful . . . distrust, doubt, diffidence or despair, sometimes furious, and sometimes merry . . . sardonian [sardonic], and false laughter . . . every serious thing for a time, is turned into a jest, and tragedies into comedies' (Timothy Bright, *Treatise on Melancholy*, 1586). How accurately does each of these words or phrases describe Hamlet?

Albrecht Dürer's engraving of *Melancholia* (1514). Dürer's engraving has often been used in programmes for stage productions of *Hamlet*. Give some reasons why you think it is frequently chosen as a powerful picture to illustrate the play.

Sin and salvation – 'What form of prayer / Can serve my turn?'

In Shakespeare's day the threat of hell and eternal damnation was much more sharply felt than it is today. Most Elizabethans cared passionately about religious belief and the state of their souls. They were obsessed by what would happen to them after death. They believed that one of three possibilities awaited them. If they died in a state of grace, with all their sins confessed, they would go to heaven and enjoy eternal peace. If none of their sins was confessed and forgiven, they would go to hell and endure eternal suffering. The third possibility was purgatory, where those who had not made full confession would go. There they suffered until their unconfessed sins were burnt away (purged). Suicides were bound for hell in whatever state they died.

Hamlet explores this obsession with the afterlife. In his first soliloquy Hamlet longs for the peace of death ('O that this too too solid flesh would melt'), but recognises that suicide is forbidden by God ('Or that the Everlasting had not fixed / His canon 'gainst self-slaughter'). In his 'To be, or not to be' soliloquy, he broods on the uncertainty of knowing what will happen after death. It is 'the dread of something after death' that makes us endure the oppressions of life (Act 3 Scene 1, lines 56–82).

Later in the play, the consequences of religious attitudes to suicide are sharply brought home as the gravediggers' talk reveals that suicides are normally denied the right to 'Christian burial' in a churchyard. Ophelia should be denied the full rites of such burial because it is thought she has taken her own life ('Her death was doubtful'). The Priest at her funeral says that only Claudius's command prevented what she should properly receive as a suicide: not 'charitable prayers', but 'Shards, flints, and pebbles should be thrown on her'. Such was the pronouncement of the Church on suicides.

The Ghost tells how he suffers in purgatory: 'confined to fast in fires, / Till the foul crimes done in my days of nature / Are burnt and purged away' (Act 1 Scene 5, lines 11–13). Because he died without having a chance to confess his sins, he must undergo torment before he can earn a place in heaven, reconciled to God. But Hamlet cannot be sure whether the Ghost is good or bad: 'Be thou a spirit of health, or goblin damned' (Act 1 Scene 4, line 40).

The question of whether the Ghost is to be trusted or not haunts Hamlet for much of the play. It reflects the Elizabethan view that some ghosts were benign, others evil, tempting humans to behave badly and so damn themselves to an afterlife of torment in hell. Hamlet fears what he has seen may be a devil who 'Abuses me to damn me'.

To test whether it is a 'damned ghost' sent to lure his own soul to eternal damnation, Hamlet contrives the play in which he hopes to 'catch the conscience of the king'. When Claudius reveals his guilt by his reaction to the Mousetrap play, Hamlet is convinced the Ghost has spoken true: 'I'll take the ghost's word for a thousand / pound' (Act 3 Scene 2, lines 260–1). And in the play's final scene Hamlet declares his conviction that heaven guides him (Act 5 Scene 2, lines 10–11).

Hamlet's delay in avenging his father's murder can be partly explained by his beliefs about sin and salvation. Shortly after the play scene, Hamlet finds Claudius at prayer, hoping God will pardon him. The fact that Claudius is praying stops Hamlet from instantly killing him. Hamlet's own father suffers after death because Claudius killed him at a moment when he was unprepared for heaven, not having confessed his sins. Now Hamlet wishes Claudius to experience the same horrible suffering after death. He therefore sheathes his sword and decides to wait, to catch Claudius at a moment 'That has no relish of salvation in't'. That moment will be when Claudius is committing a sin: 'drunk asleep, or in his rage, / Or in th'incestuous pleasure of his bed, / At game a-swearing' (Act 3 Scene 3, lines 89–91). Killing him at such a moment, when he has no thoughts of heaven in his mind, will surely send Claudius to hell, to eternal damnation. Ironically, as Claudius reveals, the king has not been successfully praying at all: 'My words fly up, my thoughts remain below. / Words without thoughts never to heaven go' (Act 3 Scene 3, lines 97–8).

Dr Johnson, an eighteenth-century essayist, poet and Shakespeare critic, believed Hamlet's thoughts when he found Claudius at prayer 'too terrible to be read or uttered'. Johnson's view influenced productions for over a hundred years. Hamlet's speech (Act 3 Scene 3, lines 73–96) was either cut in performance or interpreted as not expressing Hamlet's real intentions, but simply an excuse to procrastinate, to delay the action.

◆ Talk together about what you think of Dr Johnson's view in the preceding paragraph.
◆ Consider in turn each of the following: Polonius, Rosencrantz and Guildenstern, Ophelia, Laertes, Gertrude, Claudius. Imagine you are Hamlet and write a paragraph about each of the characters. Say whether you feel responsible for their death, whether each one deserved their death, and what you think will happen to each character after death.

Acting and theatre – 'The play's the thing . . .'

Hamlet richly displays both Shakespeare's interest in his own profession as actor and playwright, and the London theatres at the end of the reign of Queen Elizabeth I. *Hamlet* is an intensely theatrical play, with many references to playing and acting. Play-acting is concerned with a puzzle that obsesses Hamlet: the difference between appearance and reality, truth and falsehood (another way of thinking of this theme could be as 'appearance versus reality'). Hamlet uses a company of travelling players to perform a stage murder. The performance traps Claudius into revealing his guilty conscience: a fiction has discovered the truth of the Ghost's story (which is, of course, itself a fiction).

The play resonates with the language of theatre: 'play', 'act', 'show', 'perform', 'applaud', 'prologue', 'shape' (costume), and 'part' (see p. 265). Hamlet's soliloquies are like those of an actor reflecting on the part he has to play. He sees the players as 'the abstract and brief chronicles of the time', and the purpose of acting as holding 'the mirror up / to nature'. For Hamlet, the function of drama is to portray the nature of society: 'to show virtue her own feature, scorn her own image, / and the very age and body of the time his form and pressure'.

On Hamlet's first appearance he denies he is playing a part: 'I know not seems.' His grief is real. But he puts on 'an antic disposition', and throughout the play muses (or rages) about deceptive appearance: 'Smiling, damned villain!' Other characters dissemble, most obviously Claudius. Rosencrantz and Guildenstern put on an act of friendship, and even Ophelia is instructed to 'show' to enable her father and Claudius to eavesdrop on Hamlet.

The play is filled with highly dramatic scenes: the Ghost's five appearances; Hamlet's raging at Ophelia and Gertrude; the dumb-show; the fight in the grave. The final scene has abundant theatrical opportunities and references: the duel between Hamlet and Laertes; the many deaths, witnessed by 'mutes or audience to this act'; the entry of Fortinbras (preceded by '*March afar off, and shot within*'); Horatio's 'give order that these bodies / High on a stage be placèd to the view'; Fortinbras's order that 'four captains / Bear Hamlet like a soldier to the stage'; and the final stage direction: '*Exeunt marching, after the which a peal of ordnance are shot off* '.

◆ Collect quotations from the play about actors, acting or the theatre. Use them to write an essay (or dialogue in question-and-answer form) on '*Hamlet* is a tragedy dominated by the idea of the play'.

The 'tragedians of the city' Shakespeare's own company of players was sometimes forced to tour when plague closed the London theatres. The players' appearance at Elsinore echoes the experience of troupes of London actors as they toured the English provinces or Europe. On tour they performed in the great halls of country houses or on makeshift stages in inn-yards or town squares.

Around the time Shakespeare wrote *Hamlet*, an acting company of boy players was enjoying great success in London. For a short time these 'little eyases' (unfledged hawks) threatened the livelihood of some adult professional acting companies. The adult players were forced to tour because they could not attract London audiences. Hamlet's exchanges with Rosencrantz and Guildenstern in Act 2 Scene 2, lines 295–333, are thought to be about these boy players and the 'war of the theatres' (see p. 84). For a short time, there was intense rivalry between adult companies as their resident playwrights mocked each other in their plays ('much throwing about of brains').

The members of Shakespeare's acting company (The King's Men, originally The Lord Chamberlain's Men) worked together closely for over twenty years. They knew each other very well and may have contributed to Shakespeare's script. Because of his fascination with acting, Shakespeare may have put into *Hamlet* private jokes and theatrical references that would have amused his fellow players at the Globe on London's Bankside:

1.5.151 'you hear this fellow in the cellarage' (The space under the Globe stage?)

1.5.97 'this distracted globe' (The Globe Theatre? Hamlet's head? The world?)

3.2.91 'I did enact Julius Caesar' (The actor who played Polonius may well have created the title role in *Julius Caesar*, written by Shakespeare shortly before *Hamlet*.)

2.2.284–5 'this majestical roof fretted with golden / fire' (The sky, or the painted 'heavens' of the Globe's stage?)

2.2.386–90 'thy face is valanced [bearded] / since I saw thee last'; 'Pray / God your voice . . . be not cracked' (Was Shakespeare joking at his fellow actor's changed appearance, and the thought that the boy actors who played the female parts would all too soon grow up?)

See pages 272–3 for information on *Hamlet* at the rebuilt Globe on London's Bankside.

Characters

Hamlet

'. . . you would pluck out the heart of my mystery'. Hamlet's words to Guildenstern describe what thousands of books and articles have tried to do since *Hamlet* was first performed. But his character remains elusive. Hamlet plays many roles throughout the play: alienated outsider, potential suicide, actor, swordsman, joker, friend of Horatio, angry son, blood-thirsty revenger, lacerating self-critic. His mood swings from depression to elation, from extreme self-loathing to quiet acceptance of his fate in 'the readiness is all'.

Hamlet has been seen as an ironic commentator on mortality and sin, a man with acute sexual problems, a genuine madman, a clever impersonator of madness, a man tortured by irreconcilable moral dilemmas, an unhappy adolescent, a puritanical fundamentalist, a dreamer, a philosopher, a truly noble prince.

The script shows that Hamlet is a great listener. He listens intently to what is said to him and often seizes on a word or phrase to construct his own reply. His very first words: 'A little more than kin, and less than kind' (Act 1 Scene 2, line 65), imply that Claudius is too presumptuous in calling him 'son' (kin), and that his nature (kind) is unlike Claudius's. His next line 'I am too much i'th'sun' puns on Claudius's 'son'. His following two replies to Gertrude pun ironically on her use of 'common' and 'seems'.

Hamlet revels in how the slipperiness of language gives potential for bitter or comic puns or ironic retorts. He uses puns to great effect, picking up a speaker's words and giving them back with a different meaning. The Gravedigger is the only other character in the play to use this style of deliberate misunderstanding. He gives Hamlet a taste of his own medicine.

♦ Identify examples of this linguistic technique of Hamlet's. Against which characters does he use it most frequently?
♦ Hamlet not only listens carefully to others. He listens intently to himself and comments on his own thoughts. Identify passages in his soliloquies in which he comments on his own thoughts and feelings (e.g. with self-disgust or reproof).
♦ Use your findings in the two activities above to compile an assignment on what aspects of Hamlet's character are revealed by how he listens to others and to himself.

In Act 4 Scene 3, Claudius orders that Hamlet be exiled to England (where he intends Hamlet to be executed). Hamlet taunts Claudius by bidding him 'Farewell / dear mother', provoking Claudius to reply 'Thy loving father, Hamlet.' That response gives Hamlet opportunities to enrage Claudius further and to express his own loathing of his mother's sexual relationship with his uncle: 'My mother. Father and mother is man and wife, man and wife / is one flesh, and so, my mother.'

Hamlet's sexual identity

What is Hamlet's attitude towards the two women in the play? Some productions have suggested that Hamlet is sexually obsessed by his mother. Other productions imply that he truly loved Ophelia. Almost every possibility about Hamlet's sexuality has been explored on stage, on film and in print, as the following views suggest:

- **An Oedipus complex?**   Hamlet is in love with his mother, and is violently jealous of Claudius, his stepfather. This Oedipus complex makes him unable to have a loving relationship with Ophelia, whom he treats badly. His hatred for Claudius is based on sexual jealousy, since Claudius has usurped not only his father's crown, but also his mother's bed.

- **A puritan?**   Hamlet is severely puritanical about love and love-making. He is appalled by what he sees as the lust that drives the relationship between Claudius and Gertrude. His disgust at his mother's sexuality makes him despise all women. Ophelia is a victim of this loathing as Hamlet subjects her to virulent verbal abuse, full of sexual innuendo.

- **A true lover?**   Hamlet genuinely loves Ophelia. He urges her to go to a nunnery to escape the torturous, prison-like nature of love in the world that Denmark represents. His harsh words cover his deep love for her, and he is being 'cruel only to be kind'.

- **An immature boy?**   Hamlet is unready for love. His sexual bantering with Polonius, Rosencrantz and Guildenstern is immature male behaviour. He is unable to understand his mother's sexual life or to appreciate Ophelia's innocent and more mature affection for him.

- **A split personality?**   Hamlet both loves and hates Ophelia, and simultaneously admires and abhors his mother. His sexual feelings for Ophelia and his mother fight against his other feelings. His reason attempts to reconcile these sexual and emotional tensions, but thought itself makes him unable to act.

- **Private love versus public office?**   Hamlet's sexual confusion arises not from his personality but from his position as prince of Denmark. He may not choose for himself in marriage but must think first of his responsibility to the country.

- ◆ Find two or more quotations from the script to support each of the above viewpoints. Arrange the six interpretations in order of reasonableness to you, using the evidence in the play.

'I loved Ophelia'. In this Royal Shakespeare Company production, Hamlet displayed his genuine love for Ophelia by leaping into the grave for a final embrace.

Hamlet: a tragic hero?

'Tragedy' is the conventional description of a play that portrays human suffering and the decline and death of a hero or heroine. Traditionally the hero (or heroine) was of high status, and the fall from grace immense. But some modern tragedies, like Arthur Miller's *Death of a Salesman*, have an ordinary person as their tragic hero. To help your thinking about Hamlet's character, consider the following interpretations of Hamlet as a tragic hero.

- **Tragic flaw?**   The hero's downfall is caused by a tragic flaw or blemish in character. Hamlet's weakness may be that he 'thinks too much' and cannot make up his mind. The resulting inaction leads to his death. But Hamlet's tragic flaw ('vicious mole of nature', Act 1 Scene 4, line 24) may be some other feature in his character responsible for his downfall.
- **A tragedy of fate?**   The hero has no real control over his destiny. Once the spring of Hamlet's tragic narrative is released, it unwinds inevitably towards its conclusion: the death of Hamlet. His fate is predetermined. As Hamlet says, 'There's a divinity that shapes our ends . . .'.
- **A tragedy of chance?**   Accident and bad luck determine the fate of the hero. The unplanned chance encounter with the pirate ship, for example, brings Hamlet back to Denmark. Hamlet accidentally kills Polonius. The tragic hero is the victim of random uncertainty.
- **Irreconcilable opposites?**   The hero's character comprises irreconcilable sets of forces. Hamlet's mind and feelings are filled with such tensions: reason battles with passion, love is contrasted with lust, action is inhibited by thought. Hamlet struggles with a wish to die and an urge to live. *Hamlet* can be read as the tragedy of a man trapped between such contraries.
- **Hero as paragon?**   The tragic hero has an excess of virtues. This nineteenth-century Romantic view of Hamlet as a Renaissance prince suggests that he is more noble and refined than ordinary people, and that his nobility and purity carry the seeds of their own destruction. Hamlet cannot live in the world because he is too 'good' for it. His sensitivity and noble qualities lead to his downfall.

- ◆ Find evidence (quotations or actions in the play) to support each of the above viewpoints. Decide which interpretation you favour most. Then write your own view of Hamlet as a tragic hero.

'Now could I drink hot blood'. This picture shows Hamlet dressed as the typical tragic hero of Elizabethan Revenge Tragedy (see pp. 246–7). Compare it with other depictions of Hamlet in this edition, and write a paragraph on each saying how closely (and why) it matches your own imagined picture of Hamlet.

Claudius

Claudius has committed an evil deed to become king, murdering his own brother. He plans similar evil as the play unfolds, plotting to have Hamlet killed in England. When that fails, he seduces Laertes into a scheme to kill Hamlet in a deceitful duel. He lies about his 'love' for Hamlet and tells Gertrude that he tried to calm Laertes, when in fact he deliberately fuelled Laertes's rage. Hamlet condemns Claudius as a drunkard and sees him as the source of corruption in Denmark: 'this canker of our nature'.

Claudius's hypocrisy is evident throughout the play (see p. 14 on the devious eloquence of his first speech). But he seems a competent king, intelligent and quick-witted. There is no hint that the nobles of Denmark challenge his right to the throne. He appears to love Gertrude and to respect Polonius, willing to accept his advice. He knows that he does wrong, and is racked by conscience, struggling unsuccessfully to pray to find some way of absolving his murderous guilt: 'Oh my offence is rank, it smells to heaven'. He bravely stands up to Laertes's threats, but his noble words 'There's such divinity doth hedge a king' are hypocritical, because he himself has killed a king, his own brother.

What emotions are displayed by Gertrude, Hamlet and Claudius here?

What mother–son relationship is suggested here?

Gertrude

A puzzle that all productions of the play face is 'Does Gertrude know that Claudius is a murderer?' She seems in thrall to Claudius for the first half of the play, and is genuinely distressed by her son's bizarre behaviour. But Shakespeare gives Gertrude lines in and after her encounter with Hamlet in her chamber that suggest she progressively distances herself from her second husband.

Critics have often judged Gertrude as a weak, selfish and innocent woman, caught up in conflicts she does not fully understand. Her hasty marriage to Claudius so soon after her first husband's death disgusts Hamlet, and seems to indicate her pliability. That capacity to be easily persuaded is evident when she allows Polonius to use her private chamber to spy on Hamlet.

Gertrude feels compassion for both Polonius and Ophelia, and she may well love Claudius, at least for the first half of the play. She tries to protect him from Laertes's aggression. But what are Gertrude's feelings towards Hamlet? Ever since Laurence Olivier's film portrayed Hamlet's incestuous desire for his mother, productions have to decide just how to present her affection for Hamlet.

Polonius

Polonius is the king's counsellor, Claudius's chief minister of state. He is evidently filled with a sense of his own self-importance, and is proud of the service he has given to the king. Claudius acknowledges him as 'a man faithful and honourable'.

Polonius seeks to control public life. He also wishes to control his family. He hands out good advice to his son Laertes ('these few precepts in thy memory'), but then sends Reynaldo to spy on him in France. He orders Ophelia to avoid Hamlet and to return his love tokens. He even uses her as an accomplice to eavesdrop on Hamlet, an action which results in his daughter being savagely insulted by Hamlet. Polonius offers no word of comfort to the distraught Ophelia.

Polonius's concern for surveillance results in his death. He conceals himself behind the arras in Gertrude's chamber, only to be killed by Hamlet, who mistakes the hidden figure for the king.

In spite of his pomposity and authoritarianism, Polonius is loved by his children. Shakespeare enables the actor to play Polonius not simply as a spymaster and overstrict father, but also as a character who can gain audience sympathy as a well-meaning father and loyal counsellor.

Ophelia

Many critics have judged Ophelia as a beautiful, innocent but essentially passive character. But increasingly actors have sought to bring out her strength and knowledge of the world. She was often played as obedient to her father, and touchingly poignant in her madness. Modern productions tend to emphasise how she rebukes Laertes after his long catalogue of advice, and show her unwillingly or resentfully following her father's instructions.

Ophelia feels deeply for Hamlet, and his apparent rejection affects her grievously, 'Oh woe is me / T''have seen what I have seen, see what I see.' When he jokes with her at the play scene, she seems fully aware of his sexual meanings. The songs she sings in her madness reveal not simply the depth of her love for her father, but also an uninhibited sexual awareness that her mental derangement has allowed to surface.

There are parallels between Ophelia and Hamlet. Both have fathers who have been violently killed. Both feel let down by a person they deeply love. Both suffer the distress of madness, real and assumed.

'I / would give you some violets, but they withered all when my father / died.'
Ophelia, in her distraction, offers flowers to Claudius, Gertrude and Laertes.
Violets were associated with sweetness, and Ophelia's words suggest that
Polonius's death has taken all joy from her life.

The language of *Hamlet*

Imagery – 'the morn in russet mantle clad'

Hamlet abounds in imagery: vivid words and phrases that conjure up emotionally charged pictures or associations in the mind. When Hamlet thinks of how the First Player would perform if he had suffered such grief as Hamlet, he declares 'He would drown the stage with tears'. The image passionately conveys the depth of Hamlet's feelings. Similarly, Polonius abruptly dismisses Hamlet's 'holy vows' of his love to Ophelia as 'springes to catch woodcocks': merely traps to snare innocent and foolish birds.

Imagery carries powerful significance, far deeper than its surface meanings. Images enrich particular moments, as when Claudius agonises that his hand is stained with his brother's blood: 'Is there not rain enough in the sweet heavens / To wash it white as snow?' Imagery repeatedly illuminates the themes of the play such as revenge or madness (as when Gertrude describes Hamlet as 'Mad as the sea and wind, when both contend / Which is the mightier.').

Imagery gives pleasure as it stirs the audience's imagination and deepens the impact of particular moments or moods. It provides insight into character, and intensifies meaning and emotional force. In *Hamlet* the imagery is sometimes so brilliantly complex that, although it can be analysed and understood, it defies any final 'explanation', as in Hamlet's words:

Whether 'tis nobler in the mind to suffer
The slings and arrows of outrageous fortune,
Or to take arms against a sea of troubles,
And by opposing end them.   *Act 3 Scene 1, lines 57–60*

All Shakespeare's imagery uses metaphor, simile or personification. All are comparisons which in effect substitute one thing (the image) for another (the thing described).

A **simile** compares one thing to another using 'like' or 'as'. Ophelia describes Hamlet's derangement as 'Like sweet bells jangled, out of tune and harsh'. The Ghost tells how the poison spread through his body 'swift as quicksilver'.

A **metaphor** is also a comparison, suggesting that two dissimilar things are actually the same or have something in common. The distraught Hamlet speaks of his head (or the world, see p. 253) as 'this distracted globe'. He describes one play as 'caviary to the general' (caviare to ordinary people, too good for them). To put it another way, a metaphor borrows one word or phrase to express another.

Personification turns all kinds of things into persons, giving them human feelings or attributes. In the quotation on page 264 'fortune' is personified. The dying Hamlet memorably personifies death itself as a cruel officer of the law: 'this fell sergeant death / Is strict in his arrest'.

Certain image clusters recur through the play, notably those of corruption and disease, the theatre and acting.

Corruption and disease In the play's opening moments Francisco's 'I am sick at heart' is the first indication of the many images of infection that pervade *Hamlet*. Marcellus declares that 'Something is rotten in the state of Denmark.' Hamlet is haunted by the corruption of his mother's incest, seeing it as an infectious disease: 'the ulcerous place / Whiles rank corruption, mining all within, / Infects unseen.' Claudius thinks of Hamlet as a fever: 'like the hectic in my blood he rages'. Hamlet describes Claudius as 'a mildewed ear' and as 'this canker of our nature'. Watching Fortinbras's army marching towards death, Hamlet reflects that 'This is th'impostume [abscess] . . . That inward breaks, and shows no cause without / Why the man dies' (Act 4 Scene 4, lines 27–9).

Theatre and acting Page 252 gives examples of how the language of theatre and acting recurs in the play: 'play', 'act', 'cue', 'prompted', 'mutes' and so on. Shakespeare's fascination with his own profes sional world is evident in *Hamlet*: the players, the play-within-the-play which reveals Claudius's guilt, the talk of the 'little eyases' (boy actors). In Hamlet's first appearance he uses 'actions', 'play' and 'show' as he angrily denies that his grief is reflected only in his outward appearance (Act 1 Scene 2, lines 84–5):

> For they are actions that a man might play,
> But I have that within which passes show –

The notion of acting as a pretence which somehow convinces finds expression in Hamlet's amazement that an actor can weep for a fictional character: 'And all for nothing? / For Hecuba!'

◆ Identify a dozen images which especially appeal to you. Write an analysis of how they operate in *Hamlet*, both for immediate effect and on the play as a whole, reinforcing and complicating its themes.

Antithesis

Antithesis is the opposition of words or phrases against each other, as in 'To be, or not to be', and 'I must be cruel only to be kind'. This setting of the word against the word ('To be' versus 'not to be', 'cruel' versus 'kind') is one of Shakespeare's favourite language devices. He uses it extensively in all his plays. Why? Because antithesis powerfully expresses conflict through its use of opposites, and conflict is the essence of all drama. In *Hamlet*, conflict occurs in many forms. Claudius versus Hamlet, revenge versus justice, son versus mother and so on. Antithesis intensifies that sense of conflict.

Claudius's many antitheses in his first speech (Act 1 Scene 2) suggest a man attempting to balance conflicting emotions and values as he tells of his marriage to Gertrude; for example, lines 11–13:

> With one auspicious and one dropping eye,
> With mirth in funeral and with dirge in marriage,
> In equal scale weighing delight and dole . . .

For an Elizabethan audience the antithesis 'With one auspicious and one dropping eye' implied deviousness, because a contemporary proverb held that a false man looked up with one eye and down with the other. The other antitheses imply a similar two-facedness: someone who can simultaneously express joy and sorrow, or show an inappropriate emotion at a funeral or a marriage. In Act 3 Scene 1, lines 51–3, Claudius uses an image full of antitheses to acknowledge that a prostitute's use of make-up is similar to how he hypocritically conceals his evil deed behind a mask:

> The harlot's cheek, beautied with plastering art,
> Is not more ugly to the thing that helps it
> Than is my deed to my most painted word.

Laertes's passionate desire for revenge on Hamlet ('To cut his throat i'th'church') is given additional emotional power by the opposition of the bloodiness of the action with the sanctity of the holy place. In the very last moments of the play (Act 5 Scene 2, lines 380–1), Fortinbras opposes the appropriateness of dead bodies on the battlefield ('field') with their inappropriateness in the court ('here'): 'Such a sight as this / Becomes the field, but here shows much amiss.'

◆ Collect twenty examples of antithesis. Use them in an essay showing how antithesis helps create a sense of conflict and paradox in *Hamlet*.

Verse and prose

Just under three quarters of the play is in verse, just over one quarter in prose. How did Shakespeare decide whether to write in verse or prose? A rough rule of thumb is that aristocrats speak verse, and low-status and comic or mad characters speak prose. But context is very important. Thus the players (low status) speak verse in the Gonzago play (to emphasise that they are playing aristocratic characters). Hamlet and Ophelia (high status) express madness in prose.

Verse was thought more suitable than prose to moments of high dramatic or emotional intensity. So 'serious' scenes are likely to be in verse, 'comic' episodes in prose. Hamlet uses prose with Rosencrantz and Guildenstern, the Gravedigger and Osric. Hamlet's 'What a piece of work is a man' (Act 2 Scene 2, lines 286–91) is also in prose, but has all the qualities claimed for poetry.

Hamlet is written mainly in blank verse: unrhymed verse written in iambic pentameter. This is a rhythm or metre in which each line has five stressed syllables (/) alternating with five unstressed syllables (×), often expressed as de-DUM de-DUM de-DUM de-DUM de-DUM, as in Act 3 Scene 2, line 196:

    ×   / ×   /   × / ×   / × /
    But die thy thoughts when thy first lord is dead

By the time he wrote *Hamlet*, Shakespeare had become very flexible in his use of iambic pentameter. He often uses **enjambement** (running on), where one line flows on into the next, seemingly with little or no pause. Lines may have more or fewer than ten syllables.

◆ Choose a verse speech and speak it to emphasise the metre (five beats). Then speak it as if it were prose, then as you feel it should be delivered on stage. Finally, write eight lines of your own in verse.

Questions

Hamlet is full of questions. Barnardo's opening challenge 'Who's there?' symbolises the questioning tone that characterises the whole play. Virtually every character wishes to find out something. On almost every page questions are asked. Hamlet is often self-questioning.

◆ Turn to any page. Identify the questions on that page, and check how many are answered. Repeat for several more pages. Decide which questions can be answered, and which cannot. Then make up a few questions of your own about the play. Try to answer them in a small group. Put any you cannot answer to the class.

Soliloquies

Hamlet is famous for his soliloquies. A soliloquy is a kind of internal debate spoken by a character who is alone on stage (or believes themselves to be alone). Soliloquies reveal the character's true thoughts and feelings. Hamlet's soliloquies give the impression of a man discovering what he thinks as he speaks.

◆ Hamlet's soliloquies are on pages 23, 49–50, 95, 105, 133, 139 and 169. Select one and work out a dramatic presentation. You could share the lines around your group, and have several persons echoing key lines or phrases. Try speaking it as a conversation, or to the audience, or to a portrait of another character, or to a stage property. Experiment with styles of delivery (e.g. as an observer disgusted with the human condition, a bloodthirsty revenger).

Doubling language: a cause of delay?

All kinds of 'doubling' go on in *Hamlet*: the two sentries at the play's beginning; Rosencrantz and Guildenstern; Cornelius and Voltemand; two English ambassadors; two kingly brothers, Claudius and old Hamlet. Hamlet and Laertes both are students, sons, revengers, opponents.

Such doubling is strikingly reflected in the play's language. It appears in repetition of words and phrases: 'Tush tush', 'Speak, speak', 'this too too solid flesh', 'To be, or not to be' and so on. Polonius seems to say everything twice: 'You have me, have you not?' Most commonly the doubling is by means of the conjunction 'and'. When Laertes requests Claudius for permission to return to France, he uses 'leave and favour', 'thoughts and wishes', 'leave and pardon'.

Hamlet contains around 250 examples of such 'doublings'. In Act 3 Scene 1, lines 144–55, Ophelia's lines lamenting Hamlet's treatment of her ('Oh what a noble mind is here o'erthrown!') includes doubling of single words (observed/observers, quite/quite, seen/seen, see/see), together with six examples of doubles using 'and':

expectancy and rose of the fair state

glass of fashion and the mould of form

deject and wretched

noble and most sovereign reason

out of time and harsh

form and feature

A special type of such doubling is known as **hendiadys** (pronounced hen-die-a-dees), a technical term meaning 'one through two'. Here, the two words express a single idea. They duplicate the sense rather than amplify or modify each other, as these few examples show:

food and diet	grace and mercy	spark and fire
cheer and comfort	lecture and advice	flash and outbreak
pith and marrow	duty and obedience	native and indued
book and volume	heat and flame	strange or odd

This tendency to use two words when one would be sufficient to convey meaning contributes to dramatic effect. It lengthens the play, adding to the sense of delay. In its suggestion of 'one through two' it echoes the play's concern with marriage and incest (the union of separate selves).

◆ Search through the play for examples of these 'doubling' devices. Talk together about their dramatic effect and how they provide insights into character and situation.

What did Shakespeare write?

Shakespeare probably wrote *Hamlet* around 1601. But there are problems in knowing exactly what he wrote (let alone what he intended). First, he was a playwright, and undoubtedly had second thoughts as he worked with his fellow actors rehearsing and performing the play. Second, there are three versions of the play, from which all editors make their choices as they prepare their own edition for publication.

The First Quarto (Q1: the 'bad quarto'), published in 1603 and thought to be a pirated (unauthorised) version, put together by some actors and sold for a quick profit. It has 2,154 lines.

The Second Quarto (Q2: the 'good quarto'), published in 1604 and thought to be Shakespeare's response to the 'bad quarto', in order to establish the 'correct' version. It has 3,674 lines.

The First Folio (F1), published in 1623. This is thought to be Shakespeare's version of the play to make it even more suitable for the stage. But remember that Shakespeare died in 1616, and the First Folio was compiled seven years later by two of his fellow actors (see p. 276). It has 3,535 lines (including 83 that do not appear in Q2).

Some lines of the script are in square brackets [ ]. These are the lines in Q2 that were cut out of F1. It is thought that Shakespeare cut these lines to make a more actable version of the play.

◆ Find several examples of lines in square brackets (e.g. pp. 39–41, 153 and 193). Discuss possible reasons why Shakespeare cut them. But remember – no one can be certain that Shakespeare himself in fact did so. Would you cut the lines in performance? Give reasons for your decision.

Hamlet in performance

Hamlet has always been a popular play. Since it was written around 1600–1, it has rarely been absent from the stage for long. There is even a record of a version acted on a ship off the coast of Sierra Leone in 1608. Quotations from it (such as 'To be, or not to be') have become utterly familiar, even to those who have never seen the play.

But in every age the text has been cut, altered and added to. For over four hundred years audiences have watched and heard very different versions of *Hamlet*. For example, throughout the eighteenth and nineteenth centuries Fortinbras disappeared from most stagings. That tradition still influences modern productions, and occasionally performances end with Hamlet's death: 'the rest is silence'.

The example of the famous eighteenth-century actor-manager David Garrick shows there is no such thing as the 'authentic' *Hamlet*. Garrick wanted to portray Hamlet as a truly noble prince, and to make the play into what he saw as a genuine tragedy. He therefore cut anything that detracted from a heroic image of Hamlet, and removed what he called 'the rubbish of the fifth act': Ophelia's funeral and the gravediggers.

Garrick's audiences did not hear how Hamlet sent Rosencrantz and Guildenstern to their deaths, or the 'Now might I do it pat' speech (in which Hamlet wishes for Claudius to suffer in hell), because Garrick thought both speeches diminished Hamlet's noble nature. Laertes did not poison his sword, or Claudius the drink. Gertrude died off stage in guilt-ridden insanity, Fortinbras did not appear, and Laertes survived to rule over Denmark jointly with Horatio.

Nineteenth-century productions usually presented romantic interpretations of Hamlet as a sane, intellectual, sensitive prince, unable to sweep swiftly to revenge. Sets often attempted to create the illusion of a historically accurate castle of Elsinore.

Modern productions have increasingly portrayed Hamlet as disturbed and alienated, and have abandoned realistic sets. They rely more on 'symbolic' settings or bare stages with a minimum of scenery. This can be seen as a return to the conditions of Shakespeare's own Globe stage, which was not dependent on theatrical illusion.

The first mention of Hamlet in the play is as 'young Hamlet' and, from what the Gravedigger says, he seems to be about 30. But for over four hundred years Hamlet has been played by actors of all ages. Richard Burbage, the first actor ever to play Hamlet (in 1601), was

34 when he created the role. Other actors have played the part when they were well past 40. Sarah Bernhardt, a French actress, played him when she was 56. In the eighteenth century, Thomas Betterton played the part when he was over 70.

A number of features create the impression of a youthful Hamlet. He faces familiar problems of adolescence: relations with the opposite sex, coming to terms with responsibility, finding one's own personality. He seems rebellious and misunderstood, and is constantly self-questioning, unsure whom to trust, and feeling betrayed by former friends. He has problems with his mother and stepfather, and with coming to terms with the death of his own father. In the Old Vic 2004 production shown below, Hamlet was played by a very young actor as a character acutely troubled by such difficulties. The youthful appearance of his mother, Gertrude, dramatically heightened his confused feelings towards her.

Hamlet at the Globe

In Shakespeare's lifetime *Hamlet* was almost certainly performed at the Globe. It was a round theatre, open to the sky. The audience standing in the pit, the 'groundlings', got wet if it rained. Those in the galleries (who paid more), and the actors on stage, were protected from the worst of the weather.

The original Globe audiences expected and enjoyed a noisy display of drums, trumpets and the firing of cannon. *Hamlet* richly fulfils that expectation. In the play's second scene Claudius promises that 'the great cannon' will sound to heaven itself to celebrate his drinking. That boastful ritual is heard as Hamlet awaits the Ghost's appearance ('The kettle-drum and trumpet thus bray out'), and in Act 5 Scene 2 before the duel Claudius orders 'let the kettle to the trumpet speak, / The trumpet to the cannoneer without, / The cannons to the heavens'. His order is obeyed as *'Drum, trumpets sound, and shot goes off'*.

In Shakespeare's day, Gertrude and Ophelia were played by boys. Although there were no elaborate sets on the bare stage of the Globe Theatre, the actors dressed in attractive and expensive costumes, usually the fashionable dress of the times. Only a few props were used (swords, goblets etc.).

'Get thee to a nunnery'. Hamlet subjects Ophelia to a vicious tongue-lashing in the Globe 2000 production.

'. . . look how it steals away'. Gertrude is unable to see the Ghost that is all too visible to Hamlet.

The Globe Theatre has now been rebuilt on London's Bankside, close to the site on which it first stood. Each year at least one production is staged as Shakespeare's own audiences probably saw them. The Globe's 2000 production of *Hamlet* presented the play in that 'authentic' style. Actors were dressed in the fashion of the Danish court in the late sixteenth century (similar to Elizabethan costume). The royal family wore red and gold, and their coat of arms was visible on stage. To suggest the freezing cold on the gun platform, sheepskin cloaks were worn. The players in the play-within-the-play wore what Elizabethans would have thought of as Roman dress.

273

Hamlet on film

Laurence Olivier's 1948 film began with the statement 'This is the tragedy of a man who could not make up his mind', and strongly implied that Hamlet has incestuous desire for his mother. Another famous black-and-white film is the 1964 version by the Russian director, Grigori Kozintsev, which stresses the political aspects of the play. In 1990 Mel Gibson played Hamlet in a colour film which used only about one third of Shakespeare's script. In contrast, Kenneth Branagh's 1996 film lasted four hours, using virtually all the script (but a shortened two-hour version is available). Branagh's use of late nineteenth-century costumes contrasts with a 2000 modern-dress American film in which Hamlet is a New York businessman.

Film provides close-ups, tracking shots and cinematic spectacle not available on stage. In the Russian film, Fortinbras's army marches along a real sea coast (see p. 166). The sea symbolises the possibility of freedom from Elsinore's prison-like atmosphere. Film can even suggest moral perspectives, as when Olivier uses high-angle shots to look down on Claudius's court as if in moral judgement.

Modern films sometimes make sly or obvious reference to *Hamlet*, as in Arnold Schwarzenegger's 1993 *Last Action Hero*.

Hamlet on film and on stage. Two representations of the funeral of Ophelia. Make a list of the differences between Shakespeare on film and Shakespeare in the theatre. Use your list to describe how you would present Ophelia's funeral (or a scene of your choice) on film and on stage.

William Shakespeare
1564–1616

1564 Born Stratford-upon-Avon, eldest son of John and Mary Shakespeare.

1582 Marries Anne Hathaway of Shottery, near Stratford.

1583 Daughter, Susanna, born.

1585 Twins, son and daughter, Hamnet and Judith, born.

1592 First mention of Shakespeare in London. Robert Greene, another playwright, described Shakespeare as 'an upstart crow beautified with our feathers . . .'. Greene seems to have been jealous of Shakespeare. He mocked Shakespeare's name, calling him 'the only Shake-scene in a country' (presumably because Shakespeare was writing successful plays).

1595 A shareholder in The Lord Chamberlain's Men, an acting company that became extremely popular.

1596 Son Hamnet dies, aged 11.
Father, John, granted arms (acknowledged as a gentleman).

1597 Buys New Place, the grandest house in Stratford.

1598 Acts in Ben Jonson's *Every Man in His Humour*.

1599 Globe Theatre opens on Bankside. Performances in the open air.

1601 Father, John, dies.

1603 James I grants Shakespeare's company a royal patent: The Lord Chamberlain's Men become The King's Men and play about twelve performances each year at court.

1607 Daughter, Susanna, marries Dr John Hall.

1608 Mother, Mary, dies.

1609 The King's Men begin performing indoors at Blackfriars Theatre.

1610 Probably returns from London to live in Stratford.

1616 Daughter, Judith, marries Thomas Quiney.
Dies. Buried in Holy Trinity Church, Stratford-upon-Avon.

The plays and poems
(no one knows exactly when he wrote each play)

1589–95 *The Two Gentlemen of Verona, The Taming of the Shrew, First, Second and Third Parts of King Henry VI, Titus Andronicus, King Richard III, The Comedy of Errors, Love's Labour's Lost, A Midsummer Night's Dream, Romeo and Juliet, King Richard II* (and the long poems *Venus and Adonis* and *The Rape of Lucrece*).

1596–9 *King John, The Merchant of Venice, First and Second Parts of King Henry IV, The Merry Wives of Windsor, Much Ado About Nothing, King Henry V, Julius Caesar* (and probably the *Sonnets*).

1600–5 *As You Like It, Hamlet, Twelfth Night, Troilus and Cressida, Measure for Measure, Othello, All's Well That Ends Well, Timon of Athens, King Lear.*

1606–11 *Macbeth, Antony and Cleopatra, Pericles, Coriolanus, The Winter's Tale, Cymbeline, The Tempest.*

1613 *King Henry VIII, The Two Noble Kinsmen* (both probably with John Fletcher).

1623 Shakespeare's plays published as a collection (now called the First Folio).